drama

BETWEEN POETRY AND PERFORMANCE

W. B. WORTHEN

A John Wiley & Sons, Ltd., Publication

This edition first published 2010
© 2010 W. B. Worthen

Blackwell Publishing was acquired by John Wiley & Sons in February 2007.
Blackwell's publishing program has been merged with Wiley's global Scientific,
Technical, and Medical business to form Wiley-Blackwell.

Registered Office
John Wiley & Sons Ltd, The Atrium, Southern Gate, Chichester, West Sussex, PO19
8SQ, United Kingdom

Editorial Offices
350 Main Street, Malden, MA 02148-5020, USA
9600 Garsington Road, Oxford, OX4 2DQ, UK
The Atrium, Southern Gate, Chichester, West Sussex, PO19 8SQ, UK

For details of our global editorial offices, for customer services, and for information
about how to apply for permission to reuse the copyright material in this book please
see our website at www.wiley.com/wiley-blackwell.

The right of W. B. Worthen to be identified as the author of this work has been
asserted in accordance with the Copyright, Designs and Patents Act 1988.

Wiley also publishes its books in a variety of electronic formats. Some content that
appears in print may not be available in electronic books.

Designations used by companies to distinguish their products are often claimed as
trademarks. All brand names and product names used in this book are trade names,
service marks, trademarks or registered trademarks of their respective owners. The
publisher is not associated with any product or vendor mentioned in this book. This
publication is designed to provide accurate and authoritative information in regard to
the subject matter covered. It is sold on the understanding that the publisher is not
engaged in rendering professional services. If professional advice or other expert
assistance is required, the services of a competent professional should be sought.

Library of Congress Cataloging-in-Publication Data

Worthen, William B., 1955–
  Drama : between poetry and performance / W. B. Worthen.
    p. cm.
  Includes bibliographical references and index.
  ISBN 978-1-4051-5341-6 (hardcover : alk. paper) – ISBN 978-1-4051-5342-3
(pbk. : alk. paper) 1. Drama–History and criticism. 2. Drama–Technique.
3. Theater. I. Title.

  PN1655.W67 2010
  809.2–dc22

                                                                2009030391

A catalogue record for this book is available from the British Library.

Set in 10 on 13 pt Palatino by Toppan Best-set Premedia Limited
Printed in Singapore by Ho Printing Singapore Pte Ltd

1 2010

pro tebe, Hanino

Contents

Acknowledgments

It is a pleasure to have the opportunity to thank Barbara Hodgdon and Richard Abel for their inspiration, conversation, friendship, and support in the course of writing this book. My thanks, too, to LeAnn Fields, Clay Hapaz, Teresa Hartmann, Jonathan Freedman, the English Department of the University of Michigan, Elizabeth Boylan, Provost of Barnard College, and Marlena Gittleman for indispensable assistance at key points in the work; to Paula Court for the superb photographs of The Wooster Group's *Hamlet*; and long-overdue thanks to Frank Whigham for returning my attention to Burke. I'm also grateful to audiences at the Modern Language Association, the Folger Shakespeare Library, Duke University, and the Drama and Theatre Research Group at the University of Michigan for their challenging responses to some of the writing as it emerged. My sincere thanks to Emma Bennett, who asked me to think about reading drama, and to Isobel Bainton, Caroline Clamp, Brigitte Lee Messenger, and the staff at Wiley-Blackwell for their own hard work on performing my writing here. I would also like to thank Erika Fischer-Lichte, Christel Weiler, Gabriele Brandstetter, Sandra Umathum, Holger Hartung, Armin Hempel, Tina Lange, Madeleine Duchert, and the fellows, students, and staff of the "Interweaving Performance Cultures" International Research Center of the Institute for Theater Studies of the Freie Universität Berlin for their support, conversation, and critique of some of the material presented here. Finally, my deepest gratitude is to Hana Worthen, expressed in the dedication of this book to her.

The following editors and publishers have graciously allowed me to use some previously published material here, in considerably revised form: "Shakespeare 3.0," *Alternative Shakespeares 3*, edited by Diana Henderson (Routledge, 2008); "Performing Shakespeare in Digital Culture," *The Cambridge Companion to Shakespeare and Popular Culture,* edited by Robert Shaughnessy (Cambridge University Press, 2007), "Reading Performance," *Shakespeare Bulletin* 35.4 (2008): 69–83; "Antigone's Bones," *TDR: The Drama Review – The Journal of Performance Studies* 52.3 (Fall 2008): 10–33; "*Hamlet* at Ground Zero: The Wooster Group, the Archive, and Performance," *Shakespeare Quarterly* 59 (2008): 303–22; "A Quip Modest: Reply to R. A. Foakes's 'Performance Theory and Textual Theory,'" *Shakespeare* 2:2 (December 2006): 208–19 (www. informaworld.com); "Citing History: Textuality and Performativity in the Plays of Suzan-Lori Parks," *Essays in Theatre/Études théâtrales* 18.1 (November 1999): 3–22.

Preface

Drama, Poetry, and Performance

The new theatre confirms the not so new insight that there is never a harmonious relationship but rather a perpetual conflict between text and scene.

Hans-Thies Lehmann, Postdramatic Theatre *(145)*

Why would anyone want to read a play? Between the covers, the words lie dead on the page, surrounded with a strange apparatus of stage directions (usually in Latin), "speech prefixes" (as if acting were just making speeches), and artificially regimented by the rule of type in ways that utterly belie the pace and movement, the playing of the play. The theatre is a transitional space, not where we suspend disbelief, but where we are a visible and lively part of an event: in the theatre, *drama* actually takes place, and takes time too. Even in the sparest, even in the most amateur performance, the materialization of the drama should feel like *play*, involving us wittingly and unwittingly in an intensified enactment of the activities that make us most human, the visible execution of culture in our bodies. The grain of the voice, the trace of a gesture, the shape of posture, the suddenness of movement, the bite of articulation: these are at once the tenor and the vehicle, the meaning and the means of live drama. Recalling dramatic performance, it's more often the player than the play, or the player in the playing that's memorable. While everyone recalls a line "delivered" (so to speak, as if it were the actor's job to be the play's postman) with exquisite point and purpose, I don't think we remember "language" as such as the substance of our play in the theatre. How many times has an intonation, an inflection opened the play's language to completely unexpected meanings, creating a new, unanticipated event? The words await the instigation of doing. Why would anyone want to read a play?

Why would anyone want to see a play? The actors' weary flesh falls to dust but on the page, the poet's decisive invention continues to play. The page opens a transitional space, which we enter as the words enter us, a place to entertain their friction as we play them, running them back and forth, allowing them the time to do their thing, enriching, clarifying, and complicating our experience with them. As Hamlet's words insinuate themselves through my thoughts, with my thought, as my thought, their play – "To be or not to be": how to think that, say that, mean that? – becomes intimately mine; as Anna Deavere Smith puts it, the words become me ("Introduction" xxiv). Although this is surely not what Antonin Artaud had in mind, feeling the "active, plastic, respiratory sources of language," letting "the discursive, logical aspect of speech disappear beneath its physical side," takes shape more often while reading than while seeing a play (119). We don't need plays to feel the pulse of language – Yeats or Hopkins or Stevens would do as well. "Let be be finale of seem": how to think that, say that, mean that (Stevens, "Emperor")? Recalling a play, it's more often the performance of reading, how it felt to discover, take in, reflect on, return to the drama that's memorable. While everyone remembers the exquisite point and purpose of a character's line, I don't think we remember "language" alone as the substance of our play with the page. Our pleasure arises in part through the impersonated character of dramatic reading. Sitting down to read *King Lear* once again is, as Keats knew, a demanding experience to "burn through," one that burns through us in intimate, unanticipated ways. Merely seeing the play provides the profit of an audience, not of an actor – or a reader (Artaud 10). Why would anyone want to see a play?

This book explores the drama's two lives, how we understand the identity of drama at the interface between poetry and performance; it undertakes a complementary approach to reading and thinking about drama, attempting to preserve the particularity of the drama's distinct identities while suggesting some ways they may be entwined in one another. At least since the rise of print and certainly since the rise of professional modern literary studies in the last century, our understanding of drama has become more not less disjunctive, variously institutionalized in associations, concretized on campuses, disciplined in departments, and proselytized in pedagogy. *Dramatic literature, drama studies, theatre studies, theatre history, theatre research, Theaterwissenschaft, performance studies, performance theory, performance research, theory and practice, text and performance, text-based theatre, non-text-based theatre, postdramatic theatre, performance art, director's theatre, nondramatic theatre, nonmatrixed performance, liminality, restoration of behavior, surrogation, disappearance, archive and repertoire*: although our critical vocabulary and critical practice have worked to particularize the objects and methods of our inquiry, the intersection of dramatic writing and dramatic performance remains elusive.

When we are doing drama, what are we watching, reading, doing? How do we model the relationship between writing and performance, page and stage? I don't think we have a compelling way of accounting for what we say "the text" does relative to stage performance. Texts do not direct how we use them, though they may point to contemporary theatrical conventions (PROSPERO *on the top, invisible*, in *The Tempest*) and sometimes express the author's desire for the play to be imagined onstage in a specific way (the Beckett estate's controversial strictures on productions that depart from Beckett's stage directions show how hard it is to decide the theatrical warrant of authorial property).[1] Instead, "the text" functions in largely metaphorical, ideologically laden ways in most discussions of dramatic performance. Although many *texts* are variously used and discarded in a range of different kinds of performance, the habitual recourse to *the text* when attempting to characterize the meaning and purpose of dramatic performance dramatizes our critical poverty when it comes to the analysis of the work and working of drama onstage.

Dramatic writing epitomizes the interpretive dissonance posed by all poetic writing, perhaps by writing itself. On the one hand the text of the play appears as a single fabric, to have a specific shape, size, and texture, a kind of organic wholeness. Even taking its three early versions into account (the 1603 "bad" quarto, the 1604 "good" quarto, and the version published in the 1623 Folio edition of Shakespeare's plays), *Hamlet* seems to involve a relatively consistent set of events, in a more or less consistent order, and the representation of a certain set of (sometimes differently named) agents. Yet while *Hamlet* may imply both physical (the queen drinks the poisoned wine) and verbal ("To be or not to be") events, in performance the text becomes material for use, used and used up, eventually put aside in the process of making the play. And while the text may seem to direct a specific act at a specific time, the recontextualization of that "act" as performance cannot be fully specified. Do the Montagues and Capulets duel with swords or with pistols? Does Hamlet die or merely perform "dying," winking back at the audience? Is Cleopatra played by an adult woman, or by an adolescent boy?

Reading drama responds to the essential duplicity of writing: writing appears to fix a verbal object, but its signifying capacity alters with each new scene of performance. While it is sometimes thought that a critical reading of plays is merely "theoretical" as opposed to the "practical" reading undertaken by a director or actors involved in staging a play, their reading is no less "theoretical" in this sense. Rather than deriving the essential design of the play, they, too, are reading the play within a specific scene and purpose of meaning-making. As Michael Goldman suggests, scripted drama is "writing that enables acting, a kind of writing, that is, that to an unusual degree allows a performer to generate something other than a text" (*Ibsen* 30). The old cliché that a good actor can perform the telephone book points to an important truth about acting and writing: the "performative" dimension of dramatic writing, how it enables actors to "do things with words" onstage (see Austin), how it seems to afford a legible performance, arises at the intersection between the script and the embodying practices of an ambient theatricality.

Drama: Between Poetry and Performance proposes a way to read drama, one that negotiates the dialectical tension between its identity as poetry and as performance. I take "poetry" broadly: whether in prose or verse, drama imagines a distinctive experience of language, posing new challenges for using writing to create something beyond words: action. Although dramatic writing often represents a fictive world and fictive human beings acting in it, as Aristotle recognized, drama is imitation in the mode of action itself, "with all the people engaged in the *mimesis* actually doing things."[2] We see the action performed (not narrated) by its agents. The agents are, however, essentially duplicitous: in the theatre, "Oedipus" emerges through the actor's remaking of writing into something else, a performance. This performance intimately identifies "Oedipus" with and through the actor. We can only see, understand, know – *identify* – Oedipus with the ways the actor's performance uses the writing, *identifies* it with his own activities: a specific body and a way of inhabiting it; inflections of voice and movement; strategies for occupying the space it shares with us, its audience. Actors, the design and configuration of the theatre, audience expectations – since these and other features of producing the play are outside the text, beyond its control, we cannot read plays as definitive instructions for making performance. At the same time, the practices of reading – how we decode, interpret, reconstruct aspects of dramatic *language*, as Aristotle might have put it, as *plot*, *character*, *thought*, and *spectacle* – are not governed by the text, but by the interplay between the text and conventions and practices of reading we bring to it. But if the script can't control how we read its poetry or perform its actions as theatre, how can we use it to gain access to the dual identities of drama?

Dramatic writing is writing for use, and like any writing its potential uses are limitless. And yet, in learning to read drama, the play's the thing. Plays often seem attentive to specific aspects of performance. Modern plays frequently use extensive stage directions, prescribing the appearance and behavior of the characters, and most plays come to us with a highly conventional apparatus on the page – *dramatis personae*, speech prefixes, act and scene divisions, and so on. These accessories are important but hardly critical to the identity of dramatic writing. The papyri of classical Greek plays often record a change in speaker with a small mark, a dot; the early printed versions of Shakespeare's plays are very casual with regard to the consistency of speech prefixes and act/scene divisions (the 1623 Folio text of *Troilus and Cressida* begins with *Actus Primus. Scæna Prima.* – the last act/scene division in the play); stage directions become prominent in the late nineteenth century, perhaps as a way for plays to compete with novels on the platform of the printed page. But plays are often responsive to the uses of performance in more searching ways, attending to the various pressures of bodies and of space that will remake writing into doing. Armed with some understanding of theatre – both the original circumstances of a play's theatre, and subsequent stage practices – we can gain access to the drama's ways of allegorizing the action it at once encodes and enables to take place.

In the West, writing has been essential to the imagination and transmission of drama, and to the conception of dramatic performance. *Drama: Between Poetry and Performance* traces three ways the drama represents its instrumentality, its dialectical in-betweenness, using plays from the Western tradition to explore how dramatic texts reflect the encounter between writing-as-an-object (the book) and performance, between writing and embodiment, and between writing and the space of the stage. How do plays imagine the conditions of their use, implicitly challenging the polarization of poetry and performance

driving dominant models of dramatic theatre? The introductory chapter
traces the ways the polarization of "literature vs. theatre" has obstructed
a critical engagement with the drama's dynamic interplay of poetry
and performance. The transformation of Shakespearean drama from a
theatrical to a literary commodity exemplifies the historical and cultural character of the drama's dual identity. While Shakespeare is now
sometimes understood to straddle this boundary, much of the language we use to characterize the work of poetry in performance remains
conceptually rudimentary, often relying on seductive but misleading
metaphors: the *score*, the *blueprint*, and more recently, *information*, *software*. Yet writing in the theatre neither orchestrates, delineates, nor
controls performance, nor does it provide *information* unchanged by the
process of its embodied production. First considering the exemplary
role of Shakespearean drama in marking the shift from drama as a
performance commodity to drama as a textual one, and then examining
the metaphors used to regulate the proper work of writing in performance, we finally shift our attention to a more instrumental understanding of dramatic writing as a *tool* in the *technologies* of performance,
adapting Kenneth Burke's terms – *act, scene, agent, agency, purpose* – to
reconsider specific affordances of dramatic writing.

   The Introduction, then, proposes less a theory of drama than a practice of reading. The first chapter, "From Poetry to Performance," traces
the polemical commitments to poetry and performance of the two
dominant modes of the drama's critical reception in the last half-
century: literary studies and performance studies. Arising in the 1940s
and 1950s and becoming widespread as a teaching technology thereaf-
ter, the New Criticism devised an arresting practice for interpreting
poetic texts. The program of the New Criticism asserted a decontextualized reading strategy, attending to the intrinsically "literary" essence
of the poem as a verbal artifact. Yet, as the New Critics recognized,
dramatic writing is at least partly defined by the context of its theatrical
use; they saw their task, then, to define ways of attending to drama
that could isolate and examine its purely "literary" dimension. The
power of the New Criticism in the mid-twentieth century is especially
witnessed by critics working to forge a specific mode of dramatic
critique, critics recognizing, in other words, the limitations of conceiving drama in purely "textual" terms, who are nonetheless unable to
escape this perspective, one which continues to shape much of our
thinking about the poetry of drama to the present day. This chapter

places four prominent studies – Cleanth Brooks and Robert B. Heilman's *Understanding Drama*, Eric Bentley's *The Playwright as Thinker*, Francis Fergusson's *The Idea of a Theater*, and Raymond Williams's *Drama from Ibsen to Eliot* – in dialogue, books written, notably, by prominent literary scholars, a playwright and translator, a trained actor, and the founder of cultural studies. What kinds of reading strategies, inclusions and exclusions, were demanded if drama were to be read as poetry, as literature? And what kind of vision of performance did these strategies evoke?

By the 1960s, this body of critique had largely succeeded in defining the "literary" dimension of the drama apart from the stage. Enabling the widespread teaching of drama-as-literature, this paradigm defined the identity of the drama as *only* literary, fixed and identified with the text, theatrical performance serving the ministerial purpose of realizing the poetry in its proper terms. The 1970s brought many revolutions; one of them was the rise of a new "antidiscipline," performance studies. Staking out the confluence of ethnography, sociology, communications, and literary theory, performance studies brought a commanding energy to the study of *performance*. Here, we will attend to one dimension of that revolution, how a literary conception of drama provides leverage for performance studies' evocation of new analytical and political strategies. The New Critics defined a purely literary fixity for the drama, and for all its oppositional energy performance studies surprisingly echoes this view, regarding dramatic theatre as a textually legislated form of performance, and so as antithetical to the essentially destabilizing freedom of performance *per se*. The second part of the chapter outlines the function of a literary conception of drama in the shaping of the disciplinary trajectory of performance studies. It then takes up an alternative critical lineage, which has attempted to rethink the work of drama, in large part by resisting its "literary" deformations and by suggesting that *writing* need not be conceived as the antithesis of *performance* but as one instrument among many that the repertoire of enactment might deploy. Taking our cue from Diana Taylor and Richard Schechner, this section frames a second conversation, between Michael Goldman's *The Actor's Freedom*, Stanton B. Garner's *Bodied Spaces*, Herbert Blau's *The Audience*, Benjamin Bennett's *All Theater Is Revolutionary Theater*, and Hans-Thies Lehmann's *Postdramatic Theatre*, suggesting how we might resist the division of poetic from performative analysis that has consistently derailed the discussion of drama.

While the introductory chapter outlines the nature of the controversy regarding drama in literary and performance studies, the challenge of subsequent chapters is to move beyond this impasse, to trace
a way of reading drama as *agency*. Dramatic writing is writing for use,
an instrument: how we understand its utility, how we use it and what
we use it to do – its *affordance* – is partly a function of the properties of
the instrument, and partly a function of our imagination of the task we
want to perform with it. Here, then, each chapter takes up a different
aspect of the *affordance* of drama – the materiality of writing, the book;
the transformation of writing by embodiment, acting; and the mapping
of a fictive landscape onstage, space – asking how plays frame, reflect
on, *allegorize*, that agency in dramatic action. Chapter 2, "Performing
Writing," considers how our conception of dramatic writing and performance is modeled on and resistant to the book. What problems arise
from thinking about the affordance of dramatic writing in the culture
of print? Here, we will consider a notoriously "bookish" play, *Hamlet*.
Hamlet is not only suffused by texts and acts of writing, it also explores
the different ways that writing engages with performance. Beyond
that, *Hamlet* foregrounds writing in a different sense: written four
hundred years ago, much of its language is now impenetrable, incom-
prehensible by actors or audiences as a living instrument of performance. How might the archaisms of Shakespearean language provide an
index of the changing uses of dramatic writing in the history of the
stage? The chapter concludes by turning to performance itself, considering how a controversial production of *Hamlet* by the Wooster Group
interrogates the instrumentality of dramatic writing, the text, in the
event of performance.

   The third chapter turns to the question of "Embodying Writing." If
the body is always outside the play, how can we read drama as a critique, interrogation, representation of embodiment? Here, we will consider two modern playwrights, Henrik Ibsen and Suzan-Lori Parks,
and ask not only how their plays represent *bodies* as agents of dramatic
meaning, but also how the acts they assign to actors challenge a fundamentally literary notion of dramatic character as something complete, prescribed in the writing. The action of Ibsen's *Rosmersholm* turns
on its mysterious final scene, the duet between Rosmer and Rebecca
West that leads them – or in which they lead themselves – to suicide.
The scene depends on a modern sense of *character*, in which actors
motivate stage behavior by evoking a specific subtext of desire

constructed through the invention of a causal narrative, a fictive biography of the character. And yet, Ibsen seems to provide each actor with a *role* – a series of actions to perform – that challenges the stability of this sense of *character*, particularly the notion that *character* can be known merely from its history, from the refining confession of the past. Dividing the actor's work from a notion of novelistic *character*, Ibsen's play reframes the use of writing in the process of embodiment: poetry provides an instrument for use, *agency*, not a person to be, a *character*. Suzan-Lori Parks largely dispenses with the naturalistic framework of Ibsen's theatre, tending toward a more experimental use of language and dramatic structure. And yet, in their insistent reframing of history on the stage, Parks's plays – *The America Play* and *Venus* – also confront and revise the naturalistic relationship between narrative and *character*. Indeed, Parks poses the *role* not at the intersection of the actor/character's personal history, but instead within a more public discourse, where *character* emerges not as the cause but as the consequence of the practice of rewriting, "signifying" history.

The final chapter, "Writing Space," considers how dramatic writing engages with spatiality. Like the body, the space of the theatre is always outside the text. And while we might regard human bodies as having a kind of perdurable consistency across human history, the space of theatre – its social space, technological space, location in the city, the kind of space it is and does – is in constant negotiation, constant change. Here, Samuel Beckett's close attention to space in theatre, film, and television opens the question: how does writing, far from controlling space, represent the difficulties of its mapping, the play's inevitable casting and exploration of its physical milieu? A play written for four dancers and designed for the camera, *Quad* presses the question of writing dramatic space with striking power. Composed entirely of directions, *Quad* at once engages the interplay between writing and space and appears to challenge the limits of dramatic poetry itself. Yet as an allegory of the drama's encounter with theatrical space, *Quad* provocatively spatializes the *agency* of writing, showing how dramatic writing affords the occupation of a space it at once discovers and invents.

Tracing the institutional and critical fortunes of drama, allegorizing its encounter with print, with bodies, with space, I've tried to resist the temptation to provide an interpretive grid, a reading machine. Instead, I hope to model a habit of attention, pointing to some of the consequences that might flow from imagining dramatic writing as it, often brilliantly, imagines itself: as a design for doing. The following pages focus closely on the specificity of "words, words, words" and how we can address their affordance in performance, understanding performance both through the particularity of specific film and stage events, and as a more general, constantly changing technology for making dramatic writing, poetry, significant as performance behavior. Asking how plays represent the agency of writing – as books, through embodiment, in charting space – I hope to suggest how dramatic writing reflexively imagines the fluid frontier between poetry and performance.[3]

Introduction

Between Poetry and Performance

The job of interpretation – what in fact we're doing when we interpret – is to supply what the poem has appeared to omit, and our continuing interest in a poem turns on its resistance to our efforts.

James Longenbach, The Resistance to Poetry *(85)*

In the English-speaking world, the worst thing that ever happened to drama was Shakespeare (and the best, too). The densely verbal conventions of early-modern playwriting, and the cultural celebration of Shakespeare's plays as literature more or less ever since have distorted the place of writing, of scripted language in our understanding of drama and dramatic performance. Although Shakespeare is surely a special case, the centrality of Shakespeare to English-language literary and theatre studies provides a paradigm of the understanding of drama in print culture, one we can use to chart the relation between dramatic writing and dramatic performance in historical terms. Here, I want to reframe two problems in the theoretical and historical encounter between writing and performing: the impact of print on our understanding of drama, and how the metaphors commonly used to model dramatic performance – the *score*, the *blueprint*, and more recently *information* and *software* – reveal our (mis)conception of the interface between dramatic poetry and dramatic performance. Then, we'll shift ground, to consider how we might understand dramatic writing more complementarily, as a tool in the technologies of performance, and, with the assistance of Kenneth Burke, what the consequences of this way of reading drama might be.

i. Shakespeare 3.0

For the past five hundred years, drama has occupied a shifting no-man's land between print, the making of books, the social dissemination of "literature," and acting, the making of theatre, the social dissemination of performance. First inscribed in manuscript, and first published through stage performance, Shakespeare's plays dramatize the changing cultural relationship between Western drama and these two complex technologies. For Shakespeare and his fellows, the principal vehicle of drama was the stage and its players, remembering that in the sixteenth and seventeenth centuries (and well after) plays had an important, but still subsidiary life as printed texts (most plays still do). Over the next four hundred years, the ratio between poetry and performance as the cultural basis of the identity of Shakespearean drama slowly shifted, as the dissemination of printed literature and the rise of literacy assimilated the drama – however fitfully, unevenly, and incompletely – to the canons of writing, literature. And as a sense of the identity of drama became increasingly more literary, the stage itself came to be understood like the printing press, as a means to *re*produce an already existing play.

Shakespeare wrote plays for a theatre and a culture undergoing the slow transformation from orality to literacy; neither his audiences nor all of his performers could be assumed to be fully literate. The plays were handwritten in manuscript, laboriously hand copied into parts or *sides* for the actors, and this palimpsest of writing was owned by the playing company, which usually disposed of such obsolete materials after they had ceased to be of use: the great majority of plays produced in Shakespeare's era were never printed and have not survived. Despite Shakespeare's regard for literary status, well registered in the sonnets, the written play was largely an instrumental document, used and used up in the making of the play on the stage. It was the rare exception for companies to use printed texts for rehearsal; actors rehearsed only from their individual parts, and it seems likely that many learned their parts orally rather than reading them.[1] Granted, Shakespeare the literary dramatist was created by his appearance in print, and the plays may well bear the trace of Shakespeare's aspiration to a literary career through the means of print publishing.[2] Whether or not there was a significant market for the publication of individual playtexts as inexpensive quartos, the general dearth of large, expensive, folio-size editions might suggest that whatever the pretensions of playwrights whose *Works* were preserved in this form (Shakespeare, Ben Jonson, Francis Beaumont and John Fletcher), plays were at best beginning to be assimilated as "literature," and were more routinely regarded as having their principal identity onstage.[3]

Then as now, *performance* encompassed a wide range of activities, but by the late sixteenth century the use of a written script or scenario had been associated with some genres of *dramatic performance* for nearly two millennia. From Greek tragedy, inseparable from the invention of writing (see Wise), to the medieval York craft guilds whose perform-ances of individual Corpus Christi plays were checked for verbal accu-racy against the city's Register, writing enabled, preserved, and possibly instigated Western notions of drama and its performance. But plays in manuscript are nearly as vulnerable and evanescent as the theatrical performances they motivate. Rendering writing in a more robust, durable, and reproducible form, print enabled drama to gain a stable identity apart from performance, and eventually an identity in the emerging institutions of literature.

Shakespeare's plays made their way fitfully into print, and were reprinted throughout the later seventeenth century; other playwrights (Corneille, Molière, Racine, Lope de Vega, Calderón de la Barca) were printed as well, and by the publication of William Congreve's *Works* in 1710, European drama had gained a more-or-less regularized appear-ance on the page. In one sense, though, the conventions of printing plays point to the drama's unresolved conflict with the book. Some conventions – a list of *dramatis personae* before the play (characters not actors), prefixing lines to be spoken with the character's name, stage directions referring to events in the fictive narrative of the play (Laertes *Leaps in the grave*) – emphasize the text's fictional representation. Others – act and scene divisions, stage directions referring to stage business (PROSPERO *on the top, invisible*), exits and entrances – engage the play's functioning in the theatre.[4] Encoding the play rather unsystematically as poetry and as performance, print nonetheless contributed to an emerging sense of the identity of drama as arising from the page, per-formance becoming merely one instance, a kind of "edition," of its inherent complexity.

This modern, literary view of the drama took some time fully to take hold. Throughout the late seventeenth and eighteenth centuries,

Shakespeare's plays were typically rewritten for performance, their poetry revised to afford effective performance given the changing tastes of society and the stage. Famously, Nahum Tate's 1687 version of *King Lear* – Cordelia marries Edgar and Lear survives the play – held the stage *as King Lear* for over a century, and was transported both to the colonies in the Americas and Australia.[5] Such adaptations imply a comfortable slippage between the performance-based and print-based identities of Shakespearean drama.

> In the present case the publick has decided. *Cordelia*, from the time of *Tate*, has always retired with victory and felicity. And, if my sensations could add anything to the general suffrage, I might relate, that I was many years ago shocked by *Cordelia's* death, that I know not whether I ever endured to read again the last scenes of the play till I undertook to revise them as an editor. (Samuel Johnson 159)

As Samuel Johnson's famous remarks on reading Shakespeare's finale to *King Lear* may suggest, as long as the stage remained a dominant, or at least rival medium of the drama, the identity of Shakespeare's plays could be suspended between them.

The transformation of Shakespearean dramatic writing from principally performance material (Shakespeare 1.0) to literature took some time, but the now-familiar outlines of Shakespeare-the-book (Shakespeare 2.0) had clearly emerged by the early nineteenth century. Charles Lamb's well-known essay "On the Tragedies of Shakespeare, Considered with Reference to their Fitness for Stage Representation," published in 1811, is usually remembered for its astonishing, increasingly commonplace claim that the "Lear of Shakespeare cannot be acted" (136). Lamb naturally points to the inadequate and "contemptible machinery by which they mimic the storm" in productions of *King Lear*, but his hesitation regarding Shakespeare onstage finally has little to do with the verisimilitude of his theatre's ability to "represent the horrors of the real elements." A reader of Shakespeare, Lamb finds the essential dramatic action of Shakespeare's play taking place in Lear's mind, and in his own:

> It is his mind which is laid bare. This case of flesh and blood seems too insignificant to be thought on; even as he himself neglects it. On the stage we see nothing but corporal infirmities and weakness, the impotence of rage; while we read it, we see not Lear, but we are Lear, – we are in his mind [...] (136)

Lamb claims affection for the stage, but cautions against taking performance as the thing itself. Recalling the impact of seeing Shakespeare's plays performed by two of the iconic actors of the English stage, John Philip Kemble and his sister Sarah Siddons, Lamb notes how difficult it is "for a frequent playgoer to disembarrass the idea of Hamlet from the person and voice of Mr. K," or how often we "speak of Lady Macbeth, while we are in reality thinking of Mrs. S." Yet while he would never "be so ungrateful as to forget the very high degree of satisfaction" he received "some years back from seeing for the first time a tragedy of Shakespeare performed, in which these two great performers sustained the principal parts," Lamb finally sees stage performance to capture only an immature and singular impression of the myriad-minded poet. For the actors' performance "seemed to embody and realize conceptions which had hitherto assumed no distinct shape."

> But dearly do we pay all our life after for this juvenile pleasure, this sense of distinctness. When the novelty is past, we find to our cost that instead of realizing an idea, we have only materialized and brought down a fine vision to the standard of flesh and blood. We have let go a dream, in quest of an unattainable substance. (126)

Mocking flesh and blood, Lamb ignores the rich complexities of movement, gesture, intonation, acting. It might just as readily be thought that performance elaborates the inert writing on the page, materializing it in the richly ambiguous practice of social life. Instead, anticipating the values of later commentators, Lamb senses that the deepest access to the plays, our richest encounter with what Shakespearean drama *is*, takes place in reading. Shakespeare-the-book is software for reading; running Shakespeare 2.0 on a residual platform – the stage – seems to lose a significant degree of functionality.

Resistance is futile: with the rise of print as the increasingly pervasive, eventually dominant means for disseminating dramatic writing, the literary identity of Shakespeare and the primacy of fundamentally literary ways of calibrating page and stage were assured.[6] Nearly from the moment of print's achieved cultural dominance in the nineteenth century, though, its relocation of the identity of drama from the stage to the page was complicated by the rise of new technologies for making and recording performance, technologies which often came to displace

theatre altogether. Although these technologies disseminated a per
formed Shakespeare (1.0), the values of recorded performance were
plotted to the paradigmatic values (preservation, reproduction, stand-
ardization) of print (2.0).

In its first century or so, film viewing had much in common with
theatre: you could see a film several times when it was first released,
but were then reliant on "revivals" to see it again. Access to film performance participated in the occasional structure of live performance,
but the film performance remained unchanged, and so seemed to participate in the sense that the mechanical reproducibility of print guarantees the work's identity, at least until the film deteriorated. Film fixes
a performance, but while the film can be stopped and replayed, the
typically public film showing generally preserves the ritual character
of an event and temporal continuity of live performance, especially
since film is difficult to rewind and movie theatres are not economically
disposed to replay the film, or parts of it, for free. Video, more specifically the plunging price of video players, transformed this occasion,
making it easy to view Shakespeare films and recordings of stage plays
in the classroom and at home. The increasingly domestic video performance facilitates the rewinding and replaying of performance, and
adds the retemporalizing functions of fast forward and reverse; it also
relocates viewing to the private sphere. More important, widespread
access to video performance transformed recorded Shakespeare performance into a readily readable, rereadable, citable document, an
instrument of criticism and pedagogy with a perdurable and disseminated existence, like an essay or a book. The developing sense of print-
like performance is also marked by efforts to achieve and disseminate
a definitive volume of Shakespeare films, trailing the chimera of a
definitive scholarly edition, the avowed goal of the *BBC TV Shakespeare
Plays* cycle made in the late 1970s and 1980s and now available on DVD.

For all that film and video have renovated Shakespearean performance in the modern era – contributing at once to new theatricalities as
well as enabling the teaching of Shakespeare-in-performance – in some
ways the uses of recorded Shakespeare continue to echo the understanding of performance informing print culture. And yet, while
recorded Shakespeare enables a print-oriented pedagogical culture to
treat performance like a book, most often like a *critical* book offering a
narrow *interpretation* of *the text*, film and video evade and exceed
the categories of print, encoding the drama within both a technical

apparatus (the evolution of cameras, improved depth of field, color, etc.) and an ideology of the visible (perspective, camera angles, editing conventions, realism) that stand markedly outside the distinctive visualities of both early-modern and late-modern stages, and outside literature as well. With the rise of recording technologies – photography, film, television, radio, video, digital reproduction – the identity of Shakespearean drama has again undergone a cultural transformation: performance is no longer an evanescent thing, a local thing, nor even a time-bound temporal thing.

Digital Shakespeare, Shakespeare 3.0, releases performance from a single platform of production and from a single site of consumption; at the same time, though, digital Shakespeare also dramatizes our investments in earlier technologies – the page and the stage – and how we model their relationship. Shakespeare 3.0 is mobile, portable – play the DVD on your TV or computer or portable DVD player, download it to your iPhone, rip it for YouTube. At the same time, digital technology also shares a curiously familiar principle with the apparently transcended technology of the book: random access memory. Packaged in its book-like slipcase, divided into "chapters" and readily "bookmarked," enabling an instantaneous shuffling between the now-discrete moments of performance, Shakespeare 3.0 articulates dramatic performance as a commodity for personal consumption, read in a familiar private, portable, legible structure: the virtual book.

Shakespeare 3.0 is our contemporary with newly pervasive immediacy, taking shape as a virtual archive, in the bookish form of the DVD; it's so easy to page around in, to view a scene, stop, dwell on the particulars, compare to another scene, to another film. Indeed, despite the tired claims that performance is always opposed to writing, here performance is delivered through the same medium as writing, the screen, and is technically identical to writing, composed of bits of binary code. On my laptop, Shakespeare 3.0 – the Baz Luhrmann *William Shakespeare's Romeo + Juliet* – appears as a window next to a text I'm writing, sometimes with a window showing a folio or quarto page, perhaps even a digitized photofacsimile of an earlier Shakespeare release, the classic 1.1 version of 1623. Like other documents, Shakespeare 3.0 can be downloaded directly to the desktop: in the digital era, both writing and performance are virtual all the way.

Shakespeare 1.0, 2.0, 3.0 is an effort to capture the shifting historical interface between writing and performance technologies in the identity of drama. I'm laboring here to redescribe a relatively familiar history in the language of digital culture to suggest how changing technologies and the cultural relations animating them also alter our conception of writing and performance.[7] How does our understanding of drama change when drama is identified not with the material bodies of live actors (theatre), nor with the material traces of printed poetry (literature), but with the technologies of digitized *information*? Moving from Shakespeare 1.0 to Shakespeare 2.0 to Shakespeare 3.0, *is* our use of technology reflecting and enabling a dynamic change in our conception of drama, from Shakespeare-the-performance to Shakespeare-the-book to Shakespeare-the-book-like-performance? Or is this technological change, paradoxically, providing us with the means to clarify attitudes and assumptions we have held all along, even as we extend them into new ways and means of culture?

ii. Images of Writing/Metaphors of Performance

Our understanding of technologies – including the technologies of writing and performing – is often grasped metaphorically, through analogy to other, more familiar technologies. At least since the nineteenth century, the written dramatic script has appeared to prescribe the outlines of performance, a sense of the place of writing in theatre captured in several familiar metaphors: the text as *score, blueprint, information,* or *software* for performance. Metaphor is rhetorical, privileging certain elements of likeness. These metaphors reinforce a specific perspective on the practice and value of dramatic theatre, and shape attitudes about writing and performance.

The score

Nelson Goodman, with considerable resistance from musicians, has developed the most influential understanding of the *score* as a paradigm for dramatic performance. The *score* is attractive in that it appears to locate a precise model for the transmission of performance information through writing, suggesting the capacity of writing not merely to encode the semantic content of performance but the dynamic nuances of its embodiment as well. A score, for Goodman, is a notational system that specifies "the essential properties a performance must have to belong to the work; the stipulations are only of certain aspects and only within certain degrees. All other variations are permitted; and the differences among performances of the same work, even in music, are enormous" (Goodman 212).

> The text of a play, however, is a composite of score and script. The dialogue is in a virtually notational system, with utterance as its compliants. This part of the text is a score; and performances compliant with it constitute the work. The stage directions, descriptions of scenery, etc., are scripts in a language that meets none of the semantic requirements for notationality; and a performance does not uniquely determine such a script or class of coextensive scripts. (210–11)

Goodman considers dramatic texts much less carefully or critically than he does musical scores or choreographic notation, precisely because they seem less technically demanding and more transparent. But this transparency is illusory. Works that are "scored" are reversible from their compliant performances: if you could copy down all the notes played in a performance of a Brahms quartet, and carefully record tempo and dynamics, you would have a reasonable version of the score (much of the score would be equally derivable if the quartet were played on stringed instruments or kazoos). Similarly, if you could copy every spoken word heard in the theatre, you would have, in effect, a reverse-engineered score, the text of *Antigone* or *A Midsummer Night's Dream*. "Spelling" (Goodman's term) the dialogue score into speech, Beerbohm Tree's 1911 *Dream* with its live trees and rabbits, Peter Brook's 1970 circus-magic white box, Robert Lepage's 1992 multicultural swamp, and Adrian Noble's 1994 crimson fantasy, its huge umbrella cradling Titania and Bottom, may all have created compliant works. But the bunnies, the trapezes, the mud, and the umbrellas that distinguished these performances, however memorable, however essential to the specificity of the performance, stand for Goodman (like everything the actors do beyond reciting the words) outside the "essential properties" of compliance with the *score* of *A Midsummer Night's Dream*.

The dramatic text as *score* images an authoritative, constitutive role for writing in performance, framing compliant performance as the reproduction of words. Yet although the words on the page are generally spoken, actors do much more with words than simply utter them, render them as *speech*. Actors *use* the words on the page to produce an action, an event, to do something, something that's rarely if ever "having a dialogue," merely speaking. In this sense, it's not only the theatre's setting of the play that's beyond the text-as-score; what actors *do with words* – he says "Yes," but it means "No" – evades the *score* metaphor altogether. Peter Greenaway's film *Prospero's Books* visualizes just this point. Even compared to most theatrical productions, *Prospero's Books* is unusually compliant to the written text of *The Tempest*; not only are most of the words spoken, many of them are obsessively rendered on the screen. And yet, Greenaway's brilliant reframing of the play's "dialogue" – the film represents the script as dialogue between the characters through Prospero/John Gielgud's monologue, narrating the play as he writes it – in the context of an astonishing reframing of the play's visual field suggests the limits of "compliance to the score" as a productive means of negotiating between poetics and performance.

Is Bach on a piano less "compliant" than Bach on a clavier? Much as the original-instruments movement complicates the notion of "compliance," it also complicates the notion of the score as a perdurable work outside the means of its doing. For even though a score seems to inscribe the pace, volume, and intonation of music, musical performance is a social event, and "compliance," like the notion of "fidelity" common in the theatre, arises from a sense that performance conventions outside the text have been properly invoked, that the text has been used in the correct way (kazoo Brahms might be "compliant," but it's not Brahms). We no longer require masks, *kothurnoi*, and male actors to create what feels like a "compliant" *Medea*, to say nothing of flute music, an outdoor amphitheatre, a civic festival, and obligatory attendance. Deborah Warner's 2000 *Medea* for Dublin's Abbey Theatre, featuring Fiona Shaw in the title role, modern dress, Irish accents and setting, climaxed with Shaw's brilliant, brutal evisceration of the children *onstage*, blood spraying across the plexiglass wall of the "palace" – an open violation of one of the few performance conventions of classical tragedy more or less explicitly evoked by the text. Remembering that Euripides' text was translated to English, it would be fair to say that *nothing* about this production was "compliant"; yet it was, for audiences who saw it in Dublin or elsewhere around the world on tour, *Medea*, both our *Medea* and, somehow, Euripides'. Changing conventions of performance seem to bear the weight of what makes a performance appear to be compliant with the direction of the script.

In this sense, the *score* most often figures a desire to restrict performance to the imagined authority of writing. In 1994, Deborah Warner
directed Fiona Shaw in a celebrated production of Samuel Beckett's
Footfalls; although the dialogue was largely observed, rather than
having the actress pace in a thin strip of light parallel to the proscenium
as Beckett's stage directions demand, Shaw was – for part of the
production – placed on a small platform constructed in the stalls.
Responding to the production, Edward Beckett, the executor of the
Beckett estate, gave the *score* its typical phrasing, in explaining why the
estate would refuse permission for the production to tour after it closed
its brief London run:

> The estate does not seek to restrict freedom of interpretation, the very
> life blood of music and theatre. There are more than 15 recordings of
> Beethoven's late string quartets in the catalogue, every interpretation
> different, one from the next, but they are all based on the same notes,
> tonalities, dynamic and tempo markings. We feel justified in asking the
> same measure of respect for Samuel Beckett's plays. (Edward Beckett)

It's a commonplace argument, but one that nonetheless miscasts the
problem. For the instruments of theatrical performance – bodies and
space – are considerably more susceptible to ideological enrichment,
are considerably more dynamic as vehicles of signification than musical
instruments: they *mean* already, apart from their configuration in and
by the performance. Dramatic writing, by and large, fails to specify
"tonalities, dynamic and tempo markings," in part because the instrument – the entire social and material technology of dramatic theatre – is
not *re*productive, but productive, and constantly changing as well. We
expect the instrument of performance not merely to *interpret* a play that
is there on the page, but to create an event, *play*, through practices –
acting, direction, scenography – that don't merely sound the writing,
but transform it.[8]

The force of the *score* as a means of imposing a textual consistency
on the stage is nowhere more visible than in the metaphoricity of the
score itself. While the *score* seems to insist that the play is on the page,
how scores are actually used resembles the use of scripts in the theatre,
and resembles it in ways that tend to resist the force of the *score* metaphor. Most of the time there isn't one score for a musical performance,
but many, copied into parts and individually inscribed and annotated.
Stage performance is not built from *the text*, but from many texts,

scripts that are cut, rearranged, and annotated in different ways as part of the process of making the performance; a significant number of those texts – the actors' scripts – are finally left behind altogether. And for the past half-century and more, the notion of scoring music through a fully conventionalized notational system of staves, clefs, key signatures, notes, tempo and dynamic markings has itself been contested by composers, working to devise a range of ways to reshape the relationship between the score and their music, rethinking the interface of writing and performance as a means to new forms of music itself.[9] The score cannot determine what constitutes compliance. If "Bach's music" now includes the potential for performance on the piano or synthesizer, *A Midsummer Night's Dream* must, now, have a place for magic and mud, bunnies and brollies in it.

The blueprint

Perhaps more effectively than the *score*, the *blueprint* acknowledges the incompleteness of writing to the final performance, even as it – like the *score* – asserts performance as a property of the text. The dramatic script is a design for constructing something else, requiring a range of agents and materials to execute the performance: "Of the many thousands of plays written over the past couple of millenniums, only a fraction have survived, and even then they are only blueprints for three-dimensional structures that have been dismantled," as Charles Isherwood puts it ("Keeping"). Yet the *blueprint* implies a structure, not a process, a finished thing, whose tolerances can be checked against the prescriptions of the page; much as we can return to the blueprint to see whether the doorjamb should have been two or three inches to the left, the blueprint metaphor implies that we could return to the text to measure aspects of the performance. And yet, other than in relatively gross and finally uninteresting ways – must Hamlet say "To be or not to be" before he says "that is the question," if he says it at all? – the tolerances of a performance cannot be measured in this way. The affordance of performance emerges from the dynamic and changing ways writing is used by different conventions of theatrical production. Hamlet (if there is only one actor playing Hamlet) now says, does, means things in performance that could not have been imagined thirty years ago, let alone four hundred, and yet this event seems to afford us a *Hamlet*. This affordance arises from our understanding of the uses of writing in performing, and cannot be directly calibrated, *blueprint*-like, against the text "itself."

Part of the attraction of the *score* and the *blueprint* as metaphors of dramatic performance is their imaging of authorial, even artisanal, invention. The *score* and the *blueprint* image an act of inspired inscription, a writer delivering instructions for the execution of the masterwork. Violate the instructions (let's begin our *Hamlet* with "What a piece of work is a man"), violate the implied instructions (let's gut the children in Dublin, and spatter their living blood in view of the audience), violate the genre (let's make a movie instead), violate the historically implied instruments for executing the instructions (let's cast an African American actor as Mercutio, and have him cross-dress, too), and the masterwork should disappear, replaced by a self-evident fraud, P.D.Q. Bach, a Vegas Eiffel Tower, a sugar-cube Taj Mahal. In an important sense the Almereyda *Hamlet*, Warner *Medea*, and Luhrmann *Romeo + Juliet* point to the ways writing functions differently in the technologies of dramatic performance, in ways perhaps never much akin to musical or architectural notation at all.

Information/software

Writing, both as a process and a product, has been altered by digital culture, and much as digital technologies have enriched our understanding of the social technology of the book, perhaps we might ask how they model the technologies of performance, too. New technologies sometimes supplant their predecessors – remember typewriters, camera film, car phones, LP records? – but often the old and new coexist in ways that clarify the cultural implications of the activities they sustain. Much as digital technologies have provided new ways to think through the cultural impact of older forms like print, their characteristic metaphors – *information*, *software* – may also help to illuminate contemporary assumptions about dramatic performance, particularly the ways older assumptions may linger in new forms. In the privilege they accord to writing, these metaphors stand in sharp contrast to another way of modeling writing and performance, through analogy to the relationship between *tools* and *technologies*.

Writing is used in the process of dramatic performance, but is the purpose of dramatic performance to transmit the text's *information*? *Information* provides the dominant metaphor of all contemporary communications, but its technical definition – and so the work *informa-tion* does as metaphor – is not widely understood. To engineers, the problem of *information* has little to do with the content of a message, but whether, and how, to encode and decode a signal capable of being recognized *as* a message, capable of conveying any kind of *information* at all. In Claude Shannon's classic formulation, the "semantic aspects of communication are irrelevant to the engineering problems" con-fronted by digital communications technologies ("Mathematical" 27). *Information* is a function of choice, of the ability to choose from alterna-tives: *Information* happens when an isolated event in a field of variables – variation in the frequency of a signal, or turning a switch from *off* to *on* – has the probability of making a difference, of enabling a significant distinction to be made. Although all information systems require some degree of redundancy, the *value of information* is defined on the curve of probability. The possibility of information increases as the probabil-ity of mere redundancy decreases; the possibility of information decreases as the probability of mere randomness increases.

(That is, if we are choosing between two equally probable messages, then the information value of each is relatively high: since both mes-sages are equally probable, then the choice of one over the other implies a significant differentiation. Just think about reading any English sen-tence, like this one, and the "information" supplied by each letter or space in the series of marks on the page. Since the first word begins with the letter *J*, the probability that the next letter will be *b, c, d, f, g, j, k, l, m, q, s, t, v, w, x,* or *z* is zero (and the probability of *h, n, r, v* is *very* small), so the number of alternatives for filling that space is sub-stantially smaller than if the first word begins with the letter *A*, which can be followed either by a blank space or by any letter of the alphabet. *J* is most likely to be followed by one of 5 common alternatives (are we counting the names of cities in Finland, Hindu words, or abbreviations like Jr. and J.V.?), while *A* can be followed by 27. Since the possible choices after an initial *A* are so much greater than after an initial *J*, more *information* is communicated *by the letter after* the *A* than *by the letter after* the initial *J* in "Just."[10])

Digital technologies depend on this conception of "information," the probability that, as Mark C. Taylor suggests, a difference "*makes a dif-ference*. Not all differences make a difference because some differences are indifferent and hence inconsequential" (Mark C. Taylor 110), much as saying "what a storm!" during a hurricane might be a meaningful act, but too redundant to be informative. Since organization or pattern implies *difference* (an alphabet, tartans in Scotland, the American League East), the opposite of information is indistinction, what Norbert Wiener and others understand as "entropy," conceived indifferently either as utter stasis, absolute redundancy (no difference), or complete chaos (all difference). Same difference.[11]

This definition of *information* as a consistent encoding of data capable of being downloaded in different devices (performed on different platforms) sustains the contemporary digital revolution, the ability to reproduce the *same* pattern of data – the sequence of binary pulses (on/off, 1/0), *information* – on the page of a book, a laptop screen, an iPod, a mobile phone, a T-shirt. The consequences of this dissociation of meaning from information are everywhere visible, and a crucial part of our contemporary use of *information* as metaphor. But this understanding has cultural consequences as well: the notion that information has "a stable value as it [is] moved from one context to another" depends on an understanding of information as something that moves unchanged to different material means of performance. As N. Katherine Hayles argues, this abstraction of "information from context and thus from meaning" drives the reification of "information into a free-floating, decontextualized, quantifiable entity" (*Posthuman* 53–4, 9). In modern technology, *information* is not identified with *meaning*: it is a pattern *dissociated* from the contextual field of meaning, *abstracted* from a material conveyance, and then *selected* from a field of transmission. Information, in this view, is unchanged by its performance.

Information culture asserts the notion that the material platform is irrelevant to the information it displays: digital information is the same whether the photo it generates appears in a book, on a friend's mobile, or displayed on the desk of an FBI agent. This model of performance should sound familiar: it's cognate with the sense of dramatic performance as the downloading or decoding of *the text* through the transparent intermediaries of the stage, as though dramatic performances transmit the text's *information*, some better, some worse. But one of the odd consequences of information theory has been a surprising revision in our sense of the "logic" of the printed book as the realization of the work of art (Kernan 48–55). The reputed advance of print over oral and manuscript culture was twofold. Print enabled a much wider dissemination of writing and appeared to assert that *information* – the work of literature – as a stable entity apart from its specific material appearance.

The Oxford Shakespeare edition, a popular paperback, the second quarto, and the *Classics Illustrated Hamlet* might all materialize the same *information*, the same *words*. The ideology of print effectively guarantees that these books materialize the same *work* of art, despite the fact that these books in fact print many of the "same" words spelled differently, print some different words, embody the vehicle of the words in very different material (paper, ink, size, binding, covers, illustrations) and cultural terms (editorial apparatus, publishing house), and direct them to different audiences through very different social and economic processes. While *information*, in digital culture, is understood to be unchanged by its performance, digital culture has led us to revise our understanding of print-as-information: the platform creates an *information*-effect through performance. Performing *information*, the platform alters the *information*.

As Norbert Wiener suggests, "Like any form of information," textual "commands are subject to disorganization in transit" (*Human* 17). Should we understand the printed text as transparent to the information it materializes, or as performing – and so potentially changing – it? This kind of question has promoted renewed thinking about the various versions of some of Shakespeare's plays. Does Hamlet complain about his "too, too *sallied*" flesh (as he does in the 1604 second quarto version of the play, published during Shakespeare's lifetime), or about his "too, too *solid*" flesh (as he does in the 1623 Folio version, published by Shakespeare's colleagues after his death)? Or should *sallied* be corrected to the word that Shakespeare probably wrote, may have written, meant to write, should have written, but which was mispenned in Shakespeare's manuscript, and/or misread/miscopied by the playhouse copyist in his manuscript, and/or misread and/or misset in type by the print shop compositor – and is that word *solid* or *sullied*? Or is *sallied* just possibly correct; after all, Hamlet groans about "grieved and sallied" flesh in the 1603 quarto, a play that editors have often taken as more static than sense.[12]

Surprisingly, one consequence of digital technology on print has been the undoing of the implied "information-logic" of print and, in consequence, of a text-to-performance model of drama. Aspects of the early printed texts of Shakespeare that had once seemed like static, meaningless differentiae corrupting the authorial pattern – choose one: *sallied, sullied, solid* – now seem like significant differences, materializing historically distinct artworks, changing the *information* each book performs. Shakespeare's plays are full of confusing print-events. It is often hard to know who is speaking in early printed plays: sometimes a "character" appears on the page via several different speech-prefixes (as *Rob.* – for *Robin Goodfellow* – and as *Puck* in *A Midsummer Night's Dream*); sometimes the actor's name appears instead of the character's name in stage directions (*Enter Will Kemp* in *Romeo and Juliet* Q2) or even as a prefix (*Kemp* in the Folio text of *Much Ado About Nothing*); sometimes the abbreviation of the prefix makes it hard to know which character is speaking; and sometimes – in the final speech of *King Lear*, for instance – lines are assigned to one prefix (*Edg.*, for *Edgar*, in the Folio) in one version of the play, but appear under a different heading in another (*Duke*, for *Albany*, in the 1608 quarto). Sometimes stage directions bring a character into a scene in which s/he has no lines or apparent function in the action; sometimes characters are dismissed by the stage directions when they still have matter to speak. Some of these textual events are indeed mistakes, some arise from the poor transmission ("disorganization in transit") of the texts, some arise from the still fluid conventions for putting a play on the page, and some now seem to arise from revision. The irregular print-forms of early drama afford information that was once invisible to us – it is entirely invisible in modern editions, in which these features have been "corrected" – because editors did not see it *as information*, part of a potentially meaningful pattern, capable of enabling a coherent version of "Shakespeare's play" through reading or performance.[13] This recognition leads to an important insight into dramatic performance: while *information* metaphorically insists on the migration of data between platforms, dramatic *information* is changed by the systems that represent it, perform it.

Different platform, different information: this revision of the understanding of print-as-information should have important consequences for the study of dramatic performance. For the first century or so of print, the drama had two distinct platforms of realization – page and stage – that seem to have been understood as relatively distinct means of production; by the nineteenth century the modern notion that the stage can and should function as another edition, a reproduction of textual *information*, becomes increasingly dominant, common sense. *Faithful*, *straight*, *legitimate* theatre (the patriarchal and heteronormative accents underline the ideological stakes) performs the "same" words (well, many of them), and so aspires to reproduce print as performance.

In this narrow sense, the shape of the "text vs. performance" paradigm in the age of print actually anticipates the metaphor of digitized *information*, the sense that *Hamlet* should remain *Hamlet* on the various platforms of different print editions, as well as when it is produced on any successor to the wooden O, the bright box of the proscenium stage, or as lightborn images on the large, small, or pixellated screen.

While digital technologies have, paradoxically, challenged the notion of the functional stability of the book, the print-culture metaphor of the transmission of dramatic *information* from the page to the stage persists, perhaps most arrestingly in the "performance-oriented criticism" or "stage-centered reading" of Shakespearean drama that arose in the 1970s. J. L. Austin's critique of felicitous performativity in *How to Do Things with Words* located the *force* of performative speech not in the words but in their appropriate use within conventional systems of behavior. "I promise" only *performs* a promise when all necessary conditions of intention, capacity to fulfill the promise, and so on are in place: the words alone don't constitute the act, only their performance in the right animating circumstances. But "performance-oriented" reading worked in the opposite direction, constraining theatrical behavior to universalized notions of performance signaled by the words on the page. The claim that Shakespeare's "theatre was different from any we know today, but the essential act of performance was the same," and that the plays "were written for performance and reveal their true natures only in performance" seems actually to reiterate a conventionally "literary" sense of the text as abstract *information* to be decanted to the proper platform – here, stage performance rather than reading – for its display (Brown 8, 1).[14]

Burbage and Branagh are both actors, but surely the differences in training, in the social and cultural role of theatre, in the impact of performance technologies and dramatic genres (to say nothing of nutrition, film, Freud, and so on) render their work as examples of the *same* activity in something like the way the 1623 Folio *Works* and the *Norton Shakespeare* materialize the *same* conception of print, or *Pong* and *Grand Theft Auto* are both video games. In both cases, the "logic" of print is evoked as a principle for the conservation of an authentically Shakespearean drama: while the literary view regards the stage as a simplifying form of engagement, offering reduced functionality for realizing the text's richly multiple, ambiguous *information*, the "performance-oriented" view takes the universal platform of the stage to purify the signal, enabling us to distinguish the authentically Shakespearean drama from the static generated by reading.[15] Both views are sustained by the metaphor of Shakespearean *information* realized directly on the appropriate platform, itself unchanged by history and incapable of changing the information itself. Yet whether or not the "information" remains "the same" when performed through different means, in cultural terms the platform – the book, a performance – shapes our access to and valuation of the "information." You can watch *Lawrence of Arabia* on your iPhone, but even if the platform is transmitting the same signal, it's not the same event as *Lawrence of Arabia* on an IMAX.

What is the written document in performance: *information* to be transmitted or *software* for deploying the operating system – actors, space, objects, audiences – in specific ways? The *information* metaphor expresses a desire for symmetry between poetic representation and performance, one that renders the operating system of performance at once transparent and irrelevant. The *software* metaphor figures writing not as representation but as a series of instructions to drive the operating system of the theatre, and so poses other (dis)advantages: it points to the different kinds of functionality dramatic writing may have in different systems of performance (the Globe in 1600, the Royal National Theatre today, reading). It also implies that our perception of the text's functionality – what it is, might say, might do – depends on the affordances that are allowed or permitted by our operating system, our theatre. Word processing software, for instance, may have a voice-activation feature, but if the computer lacks a microphone, this potentiality doesn't exist. Yet while the *software* metaphor resists framing performance as a means of recapturing the text's representations (as the *score*, *blueprint*, and *information* do), it hardly resolves the dual identity of dramatic writing. Many of the words (*zounds!*) and gestures (kneeling, anything involving a hat) inscribed in Shakespeare's plays can still operate as *software*, drive a modern performance; yet we might well feel that such words and gestures have a different functionality in the contemporary theatre, signaling a nostalgic image of "pastness" rather than opening an immediate channel to the audience through a shared, active convention of social performance. Today, Shakespeare's Cleopatra is typically played by an adult actress. Does the greater psychological depth, sexual maturity, and professional experience that an adult actress brings to the role merely connect an unused circuit, revealing functionality already present in the *Antony and Cleopatra* software? Or does this new feature of the post-Shakespearean theatre enable the old software to gain new functionality, not so much rewriting the code as enabling the code to afford new functions the designer could not have foreseen? Like *information, software* asserts a familiar duality: the text appears to govern its representation in the appropriate operating system; new operating systems ascribe new functionality to the text.

Metaphors are interested, persuasive: their claims of identity (a play is a *score*, a *blueprint, information, software*) displace, conceal, subordinate, or smooth away the rough, complicating factors the metaphor appears to resolve. This collection of metaphors, with their overlapping edges and emphases, nonetheless charts the challenges of identifying how writing actually functions in and as performance. The dramatic script seems at once (like the *blueprint*, the *score*, and *software*) to imply a process of doing, to be instrumental to performance, even while the conduct of that performance is largely outside the instructions. At the same time, the dramatic script (again like the *score* and the *blueprint*) implies represented *information* to be transmitted or communicated through the process of playing. While many texts (Beckett's *Quad*) and playwrights (Bernard Shaw) may seem to aspire to this dual authority – the script as direction for instrumentalizing its *information* – performance necessarily subjects dramatic writing to use, to work, working it in the process of making something that is not writing at all: a performance. Like the complementarity principle in physics, in which mutually exclusive models are both required to explain a natural phenomenon (such as light), *software* and *information* dramatize an incoherence in our imagining of writing and performance, an incoherence labile in the *score* and *blueprint* as well. Can we *read* drama between poetry and performance without taking performance to be governed by the poetics of the writing? How can we conceive drama between poetry and performance unless we take the drama both as what the theatre displays and as the directions for displaying it?

Dramatic tools, performance technologies

We should first remember that reading itself is a mode of performance, a remaking of the text according to learned protocols of engagement, critique, interpretation. But I think we can also approach this question from another direction, considering how dramatic writing and stage performance are modeled by the relationship between tools and technologies. Tools always have an immediate purpose, are used to accomplish a specific task. Like tools, texts can be made to function in socially accredited ways, in illicit ways, and in ways that require a new technological adaptation, require us to rethink the technology and the work it accomplishes. You can use a screwdriver to drive a screw, or to open a paint can: while it wasn't designed for this purpose, the screwdriver is an efficient enough tool for opening cans, though over time this habit damages the blade and usually damages the lip of the can, too. Technologies, on the other hand, have a public, social character; technologies "are not limited objects present for control by individual wills. Instead they consist of patterns of conduct through which particular desires are literally incorporated and made manifest" (Hershock 21). As Peter Hershock argues, technologies are "value-driven and value-producing patterns of conduct" that create, depend on, and encode cultural relationships: "every new technology amounts to a novel biasing or conditioning of the quality of our interdependence" (22).

Driving a screw, opening a paint can, ballasting a sculpture, stealing a car, killing someone: each use of the tool engages a different sociability, a different conduct of technology – the hardware store, the gallery, the chop shop, the gang, the police. Much as "knives, forks, and spoons are not just strips of metal, but imply a whole system of eating behavior with respect to which each actual meal is a performance" (Feenberg 85), so too writing, particularly dramatic writing, implies several systems of behavior – reading, acting, watching – that enable us to use it to make identifiable performances, performances that can be recognized within the social technology of theatre, that *work*, to use the familiar language of the stage. Yet the known limits of a tool's significant utility, its *affordance*, do not lie solely in the tool itself. As Donald A. Norman suggests, "*affordance* refers to the perceived and actual properties of the thing"; while a tool has certain "fundamental properties," its instrumental properties may change as the perceived technologies of its use change (9).[16] Tools and technologies exist in a dynamic equilibrium; tools afford different acts in different technologies, which redefine the *affordance* of the tool. When the telephone was first produced it was not imagined as an essential element of domestic life; similarly, at its inception few people imagined the mobile phone as a personal data-music-Internet-banking-credit-photography-mapping-weather device. The cell phone emits a signal, and in Helsinki, you can use this signal to pay your fare on the tram. The tool gains this affordance, new forms of action within the reshaping of technology as social conduct.

While dramatic writing has properties related to its performance (certain words in a certain order, say), the utility of dramatic writing lies in the perception of what kinds of activity, performance, doing something, those properties might *afford* in the social technology of the theatre. The constraints of a play's licensed uses – as a tool for action composed of words – lie largely outside the text, in part because the theatre resignifies the properties of all its signs.[17] "A chair affords ('is for') support and, therefore, affords sitting. A chair can also be carried" (Norman 9). Fair enough; but in Ionesco's *The Chairs*, it's their *object-ness*, their portability, and their ability to represent an (invisible, possibly nonexistent but nonetheless *there*) audience that defines the chairs as tools. Rather than supporting the human body, in *The Chairs* the chairs afford a mysterious, menacing implication and displacement of the human from the stage. We might say that the *affordance* of the chair as "vehicle of existential panic" or "instrument for the materialist annihilation of the subject" is discovered by *The Chairs* through the scripted deployment of the chairs in the dramatic action, performed in the emerging social technology of absurdist theatre. Foreboding chairs, boys playing girls seducing boys (some playing girls) in Illyria, a pinpoint spot named Tinkerbelle: objects, bodies, even light onstage retain their offstage properties, and yet afford representational work invented by the drama. So, too, the affordance of performed dramatic language, whatever inherent properties it may have on the page, arises elsewhere.

iii. Agencies of Drama: Burke, Poetry, and Performance

We may be more concerned about the ways technologies appropriate the identity of tools when Shakespeare is at stake than when we are talking about a screwdriver or a chair. Dramatic writing has long been incorporated within several human technologies, the evolving practices of reading, literary critique, and performance practice. Plays are not merely inert items on the shelf; they are always used by the ongoing repertoire of the technologies of being human, used in ways that simultaneously enact, preserve, and transform them. The metaphors used to conceive text and performance – *score*, *blueprint*, *information*, *software* – polarize poetry and performance, largely by identifying the text with a representation to be authentically downloaded to the stage. Modern literary and performance theory, when applied to drama, has often tended to concretize and revalue this dichotomy: withdrawing the authority of the drama into the text provides the means either to celebrate the page's triumph over the stage, or to exile the drama from the creative immediacy of performance altogether. *Tools and technologies* shifts our perspective on the question of dramatic performance, suggesting a mobile, reciprocal relationship between the work writing might perform as *symbolic action* and the scene of its affordance, as *equipment for living* in the changing technology of the stage.

The terms are Kenneth Burke's. Associated in some ways with the emerging New Critics of the 1940s and 1950s (see chapter 1), Burke sometimes seems, like them, to contain the work that literature might do within the text, even while imagining actively useful, always changing purposes for writing: "Art forms like 'tragedy' or 'comedy' or 'satire' would be treated as *equipments for living*, that size up situations in various ways and in keeping with correspondingly various attitudes" ("Equipment" 304). Taking "literature as equipment for living" as a point of departure would seem promising as an avenue into dramatic performance: since writing provides formal "strategies" for dealing with various social situations, reading negotiates between the properties of literature and its deployment as a tool that does work, that enables performance in successive cultures. Yet despite the frequent invocation of Burke by more socially directed critique in the last thirty years – notably in Clifford Geertz's sense of interpreting culture as a readable text, in Stephen Greenblatt's related notion of literature as cultural poetics, and in Frank Lentricchia's sense of criticism as an act of social change – Burke's impact on drama and performance studies has been relatively slight.[18]

Nonetheless, the question that opens *A Grammar of Motives* remains provocative and productive, and reminds us of Burke's characteristic effort to mediate poetry and performance: "What is involved, when we say what people are doing and why they are doing it?" (xv).

> We shall use five terms as generating principle of our investigation. They
> are: Act, Scene, Agent, Agency, Purpose. In a rounded statement about
> motives, you must have some word that names the *act* (names what took
> place, in thought or deed), and another that names the *scene* (the back-
> ground of the act, the situation in which it occurred), also, you must
> indicate what person or kind of person (*agent*) performed the act, what
> means or instruments he used (*agency*), and the *purpose*. Men may vio-
> lently disagree about the purposes behind a given act, or about the
> character of the person who did it, or how he did it, or in what kind of
> situation he acted; or they may even insist upon totally different words
> to name the act itself. But be that as it may, any complete statement about
> motives will offer *some kind of* answers to these five questions: what was
> done (act), when or where it was done (scene), who did it (agent), how
> he did it (agency), and why (purpose). (*Grammar* xv)

Conceiving the significance of an action through *ratios* between this
pentad of terms, Burke's analysis usefully attends to "*the strategic spots
at which ambiguities necessarily arise*" in our understanding of an action.
Surprisingly, although Burke often illuminates "dramatism" through
the drama – *A Grammar of Motives* opens with a reading of Henrik
Ibsen's *An Enemy of the People* and Eugene O'Neill's *Mourning Becomes
Electra*, quickly landing on *Hamlet* – he rarely engages dramatic performance. And yet, dramatic performance implies two scenes of acting,
the fictive world it represents and the material scene of the theatre.
Dramatic performance might be captured as a double *pentad*, layering
dramatic action on its theatrical motives, as a fictive/material *scene* in
which character/actor *agents*, through the *agency* afforded by the material of the play and by the specific regimes of actor training, involve us
(watching both the play and the playing), in the duplicitous *purposes*
of the particularly ambiguous *act* of dramatic performance.

This interface between drama and theatre, writing as fictive representation and writing as equipment for doing, is where the engaging
"ambiguities" of drama "necessarily arise." Burke implies the warrant
for this double "dramatism" in the opening moments of his essay "The
Philosophy of Literary Form": "Let us suppose that I ask you: 'What
did the man say?' And that you answer: 'He said "yes."'" You still do
not know what the man said. You would not know unless you knew
more about the situation, and about the remarks that preceded his
answer" ("Philosophy" 1). The act performed by "yes" depends on the
context of performance, and Burke's reading of literary language may

well seem to anticipate J. L. Austin's sense of the *performative*, the notion that some spoken words (utterance) do not make statements (what Austin calls *constative* speech) but instead *do* something, when properly performed according to the culturally given constraints of a specific situation. Given the right *scene*, appropriate *agents* and *purposes*, saying the words "I promise" makes the promise happen, there and then. The deed is done in the saying, as – in Austin's terms – an *illocutionary act* of *performative* speech. The *performative* dimension came to overwhelm the *constative* in Austin's reading, and *performativity* has been adopted, adapted, and challenged in literary and social theory as a way to interpret language in/as action. Austin's sense of how speaking can perform an action when certain conventions have been satisfied has an obvious attraction as a means for thinking about drama as well. Much as "I do" performs an act only under the right conditions, the act performed by Gogo's "Nothing to be done" at the opening of Beckett's *Waiting for Godot* depends on actors, the audience, direction, design, the entire scene of theatre and how it uses Beckett's writing to make the play take place. And what happens, or happened, in a tiny theatre in the intellectual and cultural ferment of 1953 postwar Paris (where Gogo said, of course, "Rien à faire") is different than when the play was performed in Johannesburg, South Africa, under apartheid, by a cast of celebrated comedians at Lincoln Center in 1988, or during the Serbian siege of Sarajevo in 1993.

Austin was skeptical about stage performance, noting that "a performative utterance will, for example, be *in a peculiar* way hollow or void if said by an actor on the stage, or if introduced in a poem, or spoken in soliloquy"; utterance "in such circumstances is in special ways – intelligibly – used not seriously, but in ways *parasitic* upon its normal use – ways which fall under the doctrine of the *etiolations* of language" (22).[19] For Austin, the theatrical *scene* hollows out the *agency* of words, while for Burke the redoubling of the *scene* is what enables fictive words to *do things* as part of our cultural *equipment for living*. Despite their common interest in how words do things, Austin and Burke see words working differently as action. As Robert Wess argues, for Austin, a felicitous performance is "conformative," conforming to the rules of action, while for Burke, performance is "constitutive," remaking the rules and meaning of action anew (Wess 140).

This distinction helps us to address a significant problem in the historical development of dramatic performance. In both cases, the

changing technology of theatre defines the appropriate uses of its
verbal tools in shaping a successful performance. But while Austin's
"conformative" view suggests that dramatic performance "works"
when it hews closely to contemporary theatrical convention, Burke's
"constitutive" view implies that while dramatic performance must
avail itself of the rules in play, the act that performance *performs* is
original: "each act contains some measure of motivation that cannot be
explained simply in terms of the past, being to an extent, however tiny,
a *new thing*" (*Grammar* 65). Burke sharpens his difference with Austin
and clarifies the *agency* of words in the *scene* of theatre in the essay
"Words as Deeds." Noting that the US "Constitution, as a logical
'instrument,' was 'enacted' in a 'scene,' or situation, quite different
from the circumstances in which the Constitution, with its amend-
ments and often innovative judicial interpretations, is operative as
enactment now," Burke asks, "In this respect can the same utterances,
as a speech act, have the same 'meaning' they had when first declared?"
("Words as Deeds" 149). The apparent prescriptions even of revered
texts – the Constitution, *Hamlet* – are altered in their enactment: the
dialectical tension between the text as *agency* (an instrument for organizing, prioritizing, and implementing a set of values in action) and its
use in an unanticipated *scene* enlivens theatrical performance, and the
Supreme Court, too. Enacted in new *scenes* of theatrical behavior, dramatic poetry is – in another striking metaphor – the parry to the long-
gone thrust of its original environment of performance:

> But a *written text* is like the parry to a thrust. The thrust comes from
> the "context of situation" out of which the text arose. And whereas the
> thrusts of history keep undergoing changes of position and direction,
> the written text lacks corresponding immediate pliancy. The written text
> makes its particular parry statuesquely permanent, whereas the context
> of situation into which it has survived may have put forth a thrust that
> calls for a quite different parry. So I waver a bit concerning the extent to
> which we can recover the original "self-contained" meaning of a text that
> arose from a "context of situation" greatly different from ours. ("Words
> as Deeds" 152)

Burke's wavering here sounds familiar: while we may delude ourselves into believing that reading the page allows an unmediated
contact with the original scene of the poem's composition, and so with
the symbolic action it performs, theatrical performance necessarily

interrupts this fantasy. A performance must find ways to make the play's "parry" work, do work, *act*, even when we thrust at it from odd angles, with unforeseen weaponry.[20]

We are, now, partly as a consequence of Burke, more aware of the instrumental character of writing, how its *agency* changes in the changing *scenes* of its use. Shakespeare's comic play with the self-evidently seductive ambiguity of gender and sexuality was literally and figuratively rewritten in the nineteenth century to reinforce and normalize a specific politics of gender and sexual difference (Burke's "Men may violently disagree" has already alerted us to the problem of gender in the scene of Burke's own work); generations of schoolchildren in Britain's colonies – India, Nigeria – learned to admire the British landscape, and imagine themselves as admirably British subjects, through an enforced appreciation of the unseen, imaginary "host, of golden daffodils" of Wordsworth's "I wandered lonely as a cloud." Dramatic performance hovers the line between conformist and constitutive: it uses conventional means and often writing that has gained a kind of stability and familiarity through cultural reiteration to frame an act that at once depends on those conventions and transcends them. Finally, though, Burke cannot quite admit to an alteration of the artwork by its use, by the discovery of unanticipated *agencies* in the unexpected *scenes* of its performance (Wordsworth neither imagined nor intended his poem to become a set-piece either of colonial education or of its postcolonial critique). For this reason, as he suggests in alluding to the narrative logic of Constantin Stanislavski's direction of *Othello* ("in our novel-minded age" Stanislavski's methods provide the actor "something more substantial and reliable than his mood and temperament"), Burke is reluctant to grant constitutive power to the stage. So far as *"the analysis of the playwright's invention is concerned*, our proposed way of seeing the agent in terms of the over-all action would be required by a dramaturgic analysis of the characters" alone, rather than of *character* as an effect of acting ("*Othello*" 86–7).

Burke enacts the dialectical tension between tools and technologies: the tool has properties, but some of its affordance will be discovered as new *scenes* and different *agents* imagine innovative *agencies* and *purposes* for it, different ways of playing with and through it. Burke's troubled sense of the uses of literature as behavior remains unresolved, looming behind many of the key questions of contemporary performance studies: the sense of art as a process in which "implicit social processes become explicit" ("Twelve" 308); the notion of identity as *"mystification"* (308), and as emerging "by relation to groups" (311) in ways that challenge purely *"individualistic* concepts"; the "style" of performing as a means of identification (310).[21] Burke rightly proposes that the *"difference between the symbolic drama and the drama of living is a difference between imaginary obstacles and real obstacles,"* noting that *"the imaginary obstacles of symbolic drama must, to have the relevance necessary for the producing of effects upon audiences, reflect the real obstacles of living drama"* (312). In terms of dramatic performance, though, these "obstacles" are embodied in the twofold *scene* of theatre; they're both thematic/representational and processual/presentational. The symbolic action of the drama must represent thematic obstacles that can be made visibly problematic to us, the contemporary audience. At the same time, while the specific obstacles represented in a play may be distant from our everyday lives (is this ghost really my father? will Godot never arrive?), the performance must tactically engage us in grasping and working through those obstacles as part of our attention to the play, defining them in and with an evocative, contemporary, theatrically effective idiom.

Burke devised the pentad as an instrument for analyzing events in social life; as such, it also provides an instrument for analyzing the social act of dramatic performance, the act of representing the drama in the material scene of the stage. There "is implicit in the quality of a scene the quality of the action that is to take place within it. [...] Thus, when the curtain rises to disclose a given stage-set, this stage-set contains, simultaneously, implicitly, all that the narrative is to draw out as a sequence, explicitly" (*Grammar* 6–7). Burke's sense of the stage here is perhaps more inflected by Ibsen than by Shakespeare or Beckett or solo performance, but it's this sense of the rhetorical interplay between the set onstage and the setting of the play that animates dramatic performance, the assertion of likeness (what Burke calls "consubstantiality") between things that are different for suasive purposes. For the stage-set not only contains the qualities of the dramatic action, it also contains the qualities of the theatrical action. For the duration of the performance, it will be the purpose of the theatrical action to *identify* (make visible) the dramatic action *to* us by *identifying* (claiming its likeness, its consubstantiality) with the dramatic action, an action that nonetheless retains its distinctive (substantial) difference. The two *scenes* of dramatic performance are "both joined and separate, at once a distinct substance and constubstantial" (*Rhetoric* 21).[22]

Burke's discussion of *identification* should not be confused with the usual way we use the word "identify" in talking about theatre ("I really identified with Othello when he strangled Desdemona" – maybe Burke points up the obstacles to this understanding of identification in tragedy). "Metaphysically, a thing is identified by its *properties*" (*Rhetoric* 23), and drama is performed to us by the ways its "properties" are identified with and through the practice of the stage. The style of a given performance is the means by which the drama is made visible, claimed as "consubstantial" with the material events and practices of performance. In terms of acting, for instance, an urgently psychodynamic approach like Stanislavski's tends to identify actor and character through a principle of psychological and emotional likeness: using "emotion memory" the actor *identifies* (reveals) Hedda Gabler through the "consubstantiality" her performance claims between Ibsen's *"dancing of an attitude"* and the actor's own immediate, living feeling ("Philosophy" 8). "Emotion memory" is the actor's *agency* for using (*identifying*) that other *agency* of the performance, the role of "Hedda Gabler," a means of transforming the dramatic instrument, words on the page, into a specific kind of performance. A different mode of performance will deploy different identifications with and through the *agency*. When Vsevolod Meyerhold produced *Hedda Gabler* in 1906, he deployed a more symbolist rhetoric. The stage was "muffled in lace which flowed in wide streams along the sides. Vines decorated the veranda. The fairy-tale tapestry, the strange tables and chairs, the edge of the white piano covered by a real snowdrift of white fur into which Hedda would dip her rosy fingers as into snow," Hedda herself clothed in a "dress like sea water, like the scales of a sea snake" (Yu Beliaev and F. F. Komissarzhevskii, qtd. Rudnitsky 88). Here, the *scene* claims a "consubstantiality" with many of the poetic images of the play, the "vine leaves," the frozen isolation of provincial Norway, and perhaps more generally with Hedda's serpentine seductiveness. *Hedda Gabler* is a tool in different technologies of performance, technologies affording different kinds of work. The play's *agency* emerges among the *agents*, *agencies*, and *purposes* of the theatrical *scene* of its reconstitution as action.

Writing as agency: "Antony in Behalf of the Play"

Burke's admittedly *tour de force* essay (see "Foreword") on Shakespeare's *Julius Caesar*, "Antony in Behalf of the Play," begins to model some of the attractions – and challenges – of reading the play as *agency* in the *scene* of theatre. Approving a tendency to "consider literature not as a creator's device for self-expression, nor as an audience's device for amusement or instruction, but as a communicative relationship between writer and audience, with both parties actively participating" ("Antony" 329), Burke takes Antony's funeral oration – where the character speaks to the Roman public while the actor speaks to the theatrical public – as a paradigmatic site of the play's rhetoric, its "processes of appeal" (330). What makes this essay powerful and effective, however, is precisely its slippage of *ratios*. Burke impersonates the fictive *agent* of the play, who masterfully manipulates the material *scene* of performance. Granted, there's little specifically theatrical in the essay: no actual performance intrudes, and the theatrical *scene* is an imagined performance at the Globe, though Burke/Antony cannily identifies his audience with the imagined orientation of modern theatregoers (Brutus "takes on the nobility that comes of being good for private enterprise" 335). At the same time, by crossing the dramatic and the theatrical pentads, Burke touches on the dialectical character of dramatic performance, which typically depends on this exchange of registers, at times suppressing it and at others – such as Antony's oration – forcing it into view.

The purpose of "Antony in Behalf of the Play" is to suggest the second-person aspect of dramatic writing, using the means of fiction to enact suasion in the here-and-now of the theatre (or at least in the theatre-of-the-mind).

> *Antony*: Friends, Romans, countrymen … one – two – three syllables: hence, in this progression, a magic formula. "Romans" to fit the conditions of the play; "countrymen" the better to identify the play-mob with the mob in the pit – for we are in the Renaissance, at that point when Europe's vast national integers are taking shape, and all the wisdom that comes of the body is to be obscured by our putting in place of the body the political corpus … (330)

Although he doesn't address the actor's ways and means here, Burke's thumbnail metrical analysis – the syllabification (one, two, three) straining against the pentameter – identifies the power of the line. "Threeness" is a magic formula, a formula that works its magic as speech, orally. Applying the lessons of Burke's "Musicality in Verse," we might notice not only the displaced alliteration in the line, but how the sound pattern *r-m/n* is repeated thrice as well. It's not only a "magic formula" rhythmically, but its sound rhetorically compacts "fRieNds" and "countRy-MeN" into "RoMaNs." One, two, three; three into one: nothing's more magic than that. Although the "charm's *threeness*" (331) may be culturally located, it illustrates and enables the actor to put into action "the wisdom that comes of the body" (its pleasures are auditory), but also the frailty of the body as well, its readiness to be charmed – or conned.

What's most problematic here is the claim "All that I as Antony do to this play-mob, as a character-recipe I do to you." The recipe is clearly designed by "your author" to manipulate the audience: "He thinks you are as easy to be played upon as a pipe" (331). Burke presents this manipulation purely as a function of the relationship of author to reader: the "character-recipe" produces this result more or less without allusion to a performance, as effectively for readers as for spectators. Yet Burke's decision to write as, to *play* Antony in the essay, presents dramatic writing as an instrument not for representing a fictive world in front of an audience, but for enabling a specific kind of relationship, a certain kind of participation in an event, an event which identifies its participants "relationally." Like an actor, Burke speaks through "Antony," uses the role of "Antony" in ways that accomplish his own designs. We, too, are part of the recipe of the event, "actors and acters" who "establish identity by relation to groups" through the mediated duplicity of performance ("Twelve" 311).

As his remarks on Stanislavski's *Othello* suggest, Burke is little concerned with acting: the specificities of Antony's or Brutus' or Cassius' embodiment are beside the point. But in reframing the drama as *agency* – a means of constructing identifications, positions, identities – Burke transforms the *scene* of drama from the representation of a fictive Rome to the implied relations of theatre. The analysis of how the play structures the audience's appetite for blood and the simultaneous desire to be excused from culpability – "For such reasons as these you are willing to put a knife through the ribs of Caesar. Still, you are sorry for Caesar" (332) – follows a strategy T. S. Eliot had already explored in *Murder in the Cathedral*, when his twelfth-century music-hall knights address the modern audience in Canterbury Cathedral, having just murdered Thomas: "We have served your interests; we merit your applause; and if there is any guilt whatever in the matter, you must share it with us" (*Murder* 218). Or, as Burke/Antony puts it, "You have been made conspirators in a murder" (334). More recently, Anne

Carson has located the impulse of tragedy itself in a similar dialectic, translating Aristotle's fear and pity, or Burke's/Antony's murderous sympathy as the audience's rage and grief, "It is a theater of sacrifice in the true sense. Violence occurs; through violence we are intimate with some characters onstage in an exorbitant way for a brief time; that's all it is" (7, 9).

Much of Burke's concern in "Antony in Behalf of the Play" is to illustrate the notion of the character-recipe, which works its way out in the various "principles" identified with different characters and how they appeal to us and so enable our identification within the play's complex structure of culpability and compromise. As Burke's role-playing of "Antony" suggests, the character-recipe is a rhetorical, implicitly theatrical notion, and leads directly to the sense of theatre as *communion*. Like the character-recipe, *communion* also enables us to think through the represented events of the drama in terms of the sustaining identifications of theatre. The action of *Julius Caesar* not only depends on a series of ritual moments, "rites of communion, whereby one man's interests were made identical with another" (336), it insists on them in the moment of their breaching. Caesar commands Antony, running naked in the Lupercal ceremony, to touch his wife Calpurnia on the way, thereby to "Shake off" the "sterile curse." Taking Caesar's part, Antony fertilizes Calpurnia, even as the rebellious tribunes are disrobing the "images [...] decked with ceremonies" (1.2.11; 1.1.63–4). More centrally, Burke notes that Caesar's communion with his "angel" Brutus is sealed in blood as it is broken, *Et tu, Brute?* (3.1.76). But while the play is full of broken rites, Burke argues that Antony's oration, unlike Brutus', enables *communion* with and among the audience by seductively offering us the illusion of choice. While Brutus' speech told us "to choose, then stated the issue in such a way that there was no choice" (we all love Rome, so who will object?), Antony works to "awaken in you the satisfactions of authorship, as you hear me say one thing and know I mean another" (338). Disclosing the narrative of the conspiracy in such a way that we enact a subversive communion by feeling ourselves to choose to go the way Antony (and Burke) is cannily leading us, each repetition of "Brutus is an honorable man" furthers our suasion by demanding our identification as conspirators, as off-stage agents of the act Antony now sets in motion: "Now let it work. Mischief, thou art afoot. / Take thou what course thou wilt" (3.2.249–50). Charmed, to be sure.

This is a communion of blood, and the play immediately seals it with the delectable sacrifice of Cinna the poet. Burke rightly pinpoints the ambivalence of the scene, its savage comedy straining in two directions at once: "Tear him for his bad verses." For Burke, this scene signally exemplifies the communion between author and reader, "as our Great Demagogue continues to manipulate your minds" (343). But in the theatre, it's also a moment that summons the audience's performance, laughter witnessing our involuntary, physical involvement in the stage event, our identification – however resisted, knowing, or critical – with the actors' effective, brutal, play.[23] "Antony in Behalf of the Play" charts a course, without quite setting out on the journey to locate the rhetoric of drama relative to the rhetoric of theatre. The text is clearly an instrument for suasion, but the material means of that suasion in the theatre – its *scene* and *agents* – remain offstage for Burke, however much his critical performance as Antony might entail them.

Nonetheless, Burke suggests a direction for rethinking the practice of reading drama in relation to the technologies of theatre:

a. Dramatic writing is simultaneously representational and instrumental; all aspects of its verbal style and represented "fiction" are simultaneously capable of being seized as *agency* for doing, for making performance.

b. The *agency* of dramatic writing, and so the *act* it constitutes, will change with the *agent, purpose,* and *scene* in which it is performed.

c. Reading is one means of instrumentalizing writing as *agency* in a specific *scene* of performance.

d. Acting is one means of instrumentalizing writing as *agency* in a specific *scene* of performance.

e. The perceived *agency* of a text – its affordance – is shaped by the *scene, agents,* and *purposes,* what we might call the *technology,* of its use. The sense of a script's actual and potential *agency* is not a function of the text-as-tool, but of the *scene* in which it is performed, or in which we imagine it to perform.

f. Different *scenes,* different kinds of theatre, will use the drama to perform different kinds of *act;* uses afforded in one theatre may not appear in another. The writing, the text, cannot determine how it should be used or what it might mean, affordances arising in relation to specific technologies of performance.

Burke enables us to grasp some of the challenges posed by drama, its framing of a mutual contingency of poetry and performance. To the extent that dramatic technologies – gesture, behavior, reading – have a kind of *longue durée*, we may be able to feel and even to assert a kind of continuity in the work of dramatic performance over time. To the extent that these technologies change, we have only two choices: either to find new affordances in the text that enable us to use it to do new work, or to consign the drama to a forlorn heap of plays echoing in the dustbin.

What is the consequence of imagining the flux of poetics and performance along the axis of *agency*? What are the mutual affordances of writing in the practices of performance? The following chapter sets the dual identity of drama alongside the predominant critique of literary genre in the 1940s and 1950s, a paradigm for "understanding drama" surprisingly extended in the fashioning of performance studies in the 1980s. But we will also chart an alternative line of critique, stemming from the same dissatisfaction with a "literary" conception of dramatic performance driving performance studies. This critique, though, far from forsaking dramatic performance as the instrument of the hegemony of writing, instead imagines a more dynamic relationship between writing and performance, and trains our attention on some of the attractions and consequences of framing the drama between poetry and performance.

Chapter 1

From Poetry to Performance

DRAMATIC: *Having the quality of drama, that is, presented by means of characters in action and marked by the tension of conflict. Does* not *mean* surprising, unusual, shocking, striking, coincidental, *or* melodramatic. *See* theatrical.

THEATRICAL: *Literally, characteristic of the theatre. Although it might appear to be synonymous with* dramatic, *which is often mistakenly used for it (and indeed "good theatre" is always dramatic),* theatrical *has come to mean artificially contrived effects, implausible situations introduced merely because they are "striking" or spectacular, contrasts and clashes which exist for their own sake rather than as the logical products of theme and character. The theatrical situation is melodramatic rather than dramatic; it is external and showy, and often coincidental; it is "sensational" – for instance, breaking up the wedding ceremony before a church full of guests. Theatrical speech is characterized by inappropriate elevation, excessive emphasis, clichés, pompousness instead of inherent seriousness, rant instead of emotional force, the highfalutin instead of the truly poetic. Hence, a "theatrical manner" suggests exaggeration, self-consciousness, posturing. A person of perception will dismiss as "theatrical" what a naïve observer is likely to consider "so dramatic."*
Cleanth Brooks and Robert B. Heilman, *from the Glossary to*
Understanding Drama *(500, 504)*

The dramatist not only charts out a plan of procedure, he conceives and realizes a work of art which is already complete—except for technical reproduction—in his head ...
Eric Bentley, The Playwright as Thinker *(241)*

How to read drama? We can certainly read dramatic writing, though perhaps that's the answer to a different question. Drama has been read, of course, and the critical history of the past century witnesses the challenges of reading drama between poetry and performance, as dramatic writing has not only been the target for a range of interpretive strategies (feminist, Marxist, psychoanalytic, New Historical readings of Shakespeare, for instance), but has marked the interface between disciplines and the critical practices distinguishing them. If at mid-century the externality of dramatic writing, its reliance on theatrical means for its realization off the page, seemed to require a properly "literary" attention to the properties of "the text" to the exclusion of the stage, by the 1980s and 1990s the emerging field of performance studies worked to reverse this polarity, finding the scripted character of dramatic performance to violate the essentially unruly, resistant nature of performance itself. Since Aristotle, the dialectic between language and spectacle, writing and performing, has sustained inquiry into the drama, animating the strictures of neoclassical decorum, informing the iconoclasm of Nietzsche and Artaud, and marking the exploration of theatrical practice from Stanislavski to Grotowski, Bogart, and beyond. The prosecution of disciplinary inquiry a means to institutionalize the humanities in the modern university provides a sustaining framework for the narrower question of the drama's challenge to poetry and performance.

In *Professing Performance*, for example, Shannon Jackson provides a "genealogy" of the conception of "performance" in the modern academy that necessarily tracks the interlocking literary, theatrical, and performance studies engagements with "performance" – often with dramatic performance – across a wide horizon of institutional, critical, and disciplinary history. For Jackson, "drama" is rightly only part of the story of how academic disciplines and the institutions sustaining them have incorporated "performance." Taking the emergence of performance studies in the 1970s and 1980s to epitomize a more sweeping "transition from literary to cultural studies" (98), Jackson segregates the literary from the cultural or performative elements of the drama as part of "a drama-to-culture genealogy" (94). Nevertheless, while this genealogy accounts for the invention and elaboration of "performance" as an object and means of study, it also frames the challenges of reading drama as largely surpassed. Tracking the "stops and starts" of this genealogy, Jackson notices that drama studies of the mid-twentieth century legitimated the study of drama by incorporating it to the methods of the emerging canons of literary New Criticism (see 88), and at the same time proposes suggestive avatars (Francis Fergusson's invocation of "ritual," Raymond Williams's "structures of feeling") of the later achievement of cultural studies. And yet, while a more energetic and theoretically informed investment in the material work and cultural poetics of performance has enlarged and redirected performance critique (including the critique of dramatic performance), the "insights, defenses, illuminations, and confusions of mid-century drama criticism" (94) continue to haunt us, most visibly in the ways we read or misread the drama.

The modern disciplines of drama are predicated on a dichotomy between poetry and performance; reading the potential *agency* of drama in the double *scenes* of page and stage traces a slippery interface between these legitimating notions of value. In the immediate postwar period, the desire to incorporate drama, particularly modern drama, to the canons of literary study was beset by two related anxieties: how to define the purely literary character of the drama, and reciprocally how to distinguish the literary drama from theatre. Cleanth Brooks and Robert Heilman's *Understanding Drama* (1945), capitalizing on the success of Brooks's controversial *Understanding Poetry* of 1938, prescribed a means of reading plays through the practices of the New Criticism, promoting an ideological and critical practice that, however ostensibly disowned in literary studies today, however apparently displaced by "the transition from literary to cultural studies," continues to inform attitudes toward dramatic writing and performance. Moreover, in defining the literary character of drama, Brooks and Heilman necessarily conceive its potential use, its appropriate *agency*, modeling stage performance as a derivative "interpretation" of the dramatic text. This "interpretive" strategy for rehabilitating the drama was echoed by other, more theatrically oriented writers of the period: by Eric Bentley, prominent theatre critic, Brander Matthews Professor of Drama at Columbia, and indefatigable promoter of Bertolt Brecht's work in America, in *The Playwright as Thinker* (1946; 2nd ed. 1955); by Francis Fergusson's *Idea of a Theater* (1949), which deployed a blend of "ritual" theory derived from the Cambridge School with the critical strategies of the Moscow Art Theatre to open a specifically "histrionic" approach to understanding drama; and by *Drama from Ibsen to Eliot* (1952), which launched Raymond Williams's effort to track the conventional "structures of feeling" in literary and cultural work.[1] For all their sometimes vexed enthusiasm for theatre, these studies advanced a "literary" understanding of the *agency* of drama by tactically foreclosing the drama's scene of performance.

Performance, however, refused to be forsaken, even within literary studies, giving rise to a dynamic engagement with performance-oriented critique of Aeschylus, Shakespeare, Ibsen, Chekhov, Beckett, among others. But the reinvention of "performance," as an object, means, and mode of dissemination of critical study, owes itself largely to the energetic emergence of the "antidiscipline" of performance studies in the 1970s. While performance studies rightly eschews a sense of "dramatic performance" as definitive of performance itself, in many ways its representation of drama prolongs the critical inertia of the New Criticism. As the critics of the 1940s and 1950s had projected a "literary" sense of drama against the tawdry stage, performance studies urged a sense of the sedative authority of the text (sometimes called "text-based theatre" or "text theatre") to distinguish dramatic perform-ance from the transformative mobility of authentic performance. And yet while performance studies has tended to marginalize dramatic theatre as an overtly authoritarian form of performance, an alternative trajectory of critique has worked to situate the practice of dramatic performance as a more provocative field of engagement. Opening out from a subtle debate between Richard Schechner and Michael Goldman in the early 1970s, the second phase of this chapter examines the consequences of this "interpretive" paradigm, how it has been both prolonged and contested in the contemporary critique of dramatic performance. Here we will consider how some of the critical notions framing performance in contemporary performance studies – *archive* and *repertoire, restored behavior, surrogation, disappearance, liminality, effi-cacy* – have been redeployed in the critique of dramatic performance.[2] Again placing four prominent studies – Herbert Blau, *The Audience* (1990), Stanton B. Garner, Jr., *Bodied Spaces: Phenomenology and Performance in Contemporary Drama* (1994), Benjamin Bennett, *All Theater Is Revolutionary Theater* (2005), and Hans-Thies Lehmann, *Postdramatic Theatre* (1999; English translation 2006) – in dialogue with performance studies, we can track the question of the *agency* of dramatic writing and its (interpretive) implications for embodied action, the two issues that seem to set dramatic studies across this not-so-permeable disciplinary frontier.

i. Dramatic Performance and its Discontents: The New Criticism

> *Whoever wishes to share the less exhilarating sensations of an Egyptologist rifling a tomb should read the drama books of forty, thirty, even twenty years ago. It is a chastening thought for the writer on drama today.*
>
> Eric Bentley, *Foreword (1946),* The Playwright as Thinker *(xix)*

The teaching of drama, including Shakespeare, as part of modern literatures in English-speaking universities dates to the nineteenth century, marked in the United States by the appointment of Brander Matthews as the first Professor of Drama at Columbia University in 1900, and in the United Kingdom of A. C. Bradley as Professor of Poetry at Oxford in 1901. Nonetheless, it's fair to say that the disciplinary and critical tensions sustaining the study of drama took their current shape in the immediate aftermath of World War II, with the efforts to formalize principles for the reading and teaching of literature, developed in the 1930s in I. A. Richards's *Practical Criticism* (1929), disseminated in somewhat more schematic form in the US as the New Criticism, and apotheosized in a sense in Northrop Frye's *Anatomy of Criticism* (1957). The New Criticism strove, as John Crowe Ransom pointed out in 1941, to develop an "ontological account of poetry," a critical practice capable of defining and of responding objectively to the distinctive forms of poetic language (*New* 281). How did the New Criticism assimilate drama to the quintessentially literary conception of the poem?

Drama, poetry, and "interpretation"

New Criticism found drama particularly challenging to its paradigmatic critical practice, the "close reading" of the poem's verbal order, and its programmatic rejection of an appeal to social, cultural, or biographical history as a means to understanding poetry. The appearance of dramatic writing in print – all those prefixes and parentheses, exits, entrances, and stage directions – plainly gestured to a stagey life elsewhere, a life in the theatre traced on the page of the dramatic poem.

There had been shrewd efforts to integrate a sense of the stage to the practices of reading drama, in Harley Granville-Barker's brilliant *Prefaces to Shakespeare* (written by the pre-eminent British stage director of both Shakespeare and new drama, published in several volumes from the late 1920s through the 1940s), or more intermittently in G. Wilson Knight's pursuit of a spatialized "interpretation" of Shakespearean drama (again, many of his most celebrated books were published in the 1930s). This reciprocal understanding of drama and theatre was also pursued by the major poets of the era, who searchingly experimented with the ways poetry might reshape both the conventions of performance and the experience of performed drama: W. B. Yeats's plays for dancers; W. H. Auden's *Paid on Both Sides* and *The Dance of Death*, as well as the verse dramas he wrote in collaboration with Christopher Isherwood; the brilliant, pawky plays of Wallace Stevens, inspired more by Dada than by any visible mode of theatricality; the theoretically ambitious (though perhaps theatrically illegible) plays of Gertrude Stein, arguably the foundational dramatic writing of the American theatrical avant-garde in the last half of the twentieth century.[3]

"There is no official decree or supernatural intervention which graciously dispenses the theater from the demands of theoretical reflection": Roland Barthes's pronouncement of 1956 falls athwart the attitudes of Anglo-American critics of that decade, working to locate the drama as the theatre's reflective center ("Tasks" 73). The major literary critics of drama of the late 1940s and 1950s all express a characteristic concern, less about the critical impoverishment of theatre than about the challenges of assimilating drama to the values of literature and literary studies. As Bentley puts it, "The most revolutionary tenet to be advanced in this book is this: the drama can be taken seriously" (*Thinker* xx). Raymond Williams's introductory essay to *Drama from Ibsen to Eliot* makes the point more directly: "My criticism is, or is intended to be, literary criticism, [...] a working experiment in the application of practical criticism methods to modern dramatic literature" (*Ibsen to Eliot* 12). By the second revision of this book, now under the title *Drama from Ibsen to Brecht*, Williams refined the question of "whether literary criticism of the drama is appropriate" (*Ibsen to Eliot* 13), reframing the notion of "convention" as a "structure of feeling" that enables the individual work to be understood within "authentic communities of works of art," and communities of response as well

(*Ibsen to Brecht* 17). Even assuming the importance of "literature," drama could only provoke anxiety: Brooks and Heilman open the critical introduction of *Understanding Drama* by pointing to the peculiar "Problems of the Drama" (*Understanding Drama* iii).

Barthes had the example of the Berliner Ensemble performing in Paris; as we have seen, Burke offered a quasi-Brechtian alternative, a reading practice that situated poetry as a means of action, a tactical gambit in our larger *equipment for living*. Yet even the most sympathetic of the New Critics found Burke's approach too extrinsic, turning outside the poem to the "lively" sciences of psychoanalysis and sociology to find what "had better not have been there" (Ransom, "Address" 143). Imagining the theatrical function of dramatic writing in the Anglo-American tradition emerges at mid-century from a surprising quarter: the utopian attractions of "poetic drama." To the critics of the 1940s, "poetic drama" promised a more effective, thoroughgoing *agency* for language in the theatre, and a more critical theatricality as well. Williams captured the significance of this project in his title, suggestively substituting *Brecht* for *Eliot* in the second edition, and it's Eliot (rather than Brecht, Artaud, or the still-unknown Beckett) who stood as the critical paradigm for a renovated dramatic performance.

From the earliest of his dramatic monologues through the "many voices" of *The Waste Land*, Eliot's poetry had been scrupulously involved with drama, and his invocation of the plays of Webster and others, in conjunction with his own critical work on Elizabethan playwrights, inspired academic study in that field much as his interest in the "metaphysical poets" spurred widespread interest in John Donne and George Herbert. But in both popular (his 1922 obituary of the music-hall singer Marie Lloyd) and more erudite ("Poetry and Drama," 1951) essays from the 1920s on, Eliot attended to the potential for dramatic performance to restore the theatre's role as a socially engaged and engaging ritual, however etiolated ritual had become in popular culture – "O O O O that Shakespeherian rag" (*The Waste Land*). In "Tradition and the Individual Talent" (1919) Eliot defined tradition – the "existing monuments form an ideal order among themselves" (38) – in ways that underwrote the New Critical isolation of poetic analysis from contextual explanation, and perhaps "helped to define the category of the literary in specifically anti-performative terms" (Walker, "Why?" 154). Yet this sense of poetry strained against Eliot's emerging program to use dramatic writing to orchestrate and revitalize the waning social efficacy of performance.* Eliot's formal program is reminiscent of Burke's rhetorical one, and as Eliot became involved in writing plays, he recognized the variety of ways writing articulates with and in embodiment. In *Murder in the Cathedral* (1935), the Chorus' rhythmic chanting, Thomas's sermon, and the Knights' Shavian apology afford different ways of producing, attending to, and attending within dramatic performance.

As Eliot suggested in 1944, "a poet, trying to write something for the theatre, discovers first of all that it is not only a question of labouring to acquire the technique of the theatre: it is a question of a different kind of poetry, a different kind of verse, than the kind for which his previous experience has qualified him." For Eliot, poetic drama should be driven by a particular kind of action, to "remove the surface of things, expose the underneath, or the inside, of the natural surface appearance." Like other modern avant-garde revolutions – Dada, surrealism, expressionism, epic theatre, theatre of the absurd – poetic drama impelled both a rejection of naturalist theatre and a consequent refiguration of the relationship between stage and audience through the means of drama. Regardless of its spiritual thematics, this drama made specific demands as performance: "So the poet with ambitions of the theatre, must discover the laws, both of another kind of verse and of another kind of drama. The difficulty of the author is also the difficulty of the audience. Both have to be trained [...]" ("Introduction" n.p. [8–9]). Eliot's means – the adaptation of Greek drama, the Chorus in *The Family Reunion*, the festive "ritual" of *The Cocktail Party* – may now seem clumsy (though this strategy has been revived many times since, notably in Charles Mee's brilliant *Orestes* and *Big Love*), but they articulate a commitment to drama within a transformational sense of theatrical purpose, the pressure of living theatre that had, perhaps, not quite expired with Marie Lloyd: "The working man who went to the music-hall and saw Marie Lloyd and joined in the chorus was himself performing part of the act; he was engaged in that collaboration of the audience with the artist which is necessary in all art and most obviously in dramatic art" ("Marie Lloyd" 174). In "Poetry and Drama," Eliot confessed that he may merely have been chasing a mirage, the "mirage of the perfection of verse drama, which would be a design of human action and of words, such as to present at once the two aspects of dramatic and of musical order" (146). Perhaps Eliot was merely looking in the wrong direction: the mirage of a play renovating the design of action and words, the dramatic and musical order materialized the following season, on the stage of a tiny Parisian theatre, under the prosaic title *En Attendant Godot*.

Many of the most verbally innovative plays since Beckett – Sam Shepard's *Tooth of Crime*, Peter Barnes's *The Bewitched*, Suzan-Lori Parks's *The Death of the Last Black Man in the Whole Entire World*, Sarah Kane's *4.48 Psychosis*, to say nothing of the reinvention of Stein – have used writing to demand different forms of theatrical embodiment, to reorchestrate the possibilities of performance. Indeed, we shouldn't dismiss the provocative theatricality of poetic drama too readily. In the decade or so before its landmark 1963 production of Kenneth H. Brown's *The Brig*, the Living Theatre staged productions of Paul Goodman's plays, Stein's *Doctor Faustus Lights the Lights*, Eliot's *Sweeney Agonistes*, John Ashbery's *The Heroes*, Auden's *The Age of Anxiety*, William Carlos Williams's *Many Loves*, and Jackson Mac Low's *The Marrying Maiden*: perhaps poetic drama was avant-garde after all.

Poetic drama imagines a recalibration of the *agency* of writing in the process of theatre. To critics in the 1950s, Eliot provided a point of repair for rethinking the practices of writing, staging, and reading drama. Raymond Williams parallels the premiere of Ibsen's *Catilina* in 1850, written when "the drama, in most European countries other than France, was at perhaps its lowest ebb in six centuries" (*Ibsen to Eliot* 11), with the opening of Eliot's *The Cocktail Party* in London a century later: verse drama from *Peer Gynt* through Irish and English experiments to Eliot, provides a "necessary" element of the revolution of modern drama, in which "the whole art of the theatre was radically reconsidered and revised" (11). Eliot's example also confirms that "performance is an essential condition of drama": "Mr. Eliot has pointed out that to consider plays as existing simply as literature, without reference to their function on the stage, is part of the same fallacy as to say that plays need not be literature at all. No separation of drama and literature is reasonable" (16). For Williams, Eliot's achievement, like Yeats's, was to imagine a "theatre in which language should not be subordinate, as throughout the Victorian theatre it had been, to spectacle or the visual elements of acting" (209). Poetic drama imagines a recalibration of the *agency* of writing in the process of theatre. Bentley, too, taking up "the old and vexed theme of the reading of plays as opposed to seeing them in the theater," notes that while there is certainly "such a thing as undramatic poetry, as the theatricalists always remind us," there is also *"dramatic* poetry" – not to be confused with "Closet dramas, the dramas which supremely are offered to us as dramatic reading matter, are seldom good poems of any kind and therefore are seldom good reading" (*Thinker* 241–2). For Bentley, while Eliot was "provoked by the antipoetic William Archer into reaffirming that poetry is not necessarily undramatic," Bertolt Brecht "goes yet further in denying that lyric and narrative verse are necessarily out of place on the stage" (243).

Taking Eliot's dramatic writing as the inspiration for a renewed theatricality, Williams and Bentley stake out a complex position toward and against the tenets of the New Criticism: theatre should be transformed by its poetry, but the analysis of drama must be confined to the text itself. Fergusson opens *The Idea of a Theater* by invoking Eliot's "Tradition and the Individual Talent," and expressing "a more particular debt to Eliot" as "one of very few contemporary writers in English who are directly concerned with drama as a serious art" (*Idea* 8). And while Eliot, "coming to the drama from lyric poetry, starts rather with the Idealist conception of art as formally prior to the theater itself," he has nonetheless "surveyed the terrain" and "raised the crucial questions." For although Fergusson notoriously points out that drama "is not primarily a composition in the verbal medium" (*Idea* 8), he finds the "close textual analysis" of the New Criticism (he mentions John Crowe Ransom, R. P. Blackmur, and William Empson, alongside Kenneth Burke) essential to assessing "the dramatic basis of poetry," an assessment obstructed only by the fact that we "lack a theater" capable of animating the findings of such analysis in stage practice. Fergusson's invocation of the dramatic theatre's "roots in myth and ritual, its implication in the whole culture of the time" (9) evidently extends Eliot's use of the Cambridge School, though its participation in a genealogy cognate with Antonin Artaud's visceral impact on experimental theatre, or with Victor Turner's foundational role in locating a liminal/liminoid "ritual process" as the site of performance studies, is considerably more gestural than actual.[5] For Fergusson's brilliant readings of plays from *Oedipus the King* to *Murder in the Cathedral* erect a disembodied theatre on the sturdy framework of the play's "analogies of action" (236–7), a principle of the organic thematic unity of the drama meant to guide the ritual realization of theatre. While Fergusson's sense of a theatre's renewed implication in "the whole culture of the time" recalls Eliot's ritualized music-hall and jibes with Burke as well, what it most clearly anticipates is the shocking clarity with which the yet-unknown playwrights of the "theatre of the absurd" (the phrase coined by Martin Esslin in 1961) would rewrite the terms of dramatic representation, and so reimagine relations between writing, stage, audience, and world.

Eliot's poetic drama provides a chastening example of the challenges of reading the work of writing in the working of theatre. Of course, for Eliot, poetry had a value independent of the stage, never really surpassed since Shakespeare's *Romeo and Juliet*, with its "simplification to the language of natural speech, and this language of conversation again raised to great poetry, and to great poetry which is essentially dramatic: for the scene has a structure of which each line is an essential part" ("Poetry and Drama" 147). The value of "poetry," and so of drama written in verse, could be assumed, but the modern drama was rarely versified; indeed, the dominant playwrights in the European and American tradition wrote an aggressively realistic, prosaic dramatic prose. The problem engaged by Bentley, Fergusson, and Williams, and to a lesser degree by Brooks and Heilman, was to frame the "literariness" of a drama so fully dominated by the realistic theatre's emphasis on surface, on the superficial in all senses. And yet, while this critical effort seemed to require displacing the tawdry theatre from view, the absent stage continued to put pressure on the imagined *agency* of dramatic writing.[6]

"An arrangement of words"

How might dramatic writing provide the *agency* for a different kind of social ritual, reshaping the *scene* and *act* of theatrical performance? Although the example of Eliot's poetic drama implied a dynamic, instrumental relationship between writing and a revivified social technology of theatre, critics – particularly those concerned with an appropriately disciplined pedagogy – asked a slightly different question, erasing the drama as the vehicle of performance: How to restrict drama and the dramatic to the words on the page?

> Everyone knows that in drama there is little or no place for "description" or for other comment made directly by the author; that the work consists almost entirely of words spoken directly by the characters, that is, of dialogue; that the work can be read or that it can be seen in the form of

stage presentation; that plays are often written in verse form. (Brooks and Heilman 3)

Artaud had already observed – in French if not yet in English translation – that dialogue belongs "to books, as is proved by the fact that in all handbooks of literary history a place is reserved for the theater as a subordinate branch of the history of spoken language" (37). For Brooks and Heilman, though, drama is principally an order of words, representing "dialogue" between "characters" in the "printed form" of the page (3); the (unmentionable) theatre's function is "stage-presentation," syntactically and conceptually parallel with reading. As words in "printed form," arranged in "dialogue" beneath prefixes identifying the character who speaks them, dramatic writing has an intrinsic purpose: to pursue "the strait and narrow path of character-delineation" (247). Ontology recapitulates page-design: as its problems with oral poetics and with drama suggest, the New Criticism was seduced by print, taking the form of the page to embody the essence of the genre.

Reducing drama to "dialogue" provides the excuse for Brooks and Heilman's vigorous suppression of the stage. The Glossary aside, the words *theatre* or *theatrical* appear a grand total of eight times in *Understanding Drama*, and with the exception of a terse sketch of the Athenian Theatre of Dionysus (see Appendix B, 28), the "Historical Sketch of the Drama" provides no information whatsoever on the design, location, social environment, or working conditions of *any* theatre, including, surprisingly enough, Shakespeare's Globe. Despite the assumed parallel between reading and "stage-presentation" as means of realizing plays, the theatre was apparently difficult to assimilate to a "literary" critique of the drama. Fergusson, too, dwells in a very general way on the civic and festival elements of the Theatre of Dionysus, remarking only in passing on the material (as opposed to the ideological) circumstances of Shakespeare's public amphitheatre or the modern theatre's illuminated box set. In the 1950s both the actor's process and the materiality of the stage lay outside the proper sphere of "literature," even for so "dramatistic" an essay as Burke's "Antony in Behalf of the Play." Brooks and Heilman (perhaps forgetting Agamemnon's blood-red carpet, Othello's handkerchief, Miss Prism's valise) observe, "In acted drama, of course, we have costumes, settings, and 'properties'; but drama as literature has no such appurtenances."

Repressing the material theatre – even the dramatic opportunities afforded by the empty platform of the early modern stage – finally warps Brooks and Heilman's sense of the drama's intrinsic potentiality: "the Elizabethan drama, in which the use of a great variety of scenes was common" was a "marked exception" to the intrinsic design of drama, in which the "presenting of a number of places is of more trouble than value," both in terms of "practical stage-craft or of literary technique" (25). Farewell embattled Parthia, adieu bear-drawn Bohemia, let fall the ranged empire of imagined space: Shakespeare's busy stage enabled writing that simply fails to conform to the efficient rules of dramatic composition.[7]

Brooks and Heilman protest too much, but this animus against the theatre deforms the "literary" definition of drama echoed by the more theatrically savvy critics of the era. Bentley, describing *The Playwright as Thinker* as "an endorsement of the Brooks and Heilman position" (*Thinker* 309), foregrounds the manipulative use of "histrionic method" in the "commercial, political, and educational spheres," tracking the "entertainment" apotheosized in the Wagnerian *Gesamtkunstwerk* from the Broadway musical to the mass rallies of the Nazi propaganda machine (234). Drama, on the other hand, is a scripted activity (*"a drama not verbalized is a drama not dramatized"* 241), originating in the playwright's initiative: "The dramatist not only charts out a plan of procedure, he conceives and realizes a work of art which is already complete – except for technical reproduction – in his head, and which expresses by verbal image and concept a certain attitude to life" (241). Bentley's passionate defense of the literary drama depends on its distinction from the sense of theatre as mere spectacle promoted by "theatricalists," the anti-intellectual attitude that has forcibly distinguished the two essential arts of drama, "poetry and acting" (244), in the American vision of dramatic possibility. And yet, opposing "theatricalism" seems to deny dramatic performance the collaborative character implied by the drama's "uniting the two arts of poetry and acting," redirecting it instead to mere "technical reproduction." For Bentley, dramatic performance demands writing, and this writing must be conceived apart from – and be protected from – the spectacle of the stage: "Wagner of course showed that many dramatic elements can be embodied in orchestral music; silent movies showed how much can be done with the visual element alone; but if you add Wagner to Eisenstein and multiply by ten you still do not have a Shakespeare or an Ibsen" (241).

The function of writing in performance is never transparent: it emerges within the shaping social technology of the stage. But the modern theatre, distributing the playwright's presumed authority among the director and designers, making play in social and material technologies manifestly *using* the text, summons a nostalgic mirage as the essence of theatre, the fiction of a textually driven stage: "Drama, as a literary form, is an arrangement of words for spoken performance; language is the central medium of communication" (Williams, *Ibsen to Eliot* 28). Like Bentley, Williams recognizes that "there are in drama other means of communication which are capable of great richness of effect," including the individual actor's gesture, movement, and intonation; the directorial composition of bodies on stage; and the combined effects of costume, lighting, sound, and stage design. Yet Williams plots an inverse ratio between the verbal and the visual order of the stage: as the "richness of speech in drama has declined, so have the visual elements become more and more elaborated, and have even attempted individuation," tending "consistently towards autonomy" (28). Setting aside for the moment the question of whether writing implies *speech*, Williams traces a crucial recognition here, that the "visual elaboration of drama is related, in fact, not only to the impoverishment of language, but to changes in feeling." As means of materializing and resignifying social relations, dramatic performance delicately recodes our ways of imagining and inhabiting social life, including our ways of living in and through the words we use.

In 1952, Williams was still bound to the philological lineaments of a practical new criticism: "the most valuable drama is achieved when the technique of performance reserves to the dramatist primary control" (28–9). Despite the intervention of directors and designers, "when the centre of drama is language, the *form* of the play will be essentially literary; the dramatist will adopt certain conventions of language through which to work." Williams's brilliant sense of "convention" – and, later, in *Drama from Ibsen to Brecht*, its redefinition as the architecture of "structures of feeling" – proves a means to govern the stage from the page. For when the playwright succeeds in determining the form of the drama, then "the technique of performance – methods of speaking, movement, and design – is of such a kind that it will communicate completely the conventions of the dramatist, the full power of the drama is available to be deployed. This, indeed, should be the criterion of performance: that it communicates, fully and exactly, the essential form of the play. The control, that is to say, is the dramatist's arrangement of words for speech, his text" (29). Neither Williams nor Bentley articulates how stage practices should work to vivify the play: even producing Ibsen and Chekhov requires actors and audiences to engage with now-distant "conventions" of writing and performing, and it might be recalled that both Ibsen's and Chekhov's plays were initially regarded as unactable, so removed was the writing from available technologies of performance. While both playwrights clearly felt and reframed the changing "structures of feeling" of late-nineteenth-century Europe, the theatre had to find and fashion the performance conventions that would enable actors to do significant things with their words.

Given Williams's subsequent promotion of a dynamic, culturally inflected sense of the uses of literature, it is indeed surprising that the urge to promote a "literary" critique of modern drama proscribes the theatre so emphatically.[8] Arresting, too, is a similar sense of the stage machined by dramatic writing pervading Francis Fergusson's notion of the "histrionic sensibility." For Fergusson, "a drama, as distinguished from a lyric, is not primarily a composition in the verbal medium; the words result, as one might put it, from the underlying structure of incident and character" (*Idea* 8). This "underlying structure" is what Fergusson calls "action," elaborating that term as a unifying principle of dramatic design. Dramatic action is best understood in the mode of *acting*, and Fergusson takes the Moscow Art Theatre's (MAT) practice of preparation as definitive:

> If action cannot be abstractly defined, of what use is the concept in the study of the dramatic arts? [...] For this purpose practical rules may be devised, notably that of the Moscow Art Theater. They say that the action of a character or a play must be indicated by an infinitive phrase, e.g., in the play *Oedipus*, "to find the culprit." This device does not amount to a definition but it leads the performer to the particular action which the author intended. (230)

Fergusson had studied with the first protégé of the MAT to teach and direct in the United States, Richard Boleslavsky, and by 1949 the "Method" had transformed the social technology of American acting: the text could now afford a new range of theatrical opportunity, possibilities arising from new ways of using writing that were nonetheless seen as features of the script's dramatic identity, "the particular action which the author intended."[9] In performance, Fergusson's "infinitive phrase"   the Method actor's "spine" – functions like Williams's "convention," as a means of discovering and reproducing the play's authentic form, the instrument for seizing the play's underlying thematic – actualized in the plot, characters or agents, and "words of the play" (36–7) – *as action.*

Fergusson makes no apology for deriving his basic analytic principle – the "analogy of action" – from theatre practice. Instead, he argues that it enables readers and performers to grasp the fully Aristotelian principle of the organic unity of the drama, the primacy of plot as the realization of action, and the coordinating effects of character, thought, language, music, and spectacle. While invoking the authority of actors must have seemed an oxymoron to his New Critical contemporaries, the "analogy of action" that satisfies the histrionic appetite might have seemed familiar enough. The "analogy of action" at once organizes every element of the text's organic unity around a single principle (a "figure in the carpet"), and provides a technique for reproducing it in both critical discourse and theatrical performance. Far from locating stage practice in the historical specificity of a given theatre, seizing the "analogy of action" enables the actor to "play accurately the roles which dramatists of all kinds have written" (238) by training "a primitive and direct awareness," the "histrionic sensibility" (239), and so provides a "direct access to the plays of other cultures" (11). The Method was widely touted as equally applicable to Sophocles, Shakespeare, and Shaw, and despite Fergusson's emphasis on the ritual implication of theatre in a specific cultural process, the extraordinary variety of the theatre's ways of using drama, much like the extraordinary variety of poetry's relation to the cultures of its production, can be seized through a single "primitive and direct" reading strategy, one that works (like the "direct awareness" method of "close reading") by engaging the essence of the art.

Acts of speech

In some respects, both Fergusson and Williams worked to align the productive activities of the stage with the mainspring of dramatic action. The more programmatic New Critics took a narrower view, seeing the organization of the words on the page as a mimesis and projection of characters speaking, and dramatic performance as the delivery of "the text" and the characters it encodes by other means. As John Crowe Ransom put it, drama "has *characters*, who make *speeches*" (*New* 169). Understanding drama as characters-making-speeches is plainly wrong: characters speak, but they rarely – Brutus' and Antony's orations in *Julius Caesar* prove the rule – "make *speeches*." Dramatic language is "performative" in J. L. Austin's sense, a way of doing something with words (Austin's lectures were first published in 1962), but it at once uses texts and reconstitutes them in a new *scene*, "parry-ing" – as Burke put it – an evolving and unanticipatable theatrical "thrust" ("Words as Deeds" 152). Onstage, characters and the actors who play them cajole, wound, impress, persuade, reflect, romance, seduce; in Chekhov's *Three Sisters*, Vershinin may "philosophize," but in so doing he *performs* these acts, and more. Understanding the dra-matic script as a direction to "make *speeches*" enabled the New Criticism to define theatre narrowly enough that its rich embodiment (how to account for the significance of any common gesture, a shrug, a grimace, a narrowing of the eyes, onstage or off?) could be construed as the compliant execution of the text's verbal meanings.

Performance-as-speech: the foresaken stage models the New Critics' prescription of the work of drama. To take dramatic language princi-pally as "dialogue" between "characters" articulates an extraordinarily narrow understanding of dramatic and theatrical propriety. "Dialogue" implies conversation, dramatic language used to imitate or represent two or more individuals speaking together within a certain kind of dramatic fiction. And yet words are capable of being used in a variety of ways in performance, ways that have little to do either with "dia-logue" in this sense or with "character." In the classical Greek theatre, the Chorus sang/spoke/danced in unison (not conversation, not in character); today, the lines are sometimes distributed among members of the Chorus (not conversation, perhaps barely in character). In many popular theatre forms, including the great medieval cycles and the drama of Shakespeare and his contemporaries, the verbal text often (and intermittently) seems less to structure a dialogic relationship between represented "characters" than to enable an opportunity for a certain kind of byplay between the actor and the audience. One role, even a fully "characterized" role like Falstaff, might offer many oppor-tunities of this kind for the actor's immediate, physical engagement with the public (the "catechism" on honor, for instance, *1 Henry IV*, 5.1.127–39). And a given play might well provide different kinds of opportunities in different roles, as well as different means to recede into *character*: Prince Hal's soliloquies ("I know you all," *1 Henry IV* 1.2.172–95) also locate *character* between actor and audience, but imply a very different transaction than Falstaff's do.[10] Repressing the evident testimony of the stage, testimony visible enough even in the script at hand, New Criticism framed drama as the speech of characters-in-dialogue, and so articulated performance ("stage presentation") as a version of reading aloud.

What are the consequences of repressing the theatre as a means to understanding drama, and how does taking speech as "the province of the text" bear on our ways of reading plays (Gina Bloom 7)? Brooks and Heilman turn surprisingly to film to account for the role of language-as-dialogue in properly "dramatic" action. The opening moments of *The Great McGinty* have the advantage of reducing "action to the bare skeleton – indeed, to a sort of blueprint for action" (8): the drama's essentially "dialogic" character will be dramatized in contrast to action-without-speech.

SHOOTING-SCRIPT FOR *THE GREAT McGINTY*

The last title is imposed over a NIGHT shot of a drinking establishment. Now we HEAR some rumba music and we TRUCK FORWARD SLOWLY TOWARD THE CAFÉ …

DISSOLVE TO:

A PRETTY RUMBA DANCER PERFORMING IN FRONT OF A BAND

We see a few customers IN THE FOREGROUND but they are not particularly interested. In other words, they give one look then turn away. Noticing the lack of interest she bends over and grabs her skirt.

CUT TO:

THE RUMBA DANCER FROM WAIST DOWN

Slowly she starts to pull up her skirt. The CAMERA follows her

CUT TO:

LOW CAMERA SHOT UP AT THE TABLE OF MEN

They are not paying any attention. One of them is lighting a pipe. As he turns his head away to escape the cloud of smoke his eye catches the legs on the floor. There is a slight double-take, then he gives the legs his undivided attention. A second later the other men at the table follow his gaze. Now the whole table looks on stonily. In the BACKGROUND we see McGinty working at the bar but he is OUT OF FOCUS.

CUT TO:

THE GIRL'S LEGS AS SHE DANCES

CUT TO:

THE GIRL'S UPPER HALF

She looks around and is amused at the effect her legs are having. (8–9)

Lacking dialogue, the scene for Brooks and Heilman is "pure action" but "not very dramatic […] as *action* it expresses very little; and even as acted out by a competent actress whose gesture and facial expression might conceivably add a good deal to the meaning of the scene, the 'meaning' of the scene is blurred and vague"; it is mere "*pantomime* – a very old art and for certain types of material highly expressive, but an art which, deprived as it is of the use of words, can get at the inner life of its characters only very indirectly" (9).

Even in the flat language of the shooting script, though, the scene seems dynamic, *expressive*, requiring us to imagine the kinds of embodiment it might compel, even from a merely "competent" cast. Shifting perspective, the scene begins and ends with the rumba dancer expressing herself in dance, by raising her skirt, and by the hint of satisfaction when she draws the attention of the barroom. As an establishing scene, we might well think that the densely gendered opening moments of *The Great McGinty* are as "expressive" as, say, the opening moments of *Rosmersholm*, in which Mrs. Helseth busily cleans the parlor, secretly watching with Rebecca to see whether Rosmer will finally cross the bridge on his way home, or of *Hamlet*, as Barnardo and Francisco feel their way confusedly around the Danish darkness of a sunny English afternoon.

Yet while for Brooks and Heilman the absence of dialogue distinguishes the scene from true drama, it nonetheless provides a paradigm of text and performance: "This is just what is seen in plays: the meaning of the spoken lines is constantly supplemented by physical action" (7). In drama, "costume, setting, and even acting itself are, finally, secondary. It is the word which is primary" (12). Insofar as dramatic language is conceived principally as *speech*, performance becomes a subordinate means of supplementing, illustrating the text on the page. Brooks and Heilman use *The Great McGinty* to stage performance as a parasite: "we ought to observe that *what the director will add here is a kind of* commentary, a kind of interpretation which, even though it does not make use of words, still is an interpretation over and above the 'pure action' we have already considered," action coextensive with the words on the page (9). The camera, too, which we might think *creates* the scene for us, surgically dissecting the unnamed "girl" into a smile, torso, and legs, is responsible only for "sifting the material and arranging it for us in a meaningful pattern. It is making an interpretation of the scene" (10).

Understanding the director's work, the actor's work, even the camera's work as "interpretation," Brooks and Heilman take a now-familiar position: the performance is an "interpretation" of something else, the dramatic "work" that lives in the "printed form" of the text, which should be delivered to the audience by "*characters*, who make *speeches*" supplemented by action and gesture, scenography, costume and lighting. So common is this way of understanding plays on the stage (and films of stage-plays, such as Shakespeare films), that it is arresting to encounter it here about an artform – film drama – usually identified more completely with performance than with writing. The film may be called *William Shakespeare's Romeo + Juliet*, but it is Baz Luhrmann's film (screenplay by Craig Pearce and Baz Luhrmann). Regarding the film as an "interpretation" of the screenplay, Brooks and Heilman reveal how the tactical significance of performance as "interpretation" frames a misleading paradigm of theatre and drama.

For while the camera work may be "interpretive" – and while it provides the material for our further interpretation – it does not "interpret" the screenplay, the *text*, in the way Brooks and Heilman suggest. The activity of interpretation is, of course, everywhere part of the production process: the director, designers, and cinematographer will have interpreted the scene (what elements are important? should we see McGinty clearly or not? how many customers are "a few," how are they dressed, how old are they? what's the condition of the bar? is it dangerous or just dilapidated? is it dilapidated at all?), and use the camera as one means to realize the work they want the scene to do. But the scene we see is *after* interpretation. The "interpretive" activity of the director is an ongoing process, but s/he is not "interpreting" the screenplay: the screenplay is one element to be interpreted, along with the camera work, the acting, costuming, designs, in the creation of the work of performance. What the film director most directly "interprets" is performance itself ("Let's do another take"), viewing the daily rushes while shooting, and then reviewing all takes during the film's editing; so too, much of the stage director's "interpretive" work happens in rehearsal ("let's try that again"), and what is being interpreted is the developing process of the performance itself. Performance is the final cause of the director's work, and what the director and actors interpret is not the writing but the performance they are making, reading it not against the text but against what the performance might and should be, what kind of event this performance might use the text, actors, scenography to make.

We should be wary of constituting the identity of the artwork in ways that artificially disregard the range of its manifest and material instrumentalities, its use and use-value. The "interpretive" understanding of performance defines performance as "presentation" of something that already exists, a *"kind of commentary"* supplementing (or degrading) the written work of art, because it uses the work in ways that extend beyond the apparent warrant of its "printed form." To put it another way, the "interpretive" perspective arises from Brooks and Heilman's inability to read what's not there in the text, but which nonetheless makes plays legible as designs for action. Even plays that seem to put everything on the page – the misleading verbal density of Shakespeare comes to mind, as do Samuel Beckett's screenplays and mimes – dramatize the degree to which the meaning of these plays as drama will depend on unwritten, perhaps unwritable "performative" conventions, a sense of performance as a specific kind of doing that lives outside the text. As J. L. Austin argues, the linguistic, social, cultural, and theatrical systems beyond language allow us to imagine the performance of words as *illocutionary* (doing something) and *perlocutionary* (causing something to happen): the conventions of performance enable us to imagine dramatic writing as act, as deed, as doing. Burke's reading of Austin implies, though, that the *agency* of writing deployed in a new *scene* creates the possibility for new acts to take place. One of the great lessons of modern drama, and even of Shakespeare's fortunes in the modern theatre, is that plays which have seemed entirely undramatic and untheatrical – *The Seagull, The Master Builder, Ubu Roi, Waiting for Godot, The Birthday Party, Blasted,* but also *Troilus and Cressida, Measure for Measure, Titus Andronicus* – required a performative transformation, a recalibration of the Burkean "ratios" of *act, scene, agent, purpose,* and especially of the instrumental function of language as *agency*. Plays that did not seem to afford a living theatricality gained a different potential with the application of new technologies of production, understood as the entire social practice of theatrical representation. The plays required and enabled a transformation in the ways of reading dramatic language, of practicing its *agency* as a means to rendering a purposeful theatrical *agent* (actor) and dramatic *agent* (character), and so accomplishing a palpable *act* of dramatic performance. As a result, these plays became not merely stageworthy, capable of being used to create meaningful action in the *scene* of the theatre, but their performance could become a significant, critical *act* in that larger *scene*, the changing scene of social life. The theatre's makers and audiences had to learn to read, to do, and to see differently for these plays to take, or retake, the stage.

Heresy, responsibility, and performance

At first glance, isolating "the text" from the practices of the theatre in order to assess its purely "poetic" integrity and unity may not seem problematic. The New Critics promise, after all, a purely literary understanding of the play arising from the "close reading" of the words. Poetic language may be "language as gesture," but the New Criticism so thoroughly disdains the gestures with which language becomes dramatic as to falsify its defining sense of the value of poetry.[11] For this reason, Brooks and Heilman urgently discriminate between what they take to be the truly dramatic elements of the text, and those assigned a merely theatrical function. Even the most elegant and intellectually demanding comedy – such as the plays of Wilde, Sheridan, and Congreve included in *Understanding Drama* – depends for its success on the physical grace of the comic actor. The body is the palpable means and medium of comedy. Can you think of Falstaff without seeing his girth in your mind's eye, or think "Restoration Comedy" without a slight alteration in posture? This bodily summons is especially engaged by those comedies, however rich in symbolic "meaning," that depend on the physical skills of a central performer to incarnate a crucial role: Bottom in *A Midsummer Night's Dream*, or Algy and Jack contesting muffins in *The Importance of Being Earnest*. To Brooks and Heilman, though, this element of comedy stands apart from its dramatic identity. Plautus' *The Twin Menaechmi*, already part of a degraded genre, farce, "deals entirely in *amusing situations*, is little concerned with character, and not at all with ideas" (137). More alarming, Plautus'

farce depends on the (undescribed) conventions of the Roman theatre
and its performers:

> One must remember too, that the liveliness and the successfulness of
> farce depend also on the ability of the comic actor to develop the humor
> fully with his facial expression, mimicry, and gesture. By such devices,
> as we know, an able comedian can frequently make very funny a part
> which in itself may seem rather wooden and flat. [...] But though the
> dramatist has a perfect right to depend upon the actor who has such
> devices at his command, it ought to be clear that his comedy, in so far
> as it does depend upon such devices, is moving away from drama proper
> and into the realm of pantomime, vaudeville, and musical comedy. It is
> with drama proper that this book is concerned. (140–1)

The "greater the allowance which we have to make for theatrical conventions, the greater is our sense of the author's limitations" (141).
How to discriminate the theatrical convention from the dramatic?
Shakespeare's soliloquies, Wilde's epigrams, Ibsen's indirections,
Beckett's vaudevillian nonsequiturs all activate specific "conventions"
of their stages, opportunities for acting and engagement with an audience given specificity and purpose through the script. Yet for Brooks
and Heilman, the trained competence of the performer is merely a
presentational "device." The design of the drama must be insulated
from the conventionality of the stage, they suggest, for the play to be
read in the properly literary way.

As a social technology, the performance conventions of a given
theatre afford the successful use of dramatic writing; the changing
conventions of the stage are dialectically entwined with the origin and
ongoing vitality of any play. Insofar as the "form of a play is always
a convention, which it is the business of performance to express"
(*Ibsen to Eliot* 32), we can take Williams's sense of "convention" to
approximate the New Critical sense of the organic unity and compelling poesis of the literary work. In a truly dramatic theatre, performance would be like playing a musical instrument, expression "*within
certain defined limits*, open to interpretation" (30). In the absence of
convention, contemporary dramatic writing is – much as Plautus' comedies are to Brooks and Heilman – a deliquescent stream of mere
opportunity: the play becomes "a collection of events and character-
parts which require performance for completion. Often, indeed, the
play becomes a mere 'vehicle' for a particular actor" (32). For Brooks

and Heilman, the dramatic poem is split between the fully dramatic
elements and those designed to appeal to the conventions of the stage.
For Williams, the absence of informing dramatic conventions directs
the entirety of the dramatic text toward the extrinsic disciplines of the
actor, who takes "certain words into his own personality" (31). "This
discipline commands a personal respect; but it is far from the essential
discipline of drama. It is the sincere attempt at discipline of interpreta-
tive artists who have been denied adequate guidance; but it is no
substitute for that guidance, it is no substitute, in fact, for a convention"
(32). For Williams as much as for Brooks and Heilman, the appeal to
the stage is a moment of failure in the design of literary drama, a
moment that fissures the desirable integrity of the verbal order of the
text. "Convention" arises in the drama – and in mid-century drama
theory – as a means to integrate the text, and assert its control over the
interpretive spectacle of the stage.[12]

Although "drama consists of uniting the two arts of poetry and
acting" (Bentley, *Thinker* 244), performance-as-interpretation divides
the poetic from the performative aspects of drama. Indeed, understanding performance as "interpretation" surprisingly falsifies the
defining strength of the New Criticism: its tenacious account of the
intrinsically "poetic" character of poetic language. We can see the full
impact of this "interpretive" understanding of dramatic writing, and
its deformation of the fundamental values of New Criticism itself, in
Brooks and Heilman's astonishing reading of one of the masterpieces
of the Western canon, a play whose only weakness is, specifically, that
it was not written by Shakespeare, or at least by Marlowe: Ibsen's
Rosmersholm.

Rosmersholm dramatizes the degree to which the play may well lie
behind or beneath its spoken language, implicitly challenging the sense
of drama as a form of articulate speech. Perhaps for this reason, the
discussion of *Rosmersholm* is the only place where Brooks and Heilman
discuss *acting* as a means to seize, to "present," an "interpretation" of
dramatic meaning. While the play's texture is rich with explanation, its
action mainly transpires in the subtextual zone of intention, of the ter-
rible, joyous fascination that binds Rosmer and Rebecca, and binds
them to "go the way Beata went." At key moments, the dialogue is,
even for Ibsen, unusually spare, drawing on the physical delicacy and
intellectual resourcefulness of the performer. In their meticulous discussion of the play, Brooks and Heilman note one of Ibsen's stage

directions, Rebecca's "As if startled" reaction when Rosmer wonders at the end of Act 2 whether Rebecca had any inkling of Beata's suspicions of their as-yet-unacknowledged mutual attraction: "Here we see an unusual responsibility placed upon the actress; her interpretation of the line would be very important in stimulating the imagination. The words alone do not convey much" (*Understanding* 286–7). "Responsibility" is intriguing: we might think the performer's "responsibility" to the play, to the other cast members, to the audience, would be more or less uniform throughout the play. The quality of the actress's interpretation will clearly be measured – but measured against what? As Brooks and Heilman point out, it can't be measured directly against the text, since the "words alone do not convey much."

The play hinges again on the actors' responsibility toward its close, in the oblique negotiation between Rosmer and Rebecca to execute justice on themselves. Since the dialogue is evasive, Brooks and Heilman go to some lengths – uniquely in *Understanding Drama* – to explicitate the "subtext" of the action (not, of course, a word they would use), the implication that the text alone cannot convey the full significance of the event of performance. Rosmer says: "Well, then, I stand firm in our emancipated view of life, Rebecca. There is no judge over us; and therefore we must do justice on ourselves." He "evidently means: even judged by the new morality of emancipation we – that is, the individual – must do what Beata did. What I am proposing is not a reversion to my old orthodoxy. I stand firm in the emancipated view – and it is from this viewpoint that I am executing judgment on myself." That's what Rosmer means. Brooks and Heilman continue, "But, again, this view of the action may claim too much for what is in the text. Ibsen certainly, most readers will agree, has put a heavy burden of interpretation upon the actor and actress who are to play this scene" (310–11). But this "heavy burden of interpretation" placed on the actors arises from one of the most powerful and characteristic assertions of Ibsen's drama: that words fail, that the deepest currents of self-perception, self-deception, aspiration, and abjection, can only be realized (if they can be realized at all) in deeds that resist digestion in language much as they resist captivity to the stage. We never see the mill-race, nor the climax of the drama, where love and death, desire and disgust, obedience and freedom are, perhaps, consummated. The actors must shoulder the burden of realizing "this view of the action" through their "interpretation," an "interpretation" that depends, like the precise paraphrase that Brooks and Heilman develop here, on Ibsen's language, language that urgently refuses to say what it means. Indeed, like Brooks and Heilman, the actors' "interpretation" may in the end "claim too much" for Ibsen's obdurate words, more than "is in the text."

Although Brooks and Heilman fear that the actor may betray the poetic design of the text (perhaps, as Williams has it, by "taking over certain words into his own personality"), their sense of "interpretive" performance betrays something more important, the unique form and pressure of literary language itself. In *The Well Wrought Urn* (1947), Brooks maintains that the order of the poem transcends its representation in non-poetic forms, even in the language of the critical paraphrase. The "heresy of paraphrase" is to mistake the interpretive clarity of paraphrase for the experience of the poem.

> We can very properly use paraphrases as pointers and as short-hand references provided that we know what we are doing. But it is highly important that we know what we are doing and that we see plainly that the paraphrase is not the real core of meaning which constitutes the essence of the poem.
>
>   For the imagery and the rhythm are not merely the instruments by which this fancied core-of-meaning-which-can-be-expressed-in-a-paraphrase is directly rendered. Even in the simplest poem their mediation is not positive and direct. Indeed, whatever statement we may seize upon as incorporating the "meaning" of the poem, immediately the imagery and the rhythm seem to set up tensions with it, warping and twisting it, qualifying and revising it. (*Urn* 180)

The "structure of a poem resembles that of a play" (186) in that it "arrives at its conclusion through conflict"; as an event, an experience, *"an action* rather than as a formula for action or as a statement about action," the poem and the performance of the poem always stand apart from its rewriting into the logic of prose (187). The play's the thing, but is its performance the experience or the paraphrased "interpretation?" "The poem, if it be a true poem is a simulacrum of reality – in this sense, at least, it is an 'imitation' – by *being* an experience rather than any mere statement about experience or any mere abstraction from experience" (194). Yet the performed drama – which surely seems *experiential* – is oddly removed from the experience of the real, of the real drama, the thing itself. Actors *should* feel the weighty burden, the responsibility for seizing this "meaning" and conveying it to us. But to Brooks and Heilman, the burden of the responsible actor is precisely to frame the performance as a kind of "statement about action," to show what Rosmer really means, rather than enacting the harrowing effort to occupy meaning, to go where "meaning" takes him. The reasons that Ibsen's actors have an undue burden of responsibility for Brooks and Heilman, compared to, say, Shakespeare's, is because the text does not specify the content of that experience clearly enough that we can be confident in its unmediated "stage presentation."[13]

The *scene* of performance for Brooks and Heilman is, even in the theatre, not the stage, and the actors are barely its *agents*. On the one hand, Brooks and Heilman pay close attention to the verbal and ethical dimension of the plays; on the other hand, they are unable to see Ibsen's writing engaging the theatrical practices that afford its significance as performance. More to the point, they also reveal the inability of New Criticism to engage with the language of modern drama itself. In many respects the language of modern drama is specifically un-Shakespearean, impoverished in imagery, syntactically unambiguous and lexically unadventurous. Words like "gladly" in *Rosmersholm*, or "vine leaves" in *Hedda Gabler* or even properties like the wild duck and the potted forest in *The Wild Duck* stand out so sharply against the drab verbal and visual texture of Ibsen's worlds: Ibsen transformed the realistic conventions of the modern theatre, framing a world of implacable material deadness, in which the possibility of liberating action emerges only fitfully, through nuance not declaration. Setting acting outside the realm of critique – actors enact the paraphrase, not the poem – New Criticism sees the practice of acting, its precise ways of making meaning with the text as merely "interpretive," as a technology applied to the text, or more precisely, to its paraphrase, in order to "present" it onstage.

For Brooks and Heilman, Ibsen's unaccountable decision to leave the resolution of the play's most delicate meanings to the work of the performers marks his signal failure as a writer. He might, after all, have chosen a medium more adequate to the poetic design of the drama, what they call "poetic form."

> But at this point we may suggest that what Ibsen has to say would probably have come across more successfully in poetic form. Poetic language, with its suggestiveness and allusiveness, its taking full advantage of the

richness of meanings, is almost essential to the expression of so complex a conception as that of *Rosmersholm*. Here we have several levels of activity in several characters – that which appears on the surface and those which, for whatever reason, are concealed. Poetic language could represent all the levels simultaneously; prose, which is relatively flat and one-dimensional, has to do them one at a time – as in the case of Rebecca, in whom we sense ambiguities almost to the end. We are left to effect our own synthesis, which can never be as satisfactory as the author's own. Ibsen, indeed, is working toward the method of poetry when he uses such a symbol as the foot-bridge and when he has Brendel say, "slice off her incomparably moulded left ear"; he might well have gone further. When we come to the plays of Marlowe and Shakespeare, for instance, we can see how fully the poetic language supports and intensifies the dramatic meaning. (312)

Bentley complains that "Brooks and Heilman think that Ibsen is trying, or ought to have been trying, to be Shakespeare, and that he is not doing well at it" (*Thinker* 309). What would Shakespeare do had he the motive and the cue that Ibsen had? Like Rosmer and Rebecca, Othello works out his suicide onstage, and in "poetic language" that surely intensifies the scene, articulating Othello as the forceful instrument of the state's brutal justice, even as he executes that justice on its faithless enemy, himself. What is the actor's responsibility to "I kissed thee ere I killed thee. No way but this: / Killing myself, to die upon a kiss," or even to "And smote him, thus" (5.2.368–9, 365)? Is the actor's job here to communicate a paraphraseable "meaning," an "interpretation," and if so, what signs would materialize that interpretation? Or to "present" the text by making *"speeches,"* a disappearing act requiring a substantial veil of words (Shakespeare does provide more cover than Ibsen)? Does the meaning of the event lie in the words, is it clarified as language? Or is the point of acting to lend a theatrical *purpose* to the words, to seize them as *agency* toward another *act*, one transpiring not in the *scene* of the dramatic fiction, but in the *scene* of the performance? In other words, is the purpose of dramatic writing to enable the creation of an act, rather than "a formula for action or a statement about action?"

   To speak in this way is not only to echo Burke but to verge on Constantin Stanislavski or even Lee Strasberg, pointing not to the universality of their methods but to the dependency of the stage on legible means of rendering language as behavior, as *doing* that includes and exceeds *speech*. As Judith Butler reminds us, even in speaking "the act that the body is performing is never fully understood; the body is the blindspot of speech, that which acts in excess of what is said, but which also acts in and through what is said" (*Excitable* 11). The rhetorical formality of seventeenth- and eighteenth-century acting made sense, much as a production by Robert Wilson or Frank Castorf makes sense today by grounding the words in a specific way of doing. Gertrude aside, suicide in Shakespeare is a wordy affair, but perhaps it's Pyramus who gets to the bottom of the ratio between word and deed, his aria enforcing the recognition that the *performative* cannot be reduced to the *constative*, that words are used to *do* something not merely to *say* something. In the theatre, the order of language is unaccountably, unpredictably, necessarily transformed by the body's means, or had better be: "Now, die, die, die, die, die" (5.1.295).

Despite their responsiveness to ambiguity and irony as readers, Brooks and Heilman regard Ibsen's prose as incapable of resolving the ambiguities he puts into action. And yet actors do not rely on paraphrase nor on stratified "levels of activity." Acting demands a simultaneous interplay of movement and gesture, tone and expression, proximity and pace, to incarnate the "action" as experience, an *act* in the *scene* of theatre. In this sense, the summons to write in verse says less about Ibsen's failings (he had, of course, mastered the "poetic form" in the long series of plays including *Brand* and *Peer Gynt*, before forsaking it) than about Brooks and Heilman's understanding of "dramatic meaning": it is a function of language finding an illustration in performance, rather than of language that is resignified, and resignifies, the materialities it engages on the stage. They map the technology of theatre to the technology of reading, rather than taking the text as a supple tool, given the right affordance by its use in various technologies of performance.

The drama criticism of mid-century, practiced by noted critics of poetry and drama, a brilliant theatre critic and translator, a practicing actor and Shakespeare scholar, and the founder of "cultural studies," was notably successful in promoting a "literary" drama and arguing for its aesthetic complexity. And yet, in its commitment to the drama as a design for reading, it failed to read the drama, or more precisely failed to activate the range of extra-textual reading practices – spatial, visual, visceral – that locate the *agency* of the text in the *scene* of theatre, that illuminate its affordance in the social technology of the stage. This is hardly to say that the "interpretive" perspective was not influential:

we hear its accents still every time we ask how a performance interprets the play. (How do Zeffirelli's and Luhrmann's films provide different interpretations of *Romeo and Juliet*? Discuss, using specific examples from the text.) Promoting the essential ambiguity of great poetry, this vision imagined the dramatic poem as multivalent in its signification, while at the same time urging the stage as a site for the reduction of meaning, the transformation of poetic ambiguity into a single, appropriate, "responsible," actorly paraphrase. After all, while the drama "can be read or seen in the form of stage-presentation," the stage is finally not the place where the richest *experience* of the drama takes shape, at least for the New Critics. This vision of dramatic performance, perhaps not surprisingly, persists in many literary accounts of the drama; it is more surprising to find it playing a central role in an arena in which we should expect a more complex account of the work of writing in performance: performance studies.

ii. Dramatic Writing and its Discontents: Performance Studies, Drama Studies

> *What changes over time is the value, relevance, or meaning of the archive, how the items it contains get interpreted, even embodied. Bones might remain the same, even though their story may change, depending on the paleontologist or forensic anthropologist who examines them.* Antigone *might be performed in multiple ways, whereas the unchanging text assures a stable signifier.*
> Diana Taylor, The Archive and the Repertoire *(19)*

> *One aim of this study must be to develop a way of talking about drama that is not contaminated by notions derived from literature.*
> Michael Goldman, The Actor's Freedom *(4)*

Antigone's bones

Diana Taylor's superb reading of contemporary Latin American and Latino/a performance stands on a familiar dichotomy, one that emerged in its present shape in the 1970s as part of the enabling discourse of performance theory and performance studies. It is unexceptionable, now, much as it was unexceptionable to the New Criticism of the 1950s and 1960s, to regard dramatic performance as the representation and reiteration of writing, as "subordinated to the primacy of the text" (Lehmann 21). In this view, the mutable, resistant, nomadic, and carnivalesque character of textless performance stands apart from dramatic theatre, and is captured in Taylor's sense of the *repertoire*, "embodied memory: performances, gestures, orality, movement, dance, singing – in short, all those acts usually thought of as ephemeral, nonreproducible knowledge" (20).[14]

Rethinking performance required displacing paradigms – including a range of (mis)conceptions of Western dramatic performance – and performance studies has replaced the falsely "interpretive" account of dramatic performance with a series of productive paradigms for grasping the work and effect of performance more broadly: performance as *restored behavior* or *surrogation* (not the reenactment of scripted activities, but reproduced behavior); performance as a process of *disappearance* rather than presentation; performance as a *liminal* activity, posing and transgressing social and cultural thresholds; performance as a socially *efficacious* activity rather than the mere offering of an aesthetic representation for consumption.[15] Although performance studies has generally sidestepped the material critique of textuality, a sense of the *archive* of written culture defined by the fixity and stability of writing, and opposed to a *repertoire* of performance explicitly excluding dramatic performance – "performances, gestures, orality, movement, dance, singing," but not acting, theatre – should give us pause. For Taylor, theatre's use of writing associates it with the "centuries of colonial evangelical or normalizing activity" (15) characteristic of imperial expansion, and of the imperial I/eye of Western epistemology; dramatic performance is essentially assimilated to the *archive* as an instrument of oppression, one of the ways the state "sustains power" (19). As a result, "Even though the archive and the repertoire exist in a constant state of interaction, the tendency has been to banish the repertoire to the past" (21), and so the mission of *The Archive and the Repertoire* is at once to restore the repertoire's social agency to view, and to outline its ongoing political and epistemological resistance. For while the "archive and the repertoire have always been important sources of information, both exceeding the limitations of the other," and usually working "in tandem and [...] alongside other systems of transmission" (21), the *archive* is both the prison house and graveyard of active performance culture: much as bones "might remain the same, even though their story may change," so too "*Antigone* might be performed in multiple ways, whereas the unchanging text assures a stable signifier" (19).

As the limitations of the New Critics' "interpretive" understanding of theatre make clear, Taylor is surely right to urge us "to acknowledge the need to free ourselves from the dominance of the text – as the privileged or even sole object of [performance] analysis" (27), especially if we persist in regarding "the text" as determining theatrical meaning. Yet Taylor's retemporalization of *repertoire* and *archive* is cognate with a more pervasive representation of the succession of performance media and the consequent succession of licensed critical methodologies. Anticipating Taylor's dichotomy, for instance, Hans-Thies Lehmann's framing of dramatic performance as essentially "subordinated to the primacy of the text" leads to a similar temporality, the succession of a fully pre-scribed dramatic by an emerging *postdramatic* theatre. So, too, Shannon Jackson locates the emergence of performance studies in the 1970s as part of a broader "transition from literary to cultural studies" (*Professing* 98), in which the textual commitments and antitheatrical (and homophobic) resistances of a determinedly "literary" conception of theatre siderailed drama as a site of engaged critique with performance sometime in the 1950s. Despite a "humbling" (107) recognition of the possibility of alternative histories, the "drama-to-culture genealogy" (94) pursued in *Professing Performance* leaves the territory of dramatic theory and performance since then largely uncharted by simply leaving it behind.

And yet Jackson finds the "awareness of a longer, complicated disciplinary genealogy" to make "oppositions between old literary studies and new cultural studies and between old theatre studies and new performance studies less easy to maintain or to elide" (107–8); so too Taylor alludes to the "constant state of interaction" between *archive* and *repertoire*, and Lehmann takes the rupture between dramatic and postdramatic theatre as a prolonged process of negotiation, slowly and unevenly reversing the "dramatic" predominance of writing to performance: "it becomes more presence than representation, more shared than communicated experience, more process than product, more manifestation than signification, more energetic impulse than information" (Lehmann 85).[16] One way to take these gestures seriously, however, would be to resist the principal dichotomies sustaining them: the sense that, as part of the *archive*, dramatic writing determines the uses of the theatrical *repertoire*; that dramatic critique and dramatic performance must privilege a literary or "interpretive" valuation of the text; and that dramatic performance legitimates the representation, communication, product, information digested in the written script, what we might call the theatre-as-interpretive-paraphrase-by-other-means vision of performance characteristic of the New Criticism.

How might our reading of drama work at the interface between writing and embodiment, poetry and performance, rather than polarizing them? We might begin by unpacking how the distinction between *archive* and *repertoire*, for all its generative force, prevents us from seizing dramatic writing as an *agency* of performance, and so from seizing dramatic performance as performance at all. "*Antigone* might be performed in multiple ways, whereas the unchanging text assures a stable signifier" (19): for Taylor, writing ensures the unchanging transmission of the dramatic data, *information* which might be produced on different platforms, but which is unchanged by the site, means, or process of its performance. And yet Taylor's example surprisingly points to the drama's troubling place in the history of writing, and so to its troubling effect on the paradigm of *archive* and *repertoire*. First, we might ask, "What *Antigone*?" The Greek text, itself the result of the critical labors of millennia of scholarship, a text which is always plural, each individual edition differently concatenating ancient texts and commentaries, and so differing in important ways from other editions? A translation? Which translation? In what language? What "unchanging text" is *Antigone*? Few plays in Western theatre have been staged so variously, in ways that simultaneously exploit and betray the *archive*'s "stable signifier" through the unanticipated, creative immediacy of the *repertoire* as a means to generate a specific *act* of embodied resistance. This gesture even extends to the rewriting of the *archive* itself, in John Kani, Winston Ntshona, and Athol Fugard's *The Island* (1973) and Tom Paulin's *The Riot Act* (1985), for example.[17] What is the "stable signifier" *Antigone* assures? And how does that "signifier" emerge as "stable" in the changeable discourse of performance?

For Taylor, the dramatic theatre is a bland platform for the transmission of scripted data, from the dead hand of the author through the scripted performances of the archivist actors to the deadened minds of the audience. Now while some theatre certainly does work in this way,

It seems fairer to say that it's precisely the technologies of the *repertoire* that intervene, that enact the process of transmission, embodied practices such as editing, reading, memorization, movement, gesture, acting that produce both a sense of what the text *is*, and what *we might be capable of saying with and through it in/as performance, what we want to make it signify.* When performance studies emerged in the 1970s, performance theory began to part from the critique of dramatic performance, recognizing the extraordinary range and vitality of performance forms that have little to do with Western theatre, or with theatre at all.[10] At much the same time, though, dramatic critique also parted with the largely New Critical program for assimilating the drama to literary studies: a program that took the function of the stage as the interpretation of the literary character of the drama largely by framing acting as a mode of reproducing the text in speech – "*characters*, who make *speeches*" as John Crowe Ransom put it (*New* 169). In a savvy reading of the critical scene, Jon Erickson suggests that "If performance studies has a problem with theatre studies, it is that, despite its emphasis on the theatrical, it is still too literary and in thrall to a textual regime, a regime that represents the imperial power of literate cultures over oral or nonliterate cultures," and over the nontextual culture of performance as well (248). At the same time, one aspect of the impact of the access to " 'performance' as it appears in contemporary social and cultural theory," Julia A. Walker argues, is "an increasing awareness of the limitations of the metaphor of culture as text" ("Why" 157). While the "antitextualism" of performance studies is now familiar (Puchner, "Entanglements" 24), in the past three decades the critique of drama has been characterized by a complex challenge to read the drama differently by adducing a set of interlocking issues: a complex resistance to the institutions of literature and the practices of a purely "literary" analysis, requiring a reassessment of the relationship between writing and embodiment, an assessment that has also demanded a compromise with an understanding of performance as merely another kind of "text." Although there were compelling reasons for leaving traditional, literary views of dramatic performance behind in the fashioning of an emergent discipline, we might now ask whether an alternative genealogy of dramatic critique could be brought back into dialogue with the now dominant "traditions" of performance studies, and what the attractions of resuming that conversation might be.

Of course, "literary studies" itself can hardly be reduced to a narrow range of objects and activities, and dramatic writing – predominantly Shakespeare in this regard – has felt the impact of the multiplication of critical practices and perspectives characteristic of the well-known (inter)disciplinary ferment of the past thirty years. Here, though, I'm less concerned with perspectives that assume drama's likeness to other forms of literary representation, analyzing, say, the formal, ideological, psychoanalytic contingencies of a play's narrative, strategies of characterization, or fictive world. While such work has surely ramified aspects of (some) dramatic writing as cultural practice, by treating dramatic writing as textuality it confirms the drama's place in the boneyard: Antigone's bones lie near Aristotle's and Hegel's, and I suppose near Antony's and Anna Christie's too. Despite the apparent impact of "performativity and performance" in literary studies, reopening the territory between dramatic and performance studies requires a considerably more vigorous contestation of the "literary" dimension of drama, in which doing things *with* words resists the sense that it's the *words* that are doing the *doing*.[19]

The "theater of acting"

How might we read plays without conceiving stage performance as merely ministerial, "interpretive," derivative of the drama's "literary" design? More to the point, how might dramatic writing be understood in ways that reimagine the interface between *archive* and *repertoire*, text and body, in ways that could promote the affordance of dramatic writing to an emerging conception of performance? In his 1975 book *The Actor's Freedom*, Michael Goldman worked to redirect thinking about drama, attempting to "develop a way of talking about drama that is not contaminated by notions derived from literature" (4). As he suggests, this is indeed a difficult task, not least because "drama, reduced to the words connected with it – scripts – looks very much *like* literature, often has a decidedly 'literary' interest – and words are more at home talking about other words than about anything else" (4). It's a surprising gesture, in part because Goldman's frame of reference feels so familiar: T. S. Eliot casts a shadow, as does the Cambridge School, and *The Actor's Freedom* takes in the then-standard syllabus, *Oedipus* and Aristotle, *Quem Quaeritis*, Marlowe and Shakespeare, Ibsen and Chekhov, Brecht and Beckett, extending the critical outlines of

Understanding Drama or *The Idea of a Theater*. And yet, Goldman proposes a reading strategy in which the verbal organization of the script
works not to structure a literary design echoed in performance, but
something else: "the confrontation that takes place between any actor
and his audience; plays are best understood as ways of intensifying
that confrontation and charging it with meaning" (3).

Conceptualizing drama as an instrument of performance, Goldman's
work can be understood as part of a widespread movement to rethink
the "interpretation" of drama, and to resituate an "interpretive" model
of text-to-performance taking place across dramatic studies, from
Aeschylus and Sophocles, to Shakespeare and early-modern drama,
and to modern playwriting as well.[20] But *The Actor's Freedom* is also a
road not taken (and perhaps not seen), as Goldman sets dramatic performance – "the theater of acting" – at once within and against the
wider sphere of "performance."

> I use the word "theater" in these pages to refer not only to the place
> where plays are given but to the entire occasion of acted drama – that is,
> to the performance of parts by actors according to some kind of shaping
> intent. The notion is broadly inclusive, not limited to performances based
> on a written script, or even to the actor's taking on a character entirely
> separate from his own. It applies, that is, as much to the Open Theater's
> *Mutation Show* as to *Hamlet*. Most readers, I imagine, will find the defini-
> tion natural enough, but I call attention to it because some interesting
> recent criticism has approached acting under the general heading of
> "performance theory," and defined "theater" to mean any occasion of
> performance. I use "theater" in the more resricted sense partly for con-
> venience, of course, but I do insist on the difference between the theater
> of acting and other kinds of performance because I think it is a radical
> one. Acting *is* a type of performance, as speech is a type of communica-
> tion, but in both cases the subclass is so distinctive, so rich and singular,
> that it can be misleading to treat it on terms of parity with other members
> of the general classification.
>
> If anyone wishes to call a circus "theater," let him do so by all means.
> There are interesting points of similarity between circus and drama. And
> dramatic elements make their appearance in almost any kind of perform-
> ance. But my use of "theater" does keep together under a single heading
> what centuries of artists all over the world have persisted in bringing
> together – what most people commonly have in mind when they say
> "theater." More important, it points to a distinction between this kind of
> theater and circuses, demonstrations, ballet, encounter groups, sports,

religious ritual, etc., that corresponds to a widely held feeling – and the elaborate recognition of many cultures – that the theater of acting is very special, uniquely satisfying, like nothing else; that the difference is sharp, clear, and profoundly important; and that the theater of acting is as radically different from other kinds of performance as writing is from painting. (ix–x)

Implicitly countering the emerging practice of an as-yet-unnamed performance studies, Goldman's tactical "theater of acting" enables him to chart a distinctive course for dramatic theory, negotiating between a narrowly "literary" understanding of dramatic-performance-as-interpretation-of-the-text on the one hand, and the incipient force of a "performance theory" often working, appropriately enough, to marginalize dramatic performance in the wider arena of performance activity or to remove it altogether from the field.

First, Goldman counters a salient element of the "literary" view that the business of the stage is to "imitate" or "interpret" the dramatic world set out by the playwright. This rejection of performance-as-mimesis is precisely what the "theater of acting" shares with the conception of performance emerging from "performance theory." Defining the "theater of acting" as a genre of *performance*, Goldman positions *The Actor's Freedom* as a corrective to Richard Schechner's influential 1971 article, "Actuals."[21] In this foundational essay, Schechner makes a working distinction between mimetic performance events (dramatic theatre) and those – he includes Tiwi ritual, shamanistic performance, The Living Theatre's *Paradise Now*, Alan Kaprow's *Fluids*, Jerzy Grotowski's *Apocalypsis cum figuris* and *Akropolis*, and the Performance Group's *Makbeth* and *Dionysus in 69* – that refuse a conceptual "hierarchy," resist placing "any life-process 'above' any other," writing above enactment, mimetic representation above the present performance ("Actuals" 64). Yet as Goldman points out, "Schechner's distinction between the immediacy of the performer and that of the play, though 'anti-literary' in bias, actually has its roots in a distinctly literary view of drama" (32). Goldman doesn't characterize that "literary view," but perhaps he didn't need to, given the still-pervasive grip of the New Criticism in the 1970s. Seduced perhaps by the design of the printed page, for the New Criticism and an emerging performance studies, drama was principally an order of words, "dialogue" rather than action, and the function of performance was syntactically parallel with reading. Schechner's dramatic theatre is "representational" in just this way: much like Brooks and Heilman, Schechner assumes that the purpose of dramatic theatre is to subordinate the act of performance to the inherent code of the script.

Goldman was right to note that Schechner's vision of drama in the 1970s was "literary"; the gestural resistance of performance studies to the disciplines of drama depends on it. We can all agree, as Schechner has more recently suggested, that "literature and performance: they're two different subjects" ("Interview" 202), requiring different methods and attending – sometimes – to different objects of inquiry. Yet drama isn't always and only "literature": sometimes it provides a material instrument for performing, and it's precisely in this arena that Schechner's distinction between "fixed" forms – films, films of performances, writing – and the informal mutability of "behavior" begins to break down:

> Behavior is marked by qualities of presence and contingency, both contested terms. *Presence* means that the author or producer of the behavior is there actually behaving, actually doing at the same moment and in the same space with the receivers. *Contingence* means that no score is perfectly reenacted time and again. Every instance is either an original or there is no original anytime. ("Interview" 203)

Of course, in the "theater of acting" the "author or producer of behavior is there actually behaving," acting in contingent ways that both change from night to night, and have little to do with reenacting any imaginable score. There's nothing in the script of *Hamlet* that tells an actor how to act, how to use "To be or not to be" to create a significant act onstage, or what to do with and through the sounding of those words. Yet anticipating Taylor's *archive* and *repertoire*, Schechner advances an arresting hermeneutics. The purpose of "the study of literature," and so of forms of performance predicated on "literature," is to "keep the words intact, but change their meanings through interpretation" (204). Antigone's bones: Schechner isolates dramatic performance from the principal trajectories of cultural and philosophical critique of the past quarter century, which have tended to see the "interpretation" of art objects changing the objects themselves, a condition that is especially true in relation to objects, like dramatic writing, that afford behavioral, contingent, present *performances* rather than mere "interpretations."

For this reason, Schechner's sense that a "behavior-based outlook, a performative outlook, introduces the ability to change the primary text" (204) is not only not news but installs a distinction that makes little difference (think of the editions of *Hamlet* published during or shortly after Shakespeare's lifetime, Q1, Q2, F1; of the editorial tradition performing the play in print for the subsequent centuries, Rowe, Malone, Bowdler, Bevington, Oxford, *Classics Illustrated*; but also of the performance tradition itself, Burbage, Garrick, Gibson, the Wooster Group). In its representation and instigation of behavior, dramatic performance has always (already) altered the text, rewriting it and multiplying it into the many texts used in a given production (the great majority forsaken by the performance itself), as well as absorbing writing into the *repertoire*'s practices of embodiment, action resisting digestion into textuality. As John Rouse notes, the "director's control is less over performance writing than over performance discourse" (147). Although we surely cannot study performance through textual materials alone, Schechner's notion that directors have a choice whether to take the "dramatic text not as the cause or the prior authority but simply as material" (210) is slightly misframed: the text is always material, and different *repertoire*s of performance use it, stake its instrumentality in different ways.

Sharing the intellectual milieu that inspired an antidramatic performance studies – anthropology, Freud and Erikson, Artaud, Grotowski – *The Actor's Freedom* explores an attitude, a rhetoric, and a mode of critique capable of seizing dramatic writing as at once material for use conditioned by its production in/for/as theatrical work, and as representation, not of a fictional world but of the present physical process of its own performance. Goldman takes dramatic writing less to determine the theatre's representational field in opposition to the present work of performance (*archive* vs. *repertoire*, writing vs. behavior) than as a Burkean interrogation of the *agents, agencies, acts*, and *scenes* of stage performance, the "theater of acting." Resisting the New Critics' "interpretive" theatre, *The Actor's Freedom* resists offering merely a new "interpretation" of textual meanings, instead undertaking a processual reading strategy, an effort to use the "unremitting immediacy of theatrical experience" to think through the possibilities – the rather generalized possibilities to be sure – for inhabiting the drama, not as a "representation of reality," but as "reality itself, there before us in the theater" (34).

To read drama as an element of performance rather than as a complete and organic verbal expression is to challenge the sense that the
"work" inheres solely in the text, to be decanted more or less authori-
tatively to the stage, that since drama frames *"characters*, who make
speeches" (Ransom, *New* 169), good acting is a form of "responsible"
paraphrase-in-speech, as Brooks and Heilman argued in their reading
of *Rosmersholm*. Rather than taking *character* to be expressed in *speech*,
a mere enunciation of the play's verbal order, Goldman sees *character*
as a medium of interchange, and while "all dramatic characterization
has, in this sense, an iconic aspect," the purpose of the mask-like dramatic role is less to reify a mimetic fiction than to project "some motif
in the actor's repertory of emotional aggression" (50). Dramatic writing
provides the actor with a *repertoire* of potential activity to be seized by
the available *repertoire* of acting; *character* is not inscribed, a thing, but
an effect emerging consequentially from how the actor-as-character
"acts – that is, how he moves in and out of his repertory of roles" (92).
In the 1970s it was common to draw a parallel between acting and
shamanistic rituals, but though acting may resemble possession, actors
are not *possessed* by "characters": the virtual beings created in the
"theater of acting" don't exist elsewhere, awaiting their reappearance,
reanimation. This "thing" that appears "again tonight" at the opening
of *Hamlet* is ontologically complex, to be sure, but on the crowing of
the cock he returns to fast in fictive fires; but when Hamlet stops
playing Pyrrhus onstage, Pyrrhus dissolves into the trivial fond records
of sometimes misremembered words. Theatrical presentation materializes, sustains, localizes, and so betrays dramatic representation: "acting
itself is always in some sense the subject of the play" (92).

As many playwrights (Shaw, Stein, Parks, and Kane come to mind)
have recognized, the printform of plays – neat columns of type, tidily
assigning various "speeches" to various "characters" – at once impris-
ons the drama and, occasionally, provides an instrument for challenging the *repertoire* of performance practices. In the "theater of acting,"
words are incorporated through all the means of the actor's *repertoire*
for inhabiting an action, to render the contingent *behavior* of the stage
significant, to make something happen in the qualified but nonetheless
palpable event of the theatre. Far from modeling dramatic performance
(*"characters*, who make *speeches"*), "Speech is a problem in drama,"
not least because "Each line of dialogue must make up for what
it destroys" (117). Speech interrupts the presence of performance,

inserting its textuality into the lived and living enactment. The "theater of acting" must discover not the literary expressiveness of its dialogue, but its precise affordance as action within the disguise/revelation dynamic of acting: "Speech in particular, because of its mobility, its density of impressions, should always be thought of as a disguise – a disguise that slips, reveals, changes, strains to be adequate, strains even to be true or transparent to what it describes, breaks away, breaks down, stiffens, must be bolstered up" (93). And insofar as acting, acting with words in this case, is "a way of learning to think with the body" (89), it belongs to the *repertoire*'s strategies of embodiment, "performances, gestures, orality, movement, dance, singing" (Diana Taylor 20). The purpose of acting is not merely to clothe *Antigone*'s bones with new flesh – the zombie theory of drama – but to use writing as a means to render the present relation with an audience significant through the actor's shifting repertory of role-playing.

Reading drama between *archive* and *repertoire*, writing and behavior, poetry and performance demands a resistance to "literary" notions of textual fidelity and reproduction; it involves a processual engagement with *character* as a process of *doing*, of change, disguise, role-playing, performance. It means thinking "with the body" about how language can be used to specify and develop an event taking place onstage, and the significant inhabiting of that unique relationship between actor and an audience of spectators. It also means thinking with bodies in history: today's actors are trained – in New York and Johannesburg and Los Angeles and Montreal and Mumbai and London – to do things with words, to do specific and different things, and certainly do different things than Olivier or Irving or Garrick or Burbage did. Yet both Schechner and Taylor see the possibility of this kind of event taking place to be foreclosed by the essential fixity of writing, and by the ideologically reproductive function of writing sustaining the cultural *archive*. In his more recent meditation on the work of dramatic genre, *On Drama*, Goldman more directly takes on the critique of writing, the "textualization" of performance, arguing that the "mutual permeability of actor and script" addresses a "more-than-philosophical anxiety about the relation between between persons and texts." Far from endorsing either the Geertzian sense "that cultural forms can be treated as texts" (Geertz 449), or the familiar critique of the ethnocentrism of Geertz's "textualizing" perspective on performance culture developed by Conquergood and deployed by Taylor, Goldman has come to see a

"textualized" performance to be "crucially challenged by the phenomenon of theatrical performance" itself. For all the theatre's text-like
conventionality, acting is not "reducible to texts," merely providing "a
text supplementary to the script" (*On Drama* 49), what Schechner and
others call a "performance text." Much as Judith Butler underscores the
"scandalous" dimension of embodied performance, the extent to which
the speaking body "always says something that it does not intend"
(*Excitable* 10), so for Goldman, "in drama one finds inevitably an
element in excess of what can be semiotically extracted" from a reading
of performance (*On Drama* 49–50). It's precisely the dramatic text's
externality, the fact that "Contrary to Derrida, there is *always* an hors-
texte, a place from which someone at some moment needs to enter,
even to constitute the text as a text" that marks the drama's insistence
on the "mutually constitutive commerce between that which is writing
and that which is not" (51). In the theatre, "text and performance are
experienced as generating one another" (52–3), and this generative
principle animates the vitality of "the theater of acting."

I spend so much time here on Goldman's work because it marked
– at the dawn of performance studies' critical emergence – one alternative strategy for conceiving the work of drama between poetics and
performance, a strategy addressing several of the problems that both
literary studies and performance studies had with dramatic performance. Reading drama in 1975, Goldman provided a point of resistance
to the illusory dominion of "literature" in the theatre, modeling a way
to seize the specificity of dramatic writing as an encounter with embodiment, a means to reflect writing as an instrument of action rather than
as a script of subjection. Nor was Goldman alone: Bernard Beckerman's
1979 pairing of *activity* with *action* as a means of leveraging dramatic
analysis out of the text, and his articulation of performance as a holistic
activity ("an audience does not see with its eyes but with its lungs, does
not hear with its ears but with its skin. […] Nor do we have to discriminate the dramatic signals mentally in order to react") evokes a wider
effort to pursue a critical and theoretical resituation of dramatic writing
in performance (150). With the benefit of hindsight, we can see why
some of the avenues charted in *The Actor's Freedom* may not have been
pursued: many of its key terms (absence/presence) would soon be
widely foregrounded under the sign of Derridean deconstruction;
despite its attention to acting and theatre, few actual moments of acting
and theatre are brought to bear; actors, the plays they perform, and the

audiences they perform with are unmarked by gender, sexuality, race, location, politics; the Western theatre incorporates the presence of the "primitive" – drawn as much from traditional cultures as from children's play – without much explicit self-consciousness of the acts of appropriation that such cultural transfer might involve (one might well have similar hesitations regarding some of Schechner's or Victor Turner's work in the 1970s, too). And yet, even while the animating gesture of Goldman's work is to reorient a program of *reading*, what we read when we read drama is not the intrinsic relation between words on the page but the ways writing can be understood to instigate *behavior*, action *contingent* on the means of a given historical theatre and the ideologies of acting, action, spectating, and visibility it materializes. Goldman's perspective stands behind more recent work, such as Simon Shepherd's *Theatre, Body and Pleasure* (2006), which suggestively reads the demands of enacting specific roles in the history of Western theatre (Horner and Harcourt in Wycherly's *The Country Wife*, Herod in medieval cycle drama, Marlowe's *Tamburlaine*) to document how the "acting bodies" shaped by dramatic performance "are specific to particular sorts of text and theatre, and hence they are both shaped by, and contribute to, the 'dramatic rhythm' of the text" (81). Anticipating the "constant state of interaction" between *archive* and *repertoire*, Goldman, Beckerman, and others opened a means of attending to the specificities of dramatic performance that are only now beginning to be realized as their cultural and theoretical legacy.

Rethinking writing

There is hardly a dearth of writing about drama. Much of this critique, though, is concerned with making dramatic writing "perform" in a range of nontheatrical rhetorical, theoretical, and ideological venues, and even "performance-oriented" criticism frequently tracks the purpose of critique back to performance-as-interpretation. Some of the most celebrated readings of drama under the sign of "performance studies" – I'm thinking here of Joseph Roach's superb account of the 1710 visit of Iroquois ambassadors to *Macbeth* in *Cities of the Dead*, or of Timothy Raphael's surrogation of *Hamlet* in Ronald Reagan's address at a military cemetery in Bitburg, Germany, a cemetery in which members of the Waffen SS were buried ("Mo[u]rning") – primarily engage the drama's narrative and thematic dimension as an analytical

Instrument for reflecting on the cultural consequences of signal political events (Raphael) or reconstruct a specific theatrical event to ramify
and particularize the significance of deeper cultural trends (Roach). Jon
McKenzie has noted that the "liminal norm" characterizing performance studies "operates in any situation where the valorization of liminal
transgression or resistance itself becomes normative," and dramatic
writing and performance have often been constitutively positioned
across the disciplinary threshold of this "transgressive" self-conception
(*Perform* 50). Yet the impact of performance studies has been registered
in the absorption of its gestures and categories across this "liminal
norm," in ways that alter the disciplinary boundaries and what it
means to transgress them. In what we might take to be its two signal
gestures – a resistance to reading dramatic performance as the literary
illumination of the text, and a reciprocal reflection on the uses of writing
in the embodied conventionality of performance (the *performative*) –
dramatic critique, since *The Actor's Freedom* at least, has worked less to
privilege the determining function of writing than to resituate the
potential *agency* of writing in reshaping the interface of *archive* and
repertoire, the *scene* of *writing* and *behavior*.

The decisive moment in this trajectory was opened by Jacques
Derrida's celebrated essays, "La Parole Soufflée" and "The Theater of
Cruelty and the Closure of Representation" (1978), which locate
Antonin Artaud within a wider effort to unseat the logocentric hierarchy of metaphysics, and the collocation of the foundational categories
of presence and absence with speech and writing. Rather than locating
performance in a derivative, secondary, lapsed, and merely "interpretive" relation to writing, this critique charts the interaction of writing
and performance in their mutual co-creation. Contemporary dramatic
theory is not "against interpretation" exactly, but in resisting familiar
"literary" models of the priority of text-to-performance, it necessarily
resists "interpretive" accounts of theatre and the paradigms of reading,
writing, and performance they sustain, models essential to interring
drama in the *archive*. In this sense, contemporary dramatic theory
promotes alternative ways of *reading* drama, strategies that resist a
"literary" determination of dramatic theatre and the "textualization"
of performance it implies. The four influential studies considered here
– Stanton B. Garner, Jr., *Bodied Spaces: Phenomenology and Performance
in Contemporary Drama* (1994), Herbert Blau, *The Audience* (1990),
Benjamin Bennett, *All Theater Is Revolutionary Theater* (2005), and

Hans-Thies Lehmann, *Postdramatic Theatre* (1999; English translation 2006) – are hardly monovocal, yet they suggest a considerably more dynamic horizon for the reading of drama against the background of contemporary performance.

Noting the impact of performance studies – "Dramatic performance, it is often maintained, is only a subset of theatrical performance (which is itself only a subset of *performance* in its broadest meaning, a category that has grown to include other performing media arts, ritual, and various forms of social performance)" (5) – Stanton B. Garner, Jr.'s *Bodied Spaces* openly confronts the challenge "that a study concerned with the phenomenological parameters of theatrical performance should conduct its investigation largely in reference to the dramatic text, that prescriptive artifact whose traditionally literary authority contemporary performance theory has sought to overthrow" (5). Yet Garner calls for "a markedly different notion of the dramatic text from that of traditionally literary study" (6). While Goldman rejects a "literary" account of the drama in order to pursue its instrumentality in a "theater of acting," Garner urges a phenomenological mode of reading capable of describing the peculiar oscillation between the fiction onstage and the "complex participations of the dramatic event," a field including "not only the spectator and the performer who offers his or her body to view, but also the character whom this performer bodies forth" (7). This phenomenological reading, moreover, must resist "the neo-Aristotelianism that still governs much critical theory" of drama in order to "reembody, materialize the text, draw out this latency – not simply as a teleological point of realization beyond the playscript, but as an intrinsic component of dramatic textuality itself" (7).

Garner proposes a means of "reading 'through'" (6) the dramatic text to discover a range of "phenomenological configurations" it might motivate (5) within the implicit conventions of contemporary Western theatricality. Here, dramatic writing neither governs the theatrical event nor casts it as mere "interpretation," nor is it conceived principally from the actor's perspective. Instead, the text provides a means to conceive, explore, and theorize the uses of performance, the "specific bodily configurations and perceptual orientations" (7), as well as the historical record of past encounters. Charting writing's "multiple relationships to the moment of performance" (123), its operation in the "intercorporeal field" (36) of the theatre, seizing the theatre not in terms of "presence" but "in terms of *presencing*" (43), *Bodied Spaces* finally resists a logocentric role for the text in performance and also resists – strikingly, in ways resembling those of Conquergood and Taylor the application of a Geertzian "textuality" to embodied culture. For Garner, too, is impatient with the abstraction of "the body" such textualization implies, "the apparent ease with which contemporary theory has dispatched the phenomenal (or lived) body in favor of the representational (or signifying) body" (13). Transforming the body into a text-like sign, reading its meanings in purely symbolic or semiotic terms, articulates "a model of enactment and spectatorship essentially Aristotelian in outlines: in which the theater plays its meanings before the gaze of a privileged spectator who stands (or sits, as it were) outside the conditions of spectacle" (45). *Antigone* may be bones in the *archive*, but the relationships it enables us to produce, inhabit, and perform emerge in the precise configurations of specific modes of theatrical encounter. More to the point, contemporary drama encodes paradigms of spatialization that represent and so render legible the phenomenal codes with which we inhabit the world.

For Goldman, dramatic writing is the instrument of an actor's encounter with an audience; for Garner, writing similarly provides an instrument for charging the *scene* of that encounter with spatial and perceptual specificity. Garner's effort to spatialize the embodied relations of dramatic performance resonates not only with phenomenological accounts of drama, but also with efforts to engage the material functioning of space and place in dramatic performance.[22] Herbert Blau's work, difficult as it is to characterize, might be described as assimilating contemporary critique of the drama to a longer literary and philosophical tradition through the insights gained from performance itself. While Goldman uses dramatic writing to explore the action of the "theater of acting," Blau (co-founder and co-director of the Actors' Workshop of San Francisco; co-director of the Repertory Theatre at Lincoln Center; director of KRAKEN) asks how writing and its enactment might, occasionally and unpredictably, precipitate theatre, and his influential series of books constitutes "a meditation, through that experience of theater, on the dynamics of disappearance," a dynamics which, in Blau's writing, often takes place at the interface between the historicity of writing and the immediacy of doing (*Take Up the Bodies* ix).

Despite Blau's insistent contemporaneity, the history of dramatic critique reverberates through his writing, including the salient studies of the 1950s – Burke, of course, but also Francis Fergusson and Eric

Bentley jostle alongside Derrida and Butler – and one disarming and revealing element of *The Audience* is the return of T. S. Eliot to the field of dramatic theory.[23] Blau, in one sense, straddles the literary goals of an earlier generation and the resistance to textual authority character- istic of the Derridean 1970s, a tension that's palpable in his treatment of Eliot, and of the function of writing in performance more broadly. Though Blau hardly sees the dramatic text determining performance, he has no problem with poetry in the theatre: Yeats's "impatience with narrative sprawl, the mechanics of credibility in the unfolding of a plot" is brought forward as an instance of performance "at the edge of the unrepresentable" (*Audience* 160) (we might note that Blau at Stanford and Goldman at Princeton wrote PhD dissertations on the theatrical force of Yeats's plays). For Eliot, "words slip, slide, decay with impreci- sion," but "However bad-mouthed they may be, or aleatory, so long as you can make them out, there's a sticky accretion of the social that in the politics of the unconscious bears the stain of history" (125). Writing bears the "stain of history" into performance, but although (recalling Eliot's distinction in "Tradition and the Individual Talent") "the difference between art and the event is always absolute," it's pre- cisely the uptake of art*work* – writing in this case – in the event that is at stake in dramatic performance, "the indeterminable overflow of art into life reciprocated by the ceaseless incursion of life in art" (265; see Eliot, "Tradition" 42). This distinction, for Blau as for Bentley, draws Eliot into the orbit of the modern era's most pervasive theatri- cian, Bertolt Brecht, and defines the place of writing in dramatic performance. While the theatre is not predicated on language, it can – sometimes, in some forms – be precipitated through the *agency* of language, the reconstruction of art as living event.

For Blau, drama and theory permeate one another as means of thought, perhaps what Burke would call "symbolic action," and despite the theatre's use of writing, that writing is always in motion, thinking about and with performance, not in place of performance, and without predetermining performance: it's the "playing out of expectancy as *alterability* that constitutes the history of a text in performance" (47). Blau cannily notes that the moment "when performance came on the scene to posit itself *against* theater – a correlative of the antioedipal assault on logocentrism – it was in a period of body language, non- verbal or antiverbal or schizophrenically verbal, that was also against interpretation" (137). As in psychoanalysis or the Oedipus complex,

the interminable assault on language constitutes dramatic perform-
ance· "Whatever the style, hieratic or realistic, texted or untexted – box
it, mask it, deconstruct it as you will – the theater disappears under
any circumstances; but with all the ubiquity of the adhesive dead, from
Antigone's brother to Strindberg's Mummy to the burgeoning corpse
of Ionesco's *Amedée*, it's there when we look again" (137). In theatrical
performance, writing offers less a "stable signifier" than an opportunity to look again, to "take up the bodies," *our* bodies, for a renewed
assault on writing, and on history, through our means of affording it
performance.

Dramatic writing provides a means for exploring acting, for interrogating bodies, for searching the desire to perform and to watch
performance, to see "this thing" appear again tonight with the unerring
recognition that its appearance will replace the writing we may remember, and instigate remembering it anew. It's perhaps not surprising that
Blau articulates drama with performance. For Benjamin Bennett – who
is more directly drawn to the interface between drama and literature
as institutions – it's precisely performance that marks the drama's
inability to be conceived fully as "literature," and, more implicitly,
drama's status as writing that locates it differentially in the field of
"performance" as well.[24] In *Theater as Problem* (1990), Bennett argues
that drama *"as a literary type* [...] has a profound *disruptive* effect upon
the theory of literature in general" (*Problem* 1), a disruption arising
from its necessary implication in and of the stage, a productive medium
external to the process, values, and materiality of "literature." Extending
this argument in *All Theater Is Revolutionary Theater* (2005), Bennett
rejects the "interpretive" theatre of the New Criticism and its refiguration as *archive*, because any theatrical procedure for realizing the drama
stands in an exterior and arbitrary relation to the text, a necessary
means of exposing the text to performance rather than realizing it in
some definitive manner. On the one hand, the arbitrariness of performance is necessary to the category of "drama" itself, for "precisely literary tradition, the domain of the tyranny of writing, insists on a clear
generic distinction between drama and other literary forms, which
would be a meaningless distinction if it did not imply that theatrical
performance is necessary for the complete unfolding of the meaning
(or indeed for the very existence) of a dramatic work" (*Revolutionary*
66). On the other, Bennett rejects the notion that it is possible to "distinguish between possible performances and the drama 'itself,'" in the

manner both of older "literary" criticism of drama and of much recent performance-oriented critique (of, say, Shakespeare), because this distinction "would imply that performance is not strictly necessary after all, since the drama prior to performance is knowable" (67). In other words, "The 'work' itself is not available as a standard. Only the performance is available" (and here Bennett means the individual, contingent, behavioral experience of an actual performance in a theatre), performance which must always, from the perspective of "literary tradition," exhibit "strictly contradictory qualities" (67).

For this reason, "the exposure of writing to performance" (61) demanded by drama is the source of its disruptive position in the *archive* of literary genres; and – though this is not the burden of Bennett's argument – it is also the source of drama's disruptive position in the *repertoire* of performance genres, at least to the degree that we understand the always unscripted *repertoire* to gain, on many notable occasions at least, conceptual and even "revolutionary" leverage from the friction of writing. Bennett does not associate writing and textuality with oppressive Western epistemologies in the manner of Conquergood and Taylor. At the same time, his resonant critique of "interpretivity" also rejects a Geertzian "textualization" of culture while moving beyond a static dichotomy between writing and enactment. Performance resists being reduced to *hermeneusis* and cannot escape it; performance is for Bennett motivated by "interpretivity," the constitution of performance as an interpreting experience (though we should not understand "interpretation" as the New Critics did, as a paraphrase-in-performance of the dramatic text). What performance generates is a "social event," the incorporation of an "interpretivity" that finally cannot deliver an "interpretation" within the event, a closure to the hermeneutic circle, because performance "lacks the textlike focus and stability that enable an interpretation (in hermeneutic space) to serve as the text for further interpretation" (185). Interpreting a text produces another text that is itself subject to further interpretation, but the interpretation of a performance does not transform the performance into a text: the relationship between the interpretive text and the performance remains incommensurable, much as the relation between the dramatic text and the performance developed from/with/against it. Performance "introduces a nonlimitable plurality even at the starting point of the *hermeneia*" (185), excess that exceeds even the "heresy of paraphrase" (Brooks, *Urn* 180).[25]

Bennett's vision of dramatic performance resembles the most pervasive models of nondramatic performance analysis: Richard Schechner's
restored behavior and Joseph Roach's *surrogation*. Both Roach and
Schechner are concerned to model the nontextual transmission of
history through forms of performance outside of or strategically resistant to writing. Yet as Schechner notes, "Performance is not merely a
selection from data arranged and interpreted; it is behavior itself and
carries in itself kernels of originality, making it the subject for further
interpretation, the source of further study" ("Restoration of Behavior"
51): Bennett's distinction between hermeneutic and performance space
suggests, though, that by "interpretation" here we should understand
"further performance."[26] Framing an undecidable relation between
dramatic writing and its exposure to performance, Bennett implies that
the *repertoire* of performance *restores* or *surrogates* writing as behavior,
rather than being overwritten by it. The dialectic between culturally
inflected features of the text and the available (and similarly culturally
inflected) practices of embodiment is where the dramatic event
takes shape.

It has been some time since dramatic theory regarded the principal
function of dramatic performance as the *representation* of a fictive world.
In historical terms, the influential New Critical fiction of the theatre-of-
writing is, as Erika Fischer-Lichte argues, belied by the modern theatre's shift toward the sense of "performance as an autonomous work
of art" in which "No longer does the text steer, control, and legitimize
performance. Rather, the text becomes one material among other materials – like the body of the actor, sounds, objects et cetera – each of
which the performance manipulates or adapts, thereby constituting
itself as art" ("Avant-Garde" 80–1). Yet while she takes this democra-
tization of the materials of performance as typical of modernism, she
also notes, "Theater always fulfills a referential and a performative
function. While the referential function deals with the representation
of figures, actions, relationships, situations, and so forth, the performative deals with the realization of actions – through performers and
through the audience – and in this sense, with the 'eventness' of
the theater" (81–2). The history of theatre, and of modern and postmodern theatricality in particular, might be tracked through the shifting ratio between these functions, referential or performative, between
the Burkean *agency* of writing and the *scene* of theatre, between what
Julia A. Walker characterizes as the "conceptual" register of writing

and the "affective and experiential register" of embodied action ("Why" 165).[27]

This both/and understanding of theatricality drives and complicates Judith Butler's conception of the "performativity" of gender, and motivates the wider spectrum of theatrical interrogations of identity, beginning with gender, race, and sexuality and extending into a conception of transnational, globalized, and intercultural performance today. Elin Diamond even characterizes stage realism – surely the mode of theatre most evidently predicated on the production of a representation *there*, onstage, *in front of us*, derived from the loquacious direction of the text (think of Shaw or O'Neill) – at the referential/performative interface, as "more than an interpretation of reality," but a means of producing " 'reality' by positioning its spectator to recognize and verify its truths" (Diamond 4). Realism famously works to occlude the visible presence of the *theatrical*, and yet the ideological work of that occlusion is nonetheless palpable. So, too, the theatre's massive generation of alternative means of performance has used writing in a disarming variety of ways, often to expose rather than conceal the ideological constitution of *agents* and *agencies* on and off stage. If "textuality and performativity, in theory and in practice, always appear complementary and yet at the same time contestatory" (Vanden Heuvel 132) – a theoretical frame materialized in Baz Luhrmann's ironic insertion of "text" into the visual field of *Romeo + Juliet*, a gun labeled "sword" – then retaining this dynamic differentiation should be crucial to the theory of dramatic performance.

The consequences of interring dramatic performance in the *archive* extend beyond disciplinary practices along the borders between literary and performance studies; they also bear on the emerging critical practices and outlines of performance history today. In Hans-Thies Lehmann's powerful study of *Postdramatic Theatre*, theatre has entered a new epoch, defined as postdramatic precisely in its rejection of the dominance of the text and of the "representation" it puts before us. Contemporary performance surely exceeds the frontiers of the dramatic stage, which has always been a specialized form, distinguished from dithyrambic performances, the Mass, bearbaiting, dance, and even from genres like opera and musical theatre. But in *Postdramatic Theatre*, Lehmann suggests that the displacement of drama's "representational" character – fully identified with its scriptedness – motivates a contemporary transformation of the field of performance. Rather than locating dramatic performance between "the referential and the performative," for Lehmann dramatic performance is ferociously *archival*. its spectators "expect from the theatre the illustration of classic texts," leading to "a comprehensible fable (story), coherent meaning, cultural self-affirmation and touching theatre feelings" (19). Since its mode of performance is urgently derivative, "subordinated to the primacy of the text," dramatic performance consists in "the declamation and illustration of written drama" (21). Even taking various disruptive devices into account – plays within plays, choruses, prologues and epilogues, lyrical language, and epic dramaturgies – "the drama was able to incorporate all of these without losing its dramatic character" (22), namely the imposition of a textually derived representation over the presentational reality of the theatre.

Lehmann's argument arises in one sense against the landscape of European disciplinary and institutional traditions, often located under the term *Theaterwissenschaft*. In this perspective, the theatre studies/ performance studies, and theatre/drama distinctions may appear to map a distinctively North American territory; as Willmar Sauter suggests, "for northern European scholars the term 'theatre' does not designate any given genre of artistic activities" (43). For this reason, though, it's somewhat more surprising that Lehmann's vision of dramatic performance is so determinedly "literary" in character.[28] For Lehmann, "Wholeness, illusion and world representation are inherent in the model 'drama'; conversely, through its very form, dramatic theatre proclaims wholeness as the *model* of the real. Dramatic theatre ends when these elements are no longer the regulating principle but merely one possible variant of theatrical art" (22). Distinguishing between dramatic and postdramatic theatre, Lehmann – in ways reminiscent of Taylor's *archive* and *repertoire* or Schechner's *literature* and *behavior* – articulates a familiar sense of dramatic theatre as a fundamentally "literary" genre of performance. But this vision of postdramatic theatre begs the question: is a "text" always – or ever – "staged" in this way, translated in some direct manner into speech and depiction, "declamation and illustration"? Historically, the rise of print and the coordination of the representational technology of the theatre privileged a sense of the "natural" execution of certain forms of drama by the late-nineteenth- and early-twentieth-century stage. But we should note that many of the figures most associated with implementing the textually "illustrative" theatre – Stanislavski, Granville-Barker, Meyerhold – were simultaneously involved in alternative strategies for locating the work of writing in the panoply of theatrical performance, symbolism, biomechanics, and so on. Lehmann's "dramatic theatre" is hardly recognizable in the lens of contemporary drama studies, in which resisting the theatre-of-textual-interpretation also means resisting the projection of "representation" as the defining task of dramatic performance. Goldman's "theater of acting" constantly foregrounds the *process* of representation as its means, and its principal satisfaction as well: *acting* is the focus of our attention, not the *text*. Garner conceives performance as a complex "multiple positionality," deploying actual and fictive bodies and spaces in ways that constantly negotiate the "illusionistic crisis" of performance (43). Like the bodies of the actors themselves, those "self-modifying signifier[s]" (211), Bennett's theatre is "revolutionary" precisely because its "interpretivity" cannot be reduced to a reading of something else, the reproduction of textual "representation." It's the fact that dramatic performance gives "equal rights" to the "gestic, musical, visual" (Lehmann 46), and kinetic elements of performance that distinguishes it from *reading*, and the necessity of conceiving those elements that foregrounds, in Bennett's terms, the "fundamental defectiveness" (*Revolutionary* 194) of both reading plays and performing them.

While *Postdramatic Theatre* brilliantly accounts for the innovations of contemporary performance, and situates them in relation to stage modernism, the terms it brings forward might more usefully be conceived as definitive of emerging forms of dramatic performance. For example, "there are directors who may stage traditional dramatic texts but do so by employing theatrical means in such a way that a *de-dramatization* occurs" (74). Postdramatic theatre *de-dramatizes* writing (when it uses writing at all), accenting the "perpetual conflict between text and scene" (145), emphasizing the actor's "*auto-sufficient physicality*, which is exhibited in its intensity, gestic potential, auratic 'presence' and internally, as well as externally, transmitted tensions" (95), and even refiguring the status and meaning of the "*theatrical body*" which "does not exhaust itself" in signification and representation, having in performance "a value *sui generis*" (162).

Once we recognize that the "declamation and illustration" of the text is not essential to dramatic performance, then the defining principle of postdramatic theatre seems much less distinctive. Much the same might be said of Diana Taylor's heuristic for analyzing the textless performances of the *repertoire*, the *scenario*. While Lehmann assigns a purely representational force to dramatic performance, Taylor's liberating methodological alternative to the hegemony of writing over performance, the *scenario*, depends for its innovative force on the captivity of the drama and theatre to the iterative logic of print and a sense of theatre as purely representational. Taylor wants to use the *scenario* as a means to distinguish the radical energy of nonscripted performance from the normalizing force of theatre; the *scenario*, in a sense, *de-dramatizes* the narrative elements of the *repertoire*, drawing our attention primarily not to the fictive elements of representation but to the circumstances of presentational performance. The *scenario*, first, enables us to locate the performance in "a material stage as well as the highly codified environment that gives viewers pertinent information, say class status or historical period" (29). While these features of theatrical performance are often part of the dramatic scene or theatrical setting, they are of course also always features of the material historicity of performance as well. To see a performance in the Berliner Ensemble is constantly to be aware of the fin-de-siècle ornamentation of the building, and the history of warfare, political struggle, and artistic experimentation literally inscribed into its walls (the red X that Brecht painted over the Prussian coat of arms still visible before the proscenium; shrapnel marks in the banister; the Russian tank wheels that Helene Wiegel scavenged and had installed so that the stage's turntable would revolve more smoothly and quietly in support of, for example, Mother Courage's wagon). In other words, despite the fact that dramatic performances use texts, they are not in this sense any less part of the material and codified *scenario* of nonmatrixed performance. Similarly, we might find that the spectator's "need to deal with the embodiment of social actors" (29) is often a feature of dramatic performance, as is the sense that, like *scenarios*, dramatic performance offers "formulaic structures that predispose certain outcomes and yet allow for reversal, parody, change" (31).

Much as the representational fiction of dramatic performance cannot be distinguished from its presentational *agents, agencies,* and *purposes,* a *postdramatic* or *de-dramatized* emphasis on the presentational or performative aspect of performance is often haunted by the trace of representational referentiality. Dimiter Gotscheff's *Ivanov* at the Volksbühne in Berlin (which I saw in January 2005), for instance, fills the stage with smoke, framing Chekhov's drama as a series of *de-dramatized* dialogues: each character appears and disappears from the fog, apparently summoned by Ivanov from ... *where?* his mind? memory? rage? desperation? anomie? – well, summoned from somewhere else on the stage. The production plays largely to the audience, and the slowness of pace and bouts of monotone shouting characteristic of *postdramatic* German theatre enforce a constant awareness of the performance present. Even the events of the drama are staged in a way to defy the representation of a world elsewhere. For the climactic suicide, the smoke parts, Ivanov spray-paints a huge stick-figure of a man shooting himself on the upstage wall, and bodies drop one by one from the flies. And yet, while the production deflects the narrative order of a represented Chekhovian "world," it seems more adequate to say that the performance's interactive engagement of writing and performing constitutes an altered, responsive narrative, one that encodes perhaps a minimal degree of representation rather than entirely displacing it.[29] It discovers a new *agency* for Chekhov's play, fashioning a distinctive instrument for making play in the social technology of the contemporary stage.

Lehmann's brilliant and provocative book, much like Taylor's, charts the landscape of performance, reminding us that dramatic performance, for all its impact – an impact surely deepened and prolonged by print, which at once preserves the text and enables alternative means of access to it – is only a small and perhaps unrepresentative corner of performance *per se*. At the same time, as a range of dramatic critique suggests, a commitment to the work of performance need not exclude the drama on the basis of its apparently "literary" character. As Hamlet remarks, even *The Murder of Gonzago* can accommodate rewriting, a "speech of some dozen lines, or sixteen lines" (2.2.477) that marginally *de-dramatizes* or retheatricalizes its *agency* to serve present purposes. Rather than cataloguing the wide variety of ways the theory and criticism of drama have encountered the materiality of performance, I've tried here to attend to the distinctions that have in a sense positioned dramatic performance across the threshold of the "liminal norm" defining performance studies: the sense that written forms are "fixed" in a literary *archive* in contrast to the resistant multiplicity of the *repertoire* of performance, and the sense that dramatic writing exerts, like other forms of writing and like a Geertzian strategy of reading enactment as "text," a deforming pressure on both performance and our understanding of it. Although Shannon Jackson underlines the fiction of taking "dramatic literature" as an institutional dominant (it "was already outside the literary canon" 24), dramatic performance has been imag ined in performance studies as a powerful and defining antithesis to notions of a transgressive, embodied, mobile, and often subaltern reaction and resistance to authoritarian culture and its modes of historical representation. As David Román has argued of the metaphorical use of "drama" to organize "moments of institutional or disciplinary chaos" in American studies, so in fashioning performance studies, "Drama" – and dramatic performance – "is what is presumed to be known, so much so that it goes without saying" (23). Restoring complex strategies of reading drama, strategies capable of engaging the double *agency* of writing in the layered *scene* of theatre, would enable the interrogation of dramatic writing and performance to move beyond a "what is presumed to be known" that has been largely "known" as error, misrepresentation, for some time.

Even this small selection of texts suggests that there are not only powerful reasons for resisting this dichotomy, but for trying to reframe our understanding of the critical functions of writing in performance. Much as the critical projects assembled here may seem to stand apart from the "drama-to-cultural studies" genealogy, their concerns – writing as an instrument for embodiment, writing in the design of space, writing that precipitates an event, writing that abrades the conventions of experience – are readily and even necessarily inflected with specific materialities. To deploy these lines of inquiry toward their richest potential would mean asking whose bodies, which spaces, what genres of experience are being put into practice, questions that emerge at once pointedly and fitfully in this work and that demand a closer attention to the *performance* of dramatic performance. One instance of such a practice arises in Simon Shepherd's work; though Shepherd resists engaging specific performances, he charts several ways in which bodies are "culturally produced" in dramatic performance (Shepherd 12). "Theatre requires special things of bodies" (2), and dramatic analysis requires (at the least) a "generalised notion of a culture's performing technique," in order to "be alert to the particular moments at which that technique's relationship to its audience is affirmed, challenged, negotiated" (27). Though we might hesitate at Shepherd's framing of dramatic performance as a "particular scripting of the body" (27), to assess the terms of such an encounter means not only reaching across the textual horizon to seize the *repertoires* that make symbolic exchange between different forms, moods, and shapes of expression legible, but also resisting the notion that performance is captured once we can transcribe the code.

Blau takes language to bear the stain of history to the stage; writing bears an alterity of embodiment and subjection into the location and temporality of performance. If acting implies the ideological discipline of bodies toward culturally embedded means of signification, dramatic writing – with its comparable dialectic of conventionality and change, conformity and reconstitution – brings external patterns of *agency* to the production, language recording and instigating subjects in action, subjects it instigates but cannot fully represent. The material alterity of writing – like fabric or lumber, waiting to be shaped for use in/as performance – is readily perceptible in any cross-cultural event. The knotty unfamiliarity even of Shakespeare's or Jonson's or Shaw's language insists on this alterity even in the most contemporary or post-dramatic production; while our Antigones tend to speak a contemporary idiom, their words resonate with alien values, perspectives, attitudes. Recent dramatic writing also brings this alterity to the stage, a distinctive rhythm and reference to be worked into something else, the performance. Dramatic writing is writing for use; however we use it – under the sign of fidelity or betrayal, inclining toward the referential or the performative – it retains a grain, a warp given shape in the event. While this alterity is more visible and audible in some texts than others, it's always there, as much in David Mamet's scabrous nonsequiturs as in the opaque repetitions, rests, and spells of Suzan-Lori Parks.

This may sound like a return to the characters-making-speeches "literary" theatricality of the New Criticism, but that theatre only lives in the *archive*: we can find it in museified performances, often in "performance-oriented" criticism of dramatic literature, and – as Goldman pointed out in 1975 – in the framing of some of the critical instruments enabling performance studies. Dramatic performance must constantly rediscover the affordance of its tools in the changing social technology of the theatre, confronting the *archive* with the *repertoire*, or in Bennett's terms, exposing the *archive* to the *repertoire* in order to produce a unique event at the interface of art, unanticipated either by the text or by the stabilizing surrogations of restorative behavior. All the same, booking plays materializes the illusion of their *archival* stasis, or perhaps better put, fixes one form of writing as the pretext of the playing, a form of writing that's already multiple, and multiplied and forsaken in the

production process. Rather than prolonging the distracting distinction
between *archive* and *repertoire*, we might now attend to the aspect of
dramatic performance that this dichotomy fails to capture.

Writing can function as an *archive*: drama is a repository of instiga-
tions to action, software for producing significant events in the social
and cultural technology of a given theatre, and the ideologies of action,
acting, behavior, and identity it sustained. And yet, however much we
might track broad continuities in Western drama, the theatre's means
of transforming writing into performance are always under pressure.
Changing valuations of the human, of meaningful acts, of the means
and purpose of attention constantly change the shape of even the most
conventional regimes of performance. What is the affordance of different kinds of dramatic writing in different systems of production? How
does writing perform, in Anthony Kubiak's phrase, as a "lens through
which experience, thought, and emotion are excruciated" (14)? How
do we understand the warrant of "conventional" or "experimental" or
"postdramatic" production? How might we develop critical and pedagogical models for reading the drama as a site of *agency*, an instrument
for the construction of that peculiar – but not peculiarly hollow – *act*
performed by the *agents* of the stage in the *scene* of theatre?

Developing these questions requires, as Taylor indeed suggests, a
sense of the interaction between *archive* and *repertoire*, ways of reading
"the text" as open, material for use, susceptible to (re)construction
within contingent but nonetheless conventional systems of performing,
of rhetorical behavior, remembering that representation is not definitive of the rhetoric of theatre, and that the distinctive behaviors of the
"theater of acting" themselves relate to – intensify, reverse, quote,
epitomize, reduce, alienate, embody, what verb you will – the formalities of behavior in that other theatre just offstage. But, finally, it also
implies developing ways of assessing the materiality of writing, not
only in its generic formalities but how it instigates process and place,
locates the interface of representation and presentation, provides (some
of the) material for the distinctive "interpretivity" of dramatic events,
events that remain, it should be noted, a potent force of political critique, resistance, and action worldwide. It may well be, as D. J. Hopkins
and Bryan Reynolds suggest, that the "retention of the word 'drama'"
itself is the problem, or part of it, "a counterproductive vestige of
theater's fealty to a preexisting literary work" (273).[30] Fair enough:
perhaps the word "drama" is merely a distraction, incapable of being

disinterred from its connotations of a textually driven, organic, literary representation imagining its privilege over the means of the stage. But conceding that "Academic disciplines that focus on a study of 'drama,' whether that drama be read or performed, are rightly the province of literature studies," and that the "study of theater is 'theater studies'" (274), seems only to reify the problem at hand, a problem which strikes me as falling legitimately within performance studies' tradition of disciplinary intervention and disruption, a problem embraced by the dramatic conjunction of poetry and performance.

How do we, can we, articulate *writing* with/in/through *performance*? At a moment of concern with the "imperialist" potentiality of perform-ance studies (McKenzie, "Imperialist"), and of restless disenchantment "with the critical and theoretical paradigms that have dominated the field since the 1980s," one avenue of inspiration might be traced by revisiting critical openings overlooked, bypassed, or misconceived in the energetic fashioning of the field.[31] It may also imply developing ways of assessing the materiality of writing, not only in its textual formalities but how it instigates process and place, locates the interface of representation and presentation, provides (some of the) material for the distinctive "interpretivity" of dramatic events. As Peggy Phelan has suggested, "Theatre continually marks the perpetual disappearance of its own enactment" (*Unmarked* 115); it also marks the perpetual disap-pearance of drama, a fiction of significant action that becomes signifi-cant by remaining in play. As we shall see, dramatic writing often allegorizes the openness of writing as *agency*, the incomplete identity of the play with the book, of acting with character, of the fictive land-scape of the dramatic setting with the terrain of theatre. The *archive* preserves writing, enabling readers to encounter and imagine the work of drama, and the work that drama might *do*, anew. But the *repertoire* is the drama's difference engine, the machine of its (dis)appearance, and so of its distinctive survival.[32]

Chapter 2

Performing Writing: *Hamlet*

Words, words, words.

Hamlet *2.2.189*

Paper, paper, paper

Jacques Derrida, Paper Machine *(41)*

Words, words, words: As befits a play whose central character has returned from study in Wittenberg, books figure prominently in the action of *Hamlet*. Gertrude spies Hamlet "sadly" *reading on a book*, reading itself the sign of his wretchedness (Folio 2.2.164 stage direction), and Ophelia is later baited with her book, the excuse for her solitary lingering in Hamlet's way.[1] Stage and film productions often add other books to the mix; even in the 1603 quarto, the King notes Hamlet "poring upon a book" (1603 quarto, 7.110) just prior to the "To be, or not to be" soliloquy, licensing the notion that Hamlet's reflections are prompted by, perhaps even read from, a book.[2] But writing in *Hamlet* is hardly limited to books: Claudius has "here writ" (1.2.27) missives sent to Norway via Voltemand and Cornelius, who return bearing a written "entreaty" (2.2.76); Fortinbras's journey across Denmark is secured by a "license" (4.4.2); Claudius' "commission" (3.3.3) to Rosencrantz and Guildenstern is purloined and emended by Hamlet. Private letters circulate as well – Polonius sends "this money and these notes" to Laertes (2.1.1) while instructing Reynaldo on the verbal "forgeries" (2.1.20) he should lay on his son. Ophelia has received letters and other tenders from Hamlet, one of which Polonius reads to Claudius and Gertrude (along with a poem from the prince). Hamlet, famously, both reads and writes. Harrowed by the Ghost, he calls for a notebook, his "tables! Meet it is I set it down" (1.5.107).[3] He announces his return to Denmark in a letter to Horatio, and in separate letters to Claudius and Gertrude: both Horatio and Claudius perform their scripts, reading Hamlet's words aloud. Whether or not they're among the lines we hear, he writes "a speech of some dozen lines, or sixteen lines" (2.2.477) intended to lend *The Murder of Gonzago* point as performance.

Beyond material writing, the imagery of literate culture suffuses the play. Books and writing provide an essential metaphor for conscious-ness and character – Hamlet vows to wipe "all trivial fond records, / all saws of books" from the "book and volume" of his brain (1.5.103) – and writing is woven into the play's verbal texture, in Polonius' "forgeries," in the lawyer's cases, tenures, statutes, indentures that Hamlet mentions in the graveyard scene (see 5.1.93–105), in Ophelia as a "document in madness" (4.5.172). *Hamlet*, too, is rife with the canons of literary critique. Polonius is the agent of much of this critique, recit-ing the comic list of the players' capacity ("The best actors in the world, either for tragedy, comedy, history …" 2.2.333), assessing the "vile phrase" of Hamlet's poem (2.2.110), praising Hamlet's diction when he takes up Pyrrhus ("well spoken, with good accent and good discretion" 2.2.404–5) and the language of Aeneas' tale to Dido ("'The mobled queen'!" "That's good" 2.2.441–2). But Hamlet is also a critic, deriding *The Murder of Gonzago* as "a knavish piece of work," though "the story is extant and written in very choice Italian" (3.2.234, 255–6), and noting the critical "excellence" of the Trojan drama he requests from the Players. Much as the genres of "orature" – familiar proverbs, songs, and ballads – migrated to books in the early era of print, so they make their way into *Hamlet*, in Ophelia's songs, in Hamlet's japing "Jephtha judge of Israel" and perhaps "Why let the stricken deer go weep" ditty, whose "pajock" joke depends on our recognition of a suppressed rhyme, was / [ass], as Horatio points out (3.2.263–76).[4] Polonius' quot-able *sententiae* to Laertes, and his irritating quibbles with Claudius and Gertrude, mark another interface between written and oral culture, reciprocated in a sense by Laertes' ready assumption of the posture and emphasis of the stage revenger, "vows to the blackest devil, / Conscience and grace to the profoundest pit!" (4.5.130–1).[5]

Dramatic performance exemplifies the negotiation of literacy and orality in the period, and *Hamlet*'s obsession with both writing and playing locates a crucial moment of cultural transformation, inaugurating the modern dichotomies of drama between poetry and performance. *Hamlet*'s well-known interrogation of a theatricalized "world" imagines a specific kind of performance: dramatic theatre, ranging from the various scenarios devised by Polonius, Claudius, and Laertes to the formal play-within-the-play.[6] It's perhaps not surprising, then, that while Hamlet conceives his memory as "book and volume," he understands the plot that Claudius, Rosencrantz, and Guildenstern have devised to ensnare him as scripted drama ("Or I could make a prologue to my brains / They had begun the play"), a plot advanced, fittingly enough, by Hamlet's writerly recomposition of its ironic finale in a "fair" hand (5.2.29–37). Though Hamlet rebels against "actions that a man might play" (1.2.84), he's an old friend of the Players, and the speech he rehearses for them begins with a bookish false start; later, he is "as good as a chorus" commenting on *Gonzago* (3.2.238), and his graveside confrontation with Laertes "upon this theme" demonstrates his own mastery of the ranting script of grief. The Players advertise their impressive versatility in scripted drama, too – "scene indivisible or poem unlimited. Seneca cannot be too heavy nor Plautus too light" (2.2.335–7) – and Hamlet's advice evinces a writerly anxiety toward the proper enactment of "my lines" (3.2.4) out of place in an improvisational theatre, as is his irritable insistence on the appropriate division of labor between author and actor: "let those that play your clowns speak no more than is set down for them" (3.2.36–7).

Like Shakespeare's theatre itself, *Hamlet* lies across the cusp of a transformation in the technologies of drama. Obsessed with theatrical play, *Hamlet* evinces the impact of the expanding purchase of the professional theatre; obsessed with writing, it dramatizes the impact of print and the expanding literarization of the drama on and in the theatre.[7] Hamlet's manuscript additions to *The Murder of Gonzago* recall a common practice of Shakespeare's theatre; plays were not rehearsed or learned from printed books, and while Shakespeare's plays were more or less routinely published as quartos before 1600, whether drama had yet achieved fully "literary" status in the first years of the seventeenth century remains controversial. And yet, as the publication of plays in quarto, of Ben Jonson's 1616 *Works* in folio, and of Shakespeare's plays in 1623 suggests, print was assimilating the drama to the emerging canons of literary form, and *Hamlet* is an intriguing part of this story, too.[8] The short 1603 Quarto announces the play "As it hath beene diuerse times acted by his Highnesse seruants in the Cittie of London: as also in the two Vniuersities of Cambridge and Oxford, and else-where" (Irace 1); but this version was rapidly followed in press by the enlarged and improved 1604 version, advertising the authority of the book to reproduce the playwright's work: "Newly imprinted and enlarged to almost as much againe as it was, according to the true and perfect Coppie."[9]

Hamlet reads, Hamlet writes, Hamlet acts: *Hamlet* explores the dynamic exchange of performing writing. Philosophically involved in a reflexive contemplation of the ethics of theatricality, *Hamlet* signally interrogates the specific structures of dramatic theatre, the affordance of writing in performance. Rather than asking how the stage might "interpret" the text, here we will consider how *Hamlet*'s concern with writing, with books, generates a narrower inquiry into the *agency* of writing in the process of theatrical performance, in part by characterizing other ways writing is performed in the play. Scripted at the dawn of the age of print, *Hamlet* allegorizes the anxious relationship between scripted drama and its performance that continues to preoccupy drama and performance theory. The question continues to preoccupy performance practice, too, which must confront the archaic, illegible, and inaudible aspect of early-modern dramatic writing. Before turning to a recent performance that directly interrogates the play's persistence in the *archive* of performance, the 2007 *Hamlet* by the Wooster Group, we'll consider the challenges of performing writing when the words performed are simply unknown to a modern audience. While the play surely cannot answer, or answer for, the tectonic changes in Western theatre and culture, or in the technologies of writing and performance, it provides a way for asking how the drama reflects on the contested relationship between *archive* and *repertoire*, writing and performing.

i. Hamlet's Book

> "... *for the law of writ and the liberty. These are the only men."*
> (2.2.336–8)[10]

Playing the book

Hamlet's book is a striking prop, particularly when we recall how untheatrical *reading* is onstage: the book locates the play's interrogation of theatre specifically in relation to the canons of writing, of scripted drama. As Hamlet's metaphor of the "book and volume of my brain" may suggest, the sudden impact of print in early-modern Europe was the instrument of an emerging form of subjectivity: the practice of solitary, silent reading both reflected and reproduced the formation of a modern sense of inwardness, privacy, and individuality. Hamlet's initial rejection of the forms and moods of grief as "actions that a man might play" signals a withdrawal from all action as infected by the public means and manners of theatre; his isolation is marked early in 2.2 by Gertrude's "But look where sadly the poor wretch comes reading," marked in the Folio text by the preceding direction *Enter HAMLET reading on a book* (Folio, 2.2.164 s.d.). Yet while reading may be the mark of Hamlet's antitheatrical inwardness – a dramatic character asserting "that within which passeth show" (1.2.85) poses an essential challenge to signification on the stage – the *book* as a property of the action has a specific and surprising *use*, inaugurating an extended reflection on reading and doing, writing and performing.[11]

Hamlet enters the central action of the play *reading on a book*, and his response to Polonius – "Words, words, words" (2.2.189) – confirms two consequences of print's multiplication of writing and projection of reading as an act of private play: its contribution to the development of a sense of personal privacy, and the sense that as written documents multiply and circulate in increasingly inexpensive forms – quarto play-texts, for instance – the inscribed words they contain are at once privatized and devalued. Among its many other effects on language, notably the precipitation of words as things, "Print created a new sense of the private ownership of words" (Ong 131).[12] Hamlet's wordplay is typically literal-minded, scrupulously refocusing his audience's attention on words that have become soiled in their working, cheapened through blithe, manipulative repetition: *son, common, seems.* Here, the book simultaneously motivates Hamlet's multiplication of meanings and his withdrawal from public signification, as his emphasis on *words, matter, out of the air* keeps busybody Polonius at bay.

Asked what he is reading, Hamlet doesn't discuss the book, he performs it:

Slanders, sir. For the satirical rogue says here that old men have grey beards, that their faces are wrinkled, their eyes purging thick amber and plumtree gum, and that they have a plentiful lack of wit together with most weak hams – all which, sir, though I most powerfully and potently

believe, yet I hold it not honesty to have it thus set down. For yourself,
sir, shall grow old as I am – if, like a crab, you could go backward.
(2.2.193–201)

As P. K. Ayers suggests, while oral culture uses reading aloud as a
means of publication, of extending the accessibility of writing, print's
multiplication and dissemination of "identical or near-identical copies"
compromises the necessity for reading aloud and so facilitates silent
reading and its multiplication of private, subjective interpretations:
"The very conditions that generate material stability of the text, in other
words, simultaneously contribute to its hermeneutic instability" (Ayers
427, 428). Dramatic performance shares this sense of oral publication,
but *Hamlet* also signals the contemporary literarization of drama, its
preservation and publication not in the evanescence of performance
but as an alternative, permanent object, a book. Several handwritten
documents, manuscripts, are read aloud in *Hamlet*, notably all composed by Hamlet: Hamlet's letter and poem to Ophelia; his letter to
Horatio; his letter to Claudius. In these cases, performing writing is a
means to seize the "that within" of the text and its author: performing
writing is the *agency* for publicly assessing – publishing – the writing
agent. Of course, any performance represents the performer, and
Polonius' officiousness, Horatio's loyalty, Claudius' cunning are given
scope through the act of reading aloud. But the purpose of their reading
is to render Hamlet's matter public, interpretable, common knowledge.
Reading aloud, that is, is a ministerial – "text-based" – performance
genre in the play, manifestly gesturing to the authority of the text:
"What should this mean?" Claudius asks of Hamlet's letter (4.7.47).

But Hamlet's performance of the book is suggestively different.
Hamlet's book need not be printed, though its appearance for the
nonce, as a portable prop for "solo reading in a quiet corner" (Ong 131),
implies its ready availability, its lack of inherent value as an object, a
mere container of words, words, words. Its dramatic function as a
signifier of silent inwardness – both Hamlet and Ophelia apparently
read silently – is also consistent with the cultural rhetoric of print. Yet
unlike Hamlet's letters or the treaties between Denmark and Norway,
which Claudius reads privately, the book leads to a surprisingly
ambiguous performance of reading. It's just possible that the words
Hamlet speaks are in fact impressed on the pages of the book (the
words are slightly different in the Q2 and F versions), just possible that

Hamlet reads aloud from a satire on age he happens to have in hand at just the right moment (the eighteenth-century critic William Warburton suggested it might be Juvenal's tenth *Satire* and other suggestions have been made as well; see Cheney 212, and Scott 142). But it seems more probable, and more consistent with Hamlet's treatment of Polonius throughout the play ("Do you see yonder cloud ..." 3.2.367–73), to understand Hamlet inventing these words, ascribing his satirical invention to the motivation of the page. Unlike Polonius' image of the "desk or table-book," a notebook more like Hamlet's "tables," a mnemonic hiding its private matter (2.2.133), Hamlet's book is instrumental to his action here, imaging performing writing in a theatrical register: as words, words, words that gain their purchase on significant action as they are used, reinvented in the act of performance.

This is a literal instance, to be sure, of the ways performance creates the impression of scriptedness, of its reliance on writing, an impression it undoes at the moment of its doing. The players "cannot keep counsel – they'll tell all" (3.2.135), but what their performance *tells* is not, or at least not necessarily or merely, *in the book*. Hamlet enters *reading on a book*, but the book is the agency for doing something else, creating an act that establishes one (offputting) relationship to the *scene* onstage and a different (complicit) one with the larger *scene* of the theatrical audience. The book enables action, but the significance of the action is not captive to the words it may contain. Even if the words are there on the page, or Hamlet shows them to Polonius while reading, the book remains a prop, literally, a property of the action, inserted in the play for the purpose of baiting Polonius. Unlike the response to Hamlet's letters (Claudius asking "What should this mean?"), Polonius does not question the integrity of the text, but the quality of Hamlet's performance: "Though this be madness, yet there is method in't" (2.2.202–3). Hamlet's play with the book asserts the instrumental character of writing in performance. Playing the book accentuates the quality of the playing.

In Shakespeare's theatre, plays were purchased in manuscript, copied into parts or sides, and so rehearsed; printed books rarely played a part in the theatrical production process. Even now, though, the act of writing by hand plays a formative part in performance, long after the dominion of print: blocking notes, line readings, actor's notes in the scripts they use to assist them in the process of getting off book, to say nothing of the cuts, cues, commentary recorded in the director's book.[13] As Jacques Derrida suggests, at moments of the restructuring of technologies, including writing technologies, "the oldest form survives, and even survives endlessly, coexisting with the new form and even coming to terms with a new economy" (*Paper Machine* 9). *Hamlet* marks the interface of a new economy of dramatic performance – our economy – in the ways it signals different affordances, multiplies ways of performing writing.

The law of writ

Playing the book also opens *Hamlet*'s extended meditation on dramatic theatre: Rosencrantz and Guildenstern's first failed effort to play Hamlet, the arrival of the Players, a rehearsed speech, an enacted speech, a bitter soliloquy about the monstrous effectiveness of acting, and the decision to mount a play, soon to be followed by the advice to the Players and the play itself. *Hamlet*'s detailed attention to the company of players who arrive at Elsinore is particularly suggestive. Like the Lord Chamberlain's/King's Men, the Players are not a strolling band of improvisational comedians, but a professional repertory company, keeping at least two written plays, one about the fall of Troy and *The Murder of Gonzago*, ready for use. The Players may seem unremarkable, but *Hamlet* expends considerable effort placing them on the horizon of contemporary performance. Like Shakespeare's company, the Players are organized by what they sell, their lines of business: "He that plays the King shall be welcome," alongside the adventurous knight, the lover, the humorous man, the clown, and the lady (2.2.285–90). Yet despite their evident professional celerity – they can mount an effective production of *Gonzago*, with additions, "tomorrow" (2.2.473) – the troupe's fortunes have declined in the face of the "eyrie of children, little eyases" (Folio 2.2.337), children's companies performing satirical drama identified principally as a poetic, written commodity.

The vogue of children's companies at the turn of the seventeenth century outlines a familiar conflict between paradigms of theatre, perhaps amplified by print and the assimilation of (some) drama to the canons of literature. Provoked by John Marston's *Histriomastix* in 1599, facilitated by the revival of two children's companies – the Children of Paul's in 1599 and the Children of Queen Elizabeth's Chapel in 1600, playing at the Blackfriars theatre – and enflamed by Ben Jonson's *Cynthia's Revels* (1600) and *Poetaster* (1601), the plays at the center of the War of the Theatres were indeed satirical, and identified with a playwright emphatically concerned with the author's rights. *Poetaster* used the boys to parody individuals in Shakespeare's Lord Chamberlain's men (the same men playing *Hamlet*, and so playing the Players at the Globe), but the children's company was subordinate to Jonson's larger critical purpose, to assert "the poet's superiority to the player and [...] the script's priority to its enactment" (Bednarz 230).[14]

Like that of the adult companies, the repertoire of the children's companies was varied; playwrights (Jonson, Marston) wrote for both children and adult companies (*Hamlet*'s "the Humorous Man shall end his part in peace" perhaps recalls the success of Jonson's "humour" comedies with adult companies like the Lord Chamberlain's men) and the quality of the boys' performance seems not to be at issue.[15] Among its various responses to the "War," though, *Hamlet* marks a distinction between how the children and the adults deploy writing. In *Hamlet*, the children are evoked as a vehicle for writing, providing a theatrical entertainment that seems *archival* in its thorough identification with the poet's text. Through the children's performance, the writer's goose-quills intimidate the elite audience; the poets' satire on the "common stages" is so pointed that "many wearing rapiers are afraid of goose-quills and dare scarce come thither" (Folio, 2.2.340–2). The Players are, in a sense, not "textual" enough for contemporary fashion. While the boys' companies are identified with one kind of writing in *Hamlet*, the Players emphasize their generic range, "Seneca cannot be too heavy, nor Plautus too light," their comic list of dramatic genres – "tragical-comical-historical-pastoral" – dissolving literary distinction in the solution of performance. Whatever kind of script, the Players can refunction it as entertaining theatre: for "the law of writ and the liberty," these are the only men indeed (2.2.333–8).[16] While the children's performance reiterates the poet's critique, the Players' performance *is* the script, the thing itself: they are "the abstracts and brief chronicles of the time." The Players use writing, need writing, but the commodity they deliver – performance – is not writing-by-other-means. The time is surely out of joint when, "There was for a while no money bid for argument unless the poet and the player went to cuffs in the question" (Folio, 2.2.352–4), because the victory of the poet's theatre is the death of acting: "their writers do them wrong to make them exclaim against their own succession" (Folio, 2.2.348–9). After the performance of *Gonzago*, Hamlet claims "a fellowship in a cry of players" (Horatio thinks only "Half a share" 3.2.270–2), and there's little doubt which paradigm of performance Hamlet prefers: better to be badly inscribed by goose-quills, to have a "bad epitaph than their [the Players'] ill report while you live" (2.2.463–4). Finally, Hamlet aligns the boys' theatre of writing with another debased performance, the sudden popularity of images of Claudius: "for my uncle is King of Denmark, and those that would make mouths at him while my father lived give twenty, forty, fifty, a hundred ducats apiece for his picture in little" (2.2.300–3). The children's companies offer an analogous performance "in little," and their theatre is similarly delivering illegitimate wares.[17] Regardless of Shakespeare's attitude toward professional playwriting or literary authorship, *Hamlet* articulates a friction between different conceptions of the use of writing in the theatre, identified here with two different conceptions of performance.

Theatre remakes the book; it negotiates between the law of writ and the liberty, and even in a densely scripted, poetic theatre, the Players insist on their succession, the surrogation or restoration of behavior as the purpose of dramatic theatre. Hamlet develops this inquiry into the theatre's legitimate use of writing as *agency*, calling for "a taste" of the Players' "quality," "a passionate speech" (2.2.369–70). Making a speech implies the proper adjustment of the word to the action, and Hamlet's later advice to the Players to "speak the speech" as he pronounced it to them is sometimes taken as evidence of the author's – and the poem's – legitimate dominion over the whirlwind of performance. Hamlet is concerned to have "my lines" performed effectively; for the Mousetrap to work, though, the actors must both create a coherent representation, and hold the mirror up to the present tense of Claudius' unnatural court. This performance demands the proper use of language, but the words themselves provide little instruction: it's the actor's task to "acquire and beget" the "temperance that may give it smoothness" (3.2.1–10). Later in the play, the hardheaded Gravedigger's obsessive literalism will force Hamlet to "speak by the card, or equivocation will undo us" (5.1.128). This kind of constraint images an inferior, nearly inhuman act of communication, an artificial subordination of the act of speech to writing soon again ironized when the lapwing Osric – himself apparently a creature of courtly conduct literature – describes Laertes as "the card or calendar of the gentry" (5.2.95). Speaking is an embodied activity, requiring proper pronunciation ("trippingly on the tongue"), movement, and gesture, the hand "instrumental to the mouth" (1.2.48). But acting is not speaking by the card. Suiting "the action to the word, the word to the action" is not a means merely to recode the propriety of the text: proper playing holds "the mirror up" not to the script, but "to nature," showing "the very age and body of the time his form and pressure" (3.2.1–34). As Robert Weimann puts it, "What Hamlet's advice emphasizes, then, is voice and performance rather than any purely literary, let alone textual, consideration" ("Mimesis" 280). Indeed, if we lean a bit heavily on the print-culture connotations of "form" and "pressure," the theatre might be said ironically to reverse the print-to-performance logic of "literary" notions of the stage, as the theatre impresses "the image of its age" (Cheney 206). Rather than speaking "by the card," the actor creates a suitable incarnation of language as present action: the measure of its success is not whether it adequately reflects the words, but how it registers meaningfully in the form and pressure of the dual *scene* it shares with us.

The difference between "making a speech" and acting – between performing *writing* and *performing* writing – is focused by the "Pyrrhus" scene that closely follows Hamlet's performance from the book. Hamlet recalls hearing "a speech once," one that "was never acted, or, if it was, not above once," and his account stresses the formal ingenuity and the piquancy of its composition as well: "an excellent play, well digested in the scenes, set down with as much modesty as cunning. I remember one said there was no sallets in the lines to make the matter savoury nor no matter in the phrase that might indict the author of affectation, but called it an honest method, as wholesome as sweet, and by very much more handsome than fine" (2.2.372–83). By first misremembering and then recalling the lines, Hamlet underscores the "textual" aspect of his performance:

> The rugged Pyrrhus like th'Hyrcanian beast …
> – Tis not so. It begins with Pyrrhus –
> The rugged Pyrrhus, he whose sable arms (2.2.388–90)

Many productions of *Hamlet* see this scene as an opportunity to clarify the quality of Hamlet's acting. Is he better than the Player? worse? just different? more or less "stagey" or "realistic"? However a production articulates the inspired amateur and the seasoned professional, Hamlet and the Player may well give qualitatively distinct performances, because Hamlet and the Player are not engaged in the same activity. Hamlet makes a speech; the Player *plays.* This distinction is visibly registered by their audience, Polonius. Though Hamlet relentlessly derides him, Polonius "was accounted a good actor" once (3.2.96); more to the point, Polonius' response to the language ("mobled queen"), to the pace ("This is too long"), and to the force of the performance indexes the range of any audience's energy and attention. Hamlet makes a speech, and Polonius praises his facility with words: "'Fore God, my lord, well spoken – with good accent and good discretion" (2.2.404–5). But the Player's performance is not about the words, and summons a different reaction: "Look where he has not turned his colour and has tears in's eyes. – Prithee, no more" (2.2.457–8). Hamlet's speech is judged by its fidelity to its Marlovian diction; the Player's acting by its impact in the theatrical *scene* it shares with the audience, an impact that leads immediately to Hamlet's own histrionic experiment – "O vengeance!" (Folio, 2.2.576) – and the decision to deploy the well-digested "cunning of the scene" (2.2.525) to seize the cunning duplicity of that other scene, the scene of Claudius' court.

Making a speech can perform an act, but to do so the script must be used to do something more than reflect discreetly on the propriety of the speaking, the words. Claudius makes a speech when he enters the play. While morally, verbally, and syntactically complex, what's impressive about this speech is what it does. Claudius' oration brings the depth charge of his incestuous marriage to the surface before drowning it again thanks to those who "have freely gone / With this affair along" (1.2.15–16), enforcing their complicity in any impropriety; it insists on his capacity to deal both with his Norwegian opposite number and with his rebellious nephew, prioritizes the order of courtly precedence (first Laertes, then Hamlet), and attempts (less successfully) to neutralize the troublesome prince by casting him in a flattering role, "But now, my cousin Hamlet, and my son" (1.2.64). What distinguishes Claudius' performance here from Hamlet's "Pyrrhus" speech is its instrumental character, its affordance of action: Hamlet's speech is about the delivery of well-remembered, well-spoken words; Claudius' is about the accomplished assertion of power, his use of language to organize or transform the scene and its audience.

Speaking by the card

The New Critics defined drama and performance as *"characters*, who make *speeches*," but in *Hamlet* delivering a scripted speech is often a dubious activity, in which (as with the little eyases) the constraint of performing *writing* leads to a specific kind of inauthenticity, less the evacuation of merely hollow and stagey "actions that a man might play" than the inability to use the power of speech, of speaking words, to achieve a fully human *act*, *performing* writing. Speaking that is about itself, conventionalized as "speech" – speaking by the card – is unremittingly scorned in *Hamlet*: Hamlet's self-conscious rejection of his own speechifying, "Why, what an ass am I?" (2.2.517), recalls Polonius' sententious, contradictory advice to Laertes, his tedious address to Claudius and Gertrude in 2.2, and supercilious Osric as well. As Ophelia recognizes, Laertes is a speechifier like his father: his "pestilent speeches" (4.5.91) on returning from Paris proceed his confrontation of Claudius, who challenges their evocation of action: "show yourself in deed your father's son / More than in words" (4.7.123–4). Laertes prepares speeches throughout the play, but they are typically outpaced by events; "I have a speech o'fire that fain would blaze / But that this folly drowns it," he says at the news of Ophelia's drowning (4.7.188–9). And when we hear a "speech of fire" at the graveside, Hamlet – offended by Laertes' prating "phrase of sorrow" on this "theme" – outfaces, or outspeeches, him: "Nay an thou'lt mouth, / I'll rant as well as thou" (5.1.243, 255, 272–3). (Hamlet's "if thou prate of mountains" here recalls his remarks while lugging the guts of Polonius out of Gertrude's chamber – "a foolish prating knave" – suggesting perhaps a subtle recognition of family resemblance.)

Hamlet's meditation on theatricality is preoccupied with the performance of writing. As Hamlet's byplay with the book implies, transforming a mere *speech* into *acting* has less to do with fidelity to the text than with a rhetorical use of the text as *agency* to accomplish an act beyond the words.[18] This use also materializes, reveals, and conceals the *agent* (reminding us of Goldman's sense of the actor's/character's constant changing of roles), localizes his/her *purpose*, and so qualifies the action performed in the two *scenes* of the drama. But while seizing this *agency* is the proper work of dramatic performance (as distinct from the doomed succession of the children's performance of writing), *Hamlet* is also troubled by consequences of the theatre's possible "liberty" from "writ." Hamlet's advice to the Players is one example, but Claudius, too, giving the commission to Voltemand and Cornelius, restricts communication with Norway to the script, which seems to mean not transforming it at all into the slippery business of acting: "Giving you no further personal power / To business with the King more than the scope / Of these dilated articles allow" (1.2.36–8). Yet while speaking by the card prevents equivocation, it's an underling kind of behavior, fit not for mighty opposites but only for role-players like the Gravedigger, Rosencrantz and Guildenstern, Voltemand and Cornelius, dramatic functionaries so fully defined as "subjects" to the action as to lack effective subjectivity *in* action. In a sense *"characters,* who make *speeches,"* who speak by the card, never quite become *characters* at all, they're so fully subordinated to their function in the narrative. To speak by the card, by the law of writ, is to be evacuated by language, plotted and played by the words, a mere tool in the larger design: this is in a sense Laertes' tragedy, a man always speaking by someone else's card, anticipating Polonius' advice in his own to Ophelia, making pestilent and fiery speeches but failing to recognize until too late the merely instrumental role inscribed on *his* card.

   Performing writing transforms it into action, but undoing the order of writing poses other dangers, threatening to empty and theatricalize action in the world, transforming that goodly frame into a barren and sterile promontory, finally unmooring us from the records of memory, law, society, custom: Laertes can protest the "maimèd rites" of Ophelia's funeral, but enacting "more" would "profane the service of the dead" (5.1.224–5). How to locate the poem in the performance without reducing it either to inconsequent "speech" or "monstrous" misrepresentation? *Hamlet* reframes this question through its cognate critique of the language of visual representation, painting. At best, depiction in *Hamlet* registers the ambivalence of art: Pyrrhus is described as a "painted tyrant" because his blood-soaked sword pauses, imaging the revenger momentarily Hamlet-like, as "a neutral to his will and matter," before his weapon remorselessly falls on Priam (see 2.2.418– 20). More typically, though, paintings and pictures are instruments of deception: Hamlet's scorn of Claudius' "picture in little," "The harlot's cheek beautied with plast'ring art" indexing the distance from Claudius' corrupt "deed to my most painted word" (3.1.50–2), Hamlet's scorn for Ophelia's "paintings" in the "nunnery" scene (3.1.141) and for painting "an inch thick" in the graveyard (5.1.185), Claudius' barb that Laertes not be the "painting of a sorrow" (4.7.106)

Hamlet speaks of Pyrrhus with good accent and discretion, offering a verbal portrait of the "painted tyrant" that deftly images Hamlet's own cause; so too, he notes of Laertes, "by the image of my cause I see / The portraiture of his" (Folio, 5.2.77–8). Pictures freeze, moralize, conceal, epitomize, beautify the acts they represent, but like speeches they are neutral to will and matter, doing nothing. When they are used, like words, to perform an act – as Hamlet uses the two portraits to chastise Gertrude in the closet scene – they gain the undecidable duplicity of dramatic language. "Look here upon this picture, and on this" (3.4.51): conventionally staged as lockets, too small to be seen by an offstage audience, the images that Hamlet forces Gertrude to read are like his book, like the script of *Hamlet*, texts we know only through Hamlet's performance of them. Speaking daggers to Gertrude Hamlet plays the portraits, the instruments of his hypocrite instruction ("My tongue and soul in this be hypocrites," he says on his way into this scene, *hypocrite* recalling the Latin word for "actor" 3.2.387). Hamlet's reading (aloud) of the portraits drives Gertrude to remorse, but it's Hamlet's outsized performance that does the work, not the images themselves. What most stage productions confirm is that Hamlet plays the portraits as he played his book, as hypocrites. Whatever the images may symbolize about their subjects' moral character, as a play *Hamlet* seems to depend on Claudius' plausible attractiveness, and provides ample opportunity to incarnate a charismatic power onstage. Are Anthony Hopkins, Patrick Stewart, Kyle McLachlan, Derek Jacobi, Alan Bates really such mildewed ears?

On the printed page, they're just words, words, words; but when "words be made of breath" (3.4.195), they work with, through, and as action, much as Hamlet's gifts to Ophelia are transformed by the performance of their giving: "And with them words of so sweet breath composed / As made these things more rich" (3.1.97–8). Performance is not speaking by the card: it signifies beyond the image, beyond the book. The motivating, sustaining, troubling gesture of theatre is not that deeds cannot illustrate or proclaim the significance of words; they can, it's called "making a speech." But insofar as it uses words toward another *purpose*, in another *scene* of action, acting is neither subject to nor capable of violating writing. Acting – as in Shakespeare's day, when the theatres were built in the "Liberties" outside the city of

London – is beyond the "law of writ," though we may struggle (like the London city authorities) to bring performance within its governance. The desire to locate acting, performance in a fixed relation to writing is essentially frustrated by theatre. Even in its smallest details, how Hamlet moves, whether he knocks off his hat when he sees the Ghost (as Garrick did) or falls prostrate on the ground, acting exceeds the text in ways that can not be kept captive to its writ.

Hamlet's preoccupation with performing writing is perhaps registered in another way, by the repetitively excessive quality of the action itself, acts that seem to evade "discretion": Hamlet's inexplicable, volcanic cruelty to Ophelia in the "nunnery" scene (drawing many productions to "explain" it by having Hamlet discover Polonius' plot during the scene), the Mousetrap (did *you* see it, Claudius' occulted guilt unkenneling itself?), the closet scene (is Hamlet really able to control himself, his madness?), the duel. Hamlet's first appearance – "'Tis not alone my inky cloak" (1.2.77) – denies as it insists on legibility, but the paradigmatic picture of performing creating and exceeding interpretation is Hamlet's appearance to Ophelia.

> Lord Hamlet, with his doublet all unbraced,
> No hat upon his head, his stockings fouled,
> Ungartered and down-gyved to his ankle,
> Pale as his shirt, his knees knocking each other,
> And with a look so piteous in purport
> As if he had been loosed out of hell
> To speak of horrors, he comes before me. (2.1.75–81)

Hamlet methodically displays all the detail of the lovelorn prince, raising "a sigh so piteous and profound / As it did seem to shatter all his bulk / And end his being" (2.1.91–3). Yet this portrait, while legible, seems not to lead to "interpretation" but to fear. Ophelia is "affrighted" by Hamlet's performance, much as Hamlet suggests that the actor, given his motive and cue for passion, would "amaze indeed / The very faculty of eyes and ears" (2.2.500–1). The Player overwhelms Polonius with his Hecuba; here, Ophelia can read but not consolidate Hamlet's performance, his "ecstasy" (2.1.99). In performance, the language of depiction is the instrument for the performance of terror. While the words describe Hamlet's astonishing appearance, they must become the means to something else, the realization of the actress's desperation. Ophelia is the axis of histrionic excess in the play, an object lesson perhaps in the consequences of performance liberated from writ. Terrified by Hamlet here, blasted by his irrational calumny in the "nunnery" scene, humiliated by his scabrous sexual merriment – "country matters," "lie between maids' legs," "cost you a groaning" – at the play, Ophelia registers the perils of acting that can "amaze indeed / The very faculty of eyes and ears." Driven to distraction, she becomes herself a "document in madness," one that challenges legibility: "Thought and affliction, passion, hell itself / She turns to favour and to prettiness" (4.5.180–1). Performance – Hamlet's performances here and throughout the play, Ophelia's reciprocal madness, the Player's Hecuba – signifies without being fully containable as fixed signification, containable by or as a text. It offers what Benjamin Bennett might call "interpretivity," summoning a desire to interpret while frustrating reduction to writ, either to a motivating script or textualizing analysis.

Hamlet neither celebrates nor condemns the incommensurability of performing writing, though an anxiety about it runs through the play, much as it does – for both comic and tragic purposes – throughout the plays of Shakespeare and his contemporaries. *Hamlet* is deeply resonant with the specific cultural skepticism regarding the stage in seventeenth-century England, but in addition to modeling contemporary anxieties about the "monstrous," evanescent nullity of the actor's strutting and fretting, the play evidently trains a suspicious eye on the specific indeterminacies promoted by the act of performing writing.[19] To the degree that dramatic theatre is associated with writing, we might take this slippage between writing and behavior as foundational to the Western stage, a concern for the appropriate, just, ethical, moral, poetic relation between writing and performance animating the power and pleasure of drama. The contemporary sense of dramatic theatre as overscripted, of the dominion of the *repertoire* by the *archive*, merely revalues a familiar strain of antitheatricality consonant with the New Critics' reciprocal desire to limit the stage to literary reiteration. Despite its anxious regard for the "interpretive" excess of acting, *Hamlet* also refuses a vision of theatre reduced to speaking by the card. In this sense, *Hamlet* resonates less with the theatre as *archive* than with a critique of textualized performance. We can, of course, describe movement, gesture, and the larger patterns of social behavior as "texts," lending them a signifying, readily interpretable systematicity. Denis Diderot's "language of gesture" anticipates Erving Goffman's segmentation of social life into conventional "scenes," Victor Turner's "social dramas," or Clifford Geertz's influential paradigm of culture as text. But we are mistaken – as they were not – if we take the "text" for the behavior itself, Schechner's kernel of originality, what Burke calls the "constitutive" dimension of acts, their newness: "each act contains some measure of motivation that cannot be explained simply in terms of the past, being to an extent, however tiny, a *new thing*" (*Grammar* 65). *Hamlet* is rich in "textualized" performances: Osric, Laertes aping the stage revenger, Hamlet doing the same, "Pyrrhus." But the acts that seem to define performance in *Hamlet* – Hamlet's "Seems" speech, his byplay with the book and the pictures, the Player's Hecuba, *Gonzago*, the soliloquies, the duel – at once imply a script and exceed its writ.

Hamlet depends on writing, but asserts writing as only part of a process, susceptible to additions, requiring the articulate refashioning in the business of performance to be transformed from "*characters*, who make *speeches*" to performance, performance that will at once demand and frustrate "interpretive" reduction to a script. Performing writing performing: like a Moebius strip, *Hamlet* elaborates the conversion of writing, reading, performing, spectating as an undecidable process. And yet, while *Hamlet* offers a kind of essay on the dynamics of performing writing, while we can understand *Hamlet* to show the relentless use of the *archive* of writing by the *repertoire* of performance, one lesson of that critique is that it may not be part of the purpose of any specific playing of the play. After all, many performances of *Hamlet*, of Shakespeare, of scripted drama attribute their own authority to the mere reiteration of writing, even though Hamlet's playing with the book stages performance as a means of dissimulating, disguising, displacing the authority of writing (all the while insisting on the utility of the book behind the pose). Taking *Hamlet* to interrogate the dynamics of performing writing – making a speech, reading aloud, acting – we've pursued a kind of "close reading" here, one that would have been familiar to Brooks and Heilman, orchestrating a thematic consistency by tracing patterns and faultlines among the play's texture of words, words, words. And yet, this texture can only lead us in another direction, away from a sense of performance merely evoking, illustrating, confirming the script. Even this argument, so to speak, can only bear indirectly on any performance, which will use the text as one of several instruments in the making of the play, which will play the book in unique and finally unforeseeable ways.

ii. Corrupt Stuff; or, Doing Things with (Old) Words

The odd thing is, this "corrupt" stuff sounds very Shakespeare.
                                  Michael Pennington, Hamlet: A User's Guide *(25)*

Hamlet prompts us to resist performance as speaking by the card, to resist reading performance as a merely embodied "interpretation" of the text. What would Hamlet think of contemporary spectators following the action onstage along in their books? Understanding writing as one *agency* of performance requires us to adopt a different approach not only to reading plays, but also to reading performances. How can we read performances without reading them back "into" the Shakespearean text, into the *archive*?

Contemporary Shakespeare films offer a convenient archive here, enabling us to compare how an astonishingly wide range of texts has been used in performance, used to make something that is not a text at all. Granted, film is not theatre, and to take films as a kind of evidence about "performance" means setting aside much of the specificity of film itself, its technological structure, its way of addressing and positioning the audience through the work of the camera, and even its very different practices of rehearsal and production. Nonetheless, films do share a specific problem with the stage: the actor must transform often recondite and unfamiliar writing into playing; and the actor's playing will determine what we understand the writing to say.[20]

One of the problems of the dramatic archive is that it records behavior and language, storing them beyond their use in the repertoire of everyday life. Some of these gestures (bowing, kneeling, anything with a hat), even some of these words (*forsooth, zounds*) signal the *archival* dimension of classic drama: who would fardels bear, or want to be hoist with his own petard? Every time we see a production of *Hamlet* we see the work of the *repertoire* of contemporary acting on this *archive*, on the book, making these strange, unknown, words and behaviors into legible, powerful, actions that a man might play *for us*.

As J. L. Austin suggested of "performatives" in everyday life, the power of speaking as doing or action derives not from the words alone, but from the way they are deployed in the conventions of behavior that animate them, give them force as deeds. The force of performed language depends on the actor's work to locate the words in a signifying context of behavior, to animate them, give them both meaning and consequence as action. This paradigm is perhaps most visible when Shakespearean words that have a problematic contemporary meaning – or no contemporary meaning at all – are nonetheless performed. Such words, as Kenneth Burke put it, parry a thrust that no longer exists; the performance must, nonetheless, use them to parry a new thrust, to constitute a legible act in the scene of contemporary theatre. So how does performance deal with a knotty text, and what can this dealing tell us about the *agency* of the book in the playing? One way to ask this is to turn to a term that strikes dull apprehension in the hearts of both readers and actors: the *crux*.

The crux of performance

There are many different kinds of crux in Shakespeare, passages whose sense is troubled in various ways: by words we may no longer understand, by an odd repetition of phrases, by unexpected or illegible words, by words apparently assigned to illogical speakers, by different words or passages arising in different early editions. The arguments for resolving a crux can pursue several strategies, too, resorting to etymological and historical dictionaries to recover meanings gone out of use, projecting printing house practice to explain how the word on the page might logically be taken as a misprint for something else, adducing a process of textual transmission to hypothesize what the lost word of the manuscript might have been. These are appropriate and successful strategies for resolving a palpable problem in the play's material texture. And yet resolving a crux often verges on the play's performance texture, the imagination of what might be logical or consistent for a given character to speak, or what seems like it works, might work, might once have worked in performance practice. The imagination of this extended practice is, in a sense, enshrined in the Oxford edition, which reminds us that Shakespeare wrote plays not – initially, at least – for "that consortium of readers called 'the general public'; they were written instead to be read by a particular group of actors, his professional colleagues and personal friends," who could bring their "specialist knowledge about the conditions and working practices of the contemporary theatre" immediately to bear:

> The written text of any such manuscript thus depended upon an unwritten para-text which always accompanied it: an invisible life-support system of stage directions, which Shakespeare could either expect his first readers to supply, or which those first readers would expect Shakespeare himself to supply orally. (Gary Taylor, "General Introduction" 2).

It is arresting, though perhaps not surprising, that the text's perceived omissions can be addressed by imagining the working of Shakespeare's company as para*text*, a "system of stage directions" evoking its theatrical life. Gary Taylor is certainly right that Shakespeare's actors and audiences would have seized the words on the page through a relatively conventionalized understanding of the forms and moods of effective action. Suggesting that a more systematic use of stage directions would allow readers to recover that sense of theatrical possibility is perhaps more revealing of our post-print expectations of the dramatic text, as an object of novelistic description of the action rather than as an instrument for inventing it onstage.

Regardless of its imputed origin, the crux poses a moment of material textual indeterminacy, as the effervescent interpretation of the word awaits the determination of the word itself. But while a reader – a modern reader of Shakespeare, at least – can read the crux in all its multiplicity, armed with glosses, textual notes, and so on, an actor will generate the rich palimpsest of intonation, emphasis, insinuation – action – by performing *one* word, once.[21] "O that this too, too, *something* flesh would melt ..." (1.2.129): the word is *sallied* in Ann Thompson and Neil Taylor's recent edition of the second quarto; onstage, Hamlet's flesh is now usually *sallied* or *solid*, just occasionally *grieved and sallied*, but never all three.[22] In this sense, the crux emblematizes a familiarly bookish paradigm of text and performance in Shakespeare studies, the notion that reading engages the play as the site of multiple simultaneous significations, while performance betrays that infinite space into the nutshell of a single meaning. To think in this way, though, is to ignore one of the lessons of *Hamlet*, that dramatic performance confronts and remakes writing rather than illustrating it. Since acting isn't speaking by the card, the word becomes the site for the rich, potentially limitless play of embodied ambiguity. Rather than seeing the task of performance as either resolving or betraying the complexity of the crux – reaffirming the *archive* or dissolving its richness into the fluid *repertoire* – we might pose the question differently. A crux often demands an imaginative, speculative rethinking of what we mean by the text and the process of its transmission. What kind of affordance might a crux provide in the social technology of performance? Short of having Falstaff babble about tables, how might the crux dramatize the changing ways performance affords the materiality of writing?

Let's consider a line from *Hamlet* that is really not a textual crux at all.[23] In the closet scene, just after he has compared Gertrude's two husbands, and she has admitted the "black and grained spots" of guilt, Hamlet graphically assaults his mother:

> … Nay, but to live
> In the rank sweat of an enseamed bed,
> Stewed in corruption, honeying and making love
> Over the nasty sty – (3.4.89–91)

Q2 and F are largely in agreement here, and the sense of the passage is moist enough even in Q1, "Nay, but still to persist and dwell in sin, / To sweat under the yoke of infamy" (11.47–8). The most challenging word here is *enseamed*, which appears as such in F, and as *inseemed* in Q2. Most editions quickly gloss *enseamed* as meaning *greasy*, pointing to *Troilus and Cressida* 2.3, where Ulysses describes Achilles as "the proud lord / That bastes his arrogance with his own seam" (2.3.173–4), though Harold Jenkins has a fuller reading:

> saturated with *seam* (c.f. *Troil.* ii.iii.180), i.e. animal fat, grease. The word combines with others in the context to suggest the grossness of sexual behaviour through physical metaphors of disgusting exudations. Explanations making it out to be a technical term from falconry (Schmidt, etc.) or the woolen industry (Dover Wilson) are quite beside the point. (Jenkins, gloss to 3.4.92)[24]

In a longer note on 5.2.90, Jenkins takes Gertrude's concern for Hamlet – "He's fat and scant of breath" – as a parallel, noting a strong "equation of *fat* with sweating" elsewhere in Shakespeare and proverbially, and presumably with the *greasy* residue of perspiration: "It seems likely, however, that an ancient usage was preserved by the farmer's wife in Wisconsin in 1923 who is reported to have greeted perspiring visitors with 'How fat you all are!' (*TLS*, 1927, p. 375)."

The OED suggests something of the term's complexity, and of the difficulty of glossing Hamlet's slimy sense here. Deriving from Old French, to *enseam* could mean one of two opposed activities, either to cleanse a horse or a hawk of fat or grease, or "to load with grease," though the OED and other dictionaries note that this sense is obsolete, and that "The French word is now used only in the sense 'to grease (cloth)', whence perh. the fig. use in Shaks.," citing this line from *Hamlet*. (To *enseam* is perhaps related to the transitive sense of to *seam*, to dress wool with grease.) This fatty sense persists, traceable through any number of gentlemanly conduct books of the seventeenth century, particularly those preoccupied with hawking and horses. *Enseaming* – the overnight cleansing of the digestive track of a hawk or falcon before flight to make the bird both lighter and hungrier – remains a subject of rather surprisingly contentious online discussion in falconry associations.[25] Our gorge rises at it indeed (*Hamlet* 5.1.174).

So, not much of a crux at all. The only problem is, we know not *seams*. The *greasy* meaning is not terribly audible for us in the *enseamed bed*, however closely the rank sweat and the nasty sty may remind us of it. Except for the people reading along with the play, Hamlet's gross assault on his mother is, well, grosser, because the "disgusting exudations" we *hear* have less to do with *grease* than with something else: *enseamed bed* sounds like a bed stained with *semen*. Perhaps it's even a pun. In their recent edition of Q2, Anne Thompson and Neil Taylor suggest "stained with semen seems another possibility": not a very strong endorsement.[26] Shakespeare doesn't use the word *semen* or variants, nor did many writers of his era, who preferred the homely English *seed* (the very few OED citations are to natural philosophy – biology – or animal husbandry texts, or to Latin, whence the word made its way into English). Indeed, as Margreta de Grazia suggests, it's precisely to the point that the "seminal fluids exchanged '[i]n the rank sweat of an enseamed bed' are greasy waste-matter – *seam* rather than *semen*, secreting fat rather than germinating seed" (*Hamlet without Hamlet* 102).

There are other uses of *enseam* and its derivatives with the sense of *including* or *joining together*, related to the sartorial sense of the verb, to make a seam, join two pieces of fabric. Spenser uses it in this sense in *The Faerie Queene*, "And bounteous Trent, that in himselfe enseames / Both thirty sorts of fish and thirty sundry streames" (IV.xi.35). More engaging, though, are two dramatic uses of the word. In Chapman's

Bussy D'Ambois (1607), Monsieur introduces Bussy to a brace of ladies – "See here's the Guise's Duchess. The Countess of Mountsurreaue; Beaupres, come I'll enseame thee" (1.2.70).[27] Maurice Evans glosses *enseame* as "introduce to company, usually with sexual implication," though this implication can hardly have been that usual; Jonathan Hudston joins the tailor image, "bring together, introduce (with sexual implications)."[28] But it's hard not to think that the "sexual implications" arise largely from what follows, the overtly flirtatious double-entendres that arise when Bussy is *enseamed* to the Duchess.

A more intriguing usage occurs in Nathaniel Richards's *Tragedy of Messallina, the Roman Empress*, published 1640. Early in the second act, after we've seen the actor Menester racked onstage for refusing to satisfy Messallina's lust (he eventually gives in), as well as witnessing her order the virtuous Silius to execute his wife Sylvana and hurry back, the Empress is confronted by her honest, outraged mother Lepida. Messallina's sidekick and procurer Saufellus ridicules Lepida and hustles her off, and in gratitude, Messallina calls him her favorite and bids his "fortunes rise." He replies:

> And all those fortunes, favours, life and all,
> Shall like an *Atlas* undergoe the weight
> Of your imperious will, be it toth' death
> Of Parents, massacre of all my kin,
> To exceede the divell, act any sinne.
> *Messallina.* For which we thus enseame thee.
> *Kisses him.* (Richards, *Messallina*)

The situation is seamy enough (*seamy*, by the way, refers to clothes with the seams showing outward; ill-made, "seamy" clothes more generally suggest poverty, a lower social class, and so social crudeness), but rather than "let me grease you," Messallina probably means to join their lips together like a seam, though "Those delicate delicious rubie lips" do seem to apply some sort of balm, to "quench, quench" Saufellus' "burning heat."

While the word – whether with regard to fat, sweat, or stitches – may have been used, clearly on very rare occasions, with some kind of salacious intent, Hamlet's use is by far the most vulgar, part of what is often one of the actor's most demanding, outsized scenes in the play. More to the point, for us *enseamed* produces a crux nowhere but in performance: readers quickly find an annotation, but spectators hear an unfamiliar word they think they understand. Hamlet's greasy sheets are replaced instead by a suitably Shakespearean-sounding faux-archaism, *enseamèd*, stained with semen. As Michael Pennington suggests, "this 'corrupt' stuff sounds very Shakespeare."

Any production of a Shakespeare play will read differently to a contemporary audience than it did to its first public: even our posture and gestures are differently articulated with social meaning. But *enseamed* locates a different kind of problem, dramatizing how – like Hamlet's book – the text is not the repository of meaning but lends significance to action through its affordance by the action. Hearing a modern sense in an early-modern word is perhaps definitive of the process of performance, akin in this respect to the editorial problem of modern spelling, which may simplify or falsify the complexity signaled by a word's early-modern orthography (of which kind of "metal" is Regan made?) in order to render an audible *word* at all.[29] What uses have productions made of this word, and how might we read that use to specify their way of claiming the words as *agency* of the action?

Enseamed beds

Laurence Olivier's 1948 film had little problem with editing the play: Voltimand and Cornelius, Reynaldo, the Second Gravedigger, and, more famously, Fortinbras, Rosencrantz, and Guildenstern are all absent. Olivier's avowed "aim and purpose" to "make a film of 'Hamlet' as Shakespeare himself, were he living now, might make it" (Olivier, "Foreword") is executed in this way in order to bring the performance into the "one hundred and sixty minutes at the very outside" limit required by "film management" (Dent, "Text-Editing"). As the film's textual editor Alan Dent put it, "*Obsolete and obscure phrases in* HAMLET *give the scholar a pleasurable headache. But it is, I contend, quite the wrong sort of headache which they occasion in the workaday playgoer (or filmgoer).*" More to the point, a "West End of London audience" is one thing, but a global audience – and a markedly *classed* audience – is quite another. Olivier's version "intended to surprise and storm remote and un-Shakespeare-minded audiences throughout the habitable globe – not only Peru but Poole, and Blackpool, and Ullapool, not only China but Chepstow and Chorley and Chipping Sodbury." Though "Sir Laurence takes a higher view of humanity," and "wanted to keep far more of the text's obscurities," it's clear that some matters were simply not to be spoken, or in this case heard, in Chipping Sodbury let alone China.

Dent lists thirty-two *"noteworthy simplifications for words or phrases that must reasonably be considered 'caviare to the general'. In almost every case it will be observed, and it must be granted, that the Shakespearean word or phrase has become obsolete or has totally changed its meaning."* For this reason, perhaps, in Olivier's film, Gertrude and Claudius are a little less greasy, honeying "in the rank sweat of a lascivious bed." Onscreen, the line is instrumentalized as Hamlet creeps on to the bed on all fours; on the phrase "nasty sty" Eileen Herlie's youthful Gertrude – who has been wringing her hands in the (apparently clean) bedcovers – rises, turns, and clings to Hamlet's neck, where she remains until we hear the amplified heartbeat signaling the Ghost's return. Notably, though Gertrude had thrown herself on the bed, when she turns to touch Hamlet she rises, and they remain vertical (though, to be fair, the black and grainèd spots of her guilt don't "lose their tinct," but "lose their stain"). Dent's emendation implies that *enseamed* would have been heard as one of those words *"totally changed"* in *"meaning,"* slipping from one disgusting exudation to another, a sense violating the propriety of the production, and perhaps raising a salacious grin among the lads of Chipping Sodbury. This famously Freudian production hinges on a scene in which, in this tiny matter, the expense of spirit is abstracted and to some degree etherealized, as though things rank and gross in nature are not to be thought upon too closely. And, as an aside, while Gertrude and Claudius rankly sweat, the Prince is himself cleansed of perspiration. In the duel scene, when Gertrude expresses her concern for her Hamlet, he's not "fat," but merely "hot and scant of breath." Danish princes, like Southern belles, don't perspire; they glow.

Replacing *enseamed* with *lascivious*, Olivier elevated and remoralized Hamlet's language here; it's fitting, perhaps, that Kenneth Branagh – wearing Olivier's bleach blond – takes a similarly rhetorical approach to the line, in a production that Lisa Starks rightly describes as sanitizing unruly sexualities. After discovering dead Polonius, Branagh moves "slowly to her. Talks as if he were a priest about to pronounce eternal damnation" (Branagh 105).[30] Kneeling and embracing Gertrude from behind to "read" the portraits of Old Hamlet and Claudius to her, Hamlet "throws her back down on the bed and leaps off to pace the room" (Branagh 106). Hamlet paces, lecturing Gertrude; for these lines he drops to her eye level, but *enseamed* comes and goes, without particular emphasis: we get it, get something, or we don't. Julie Christie's "These words like daggers enter into mine ears" emphasizes the rhetorical more than the physical dimension of Hamlet's lecture, the success of Hamlet's plan to "speak daggers to her." Olivier's *lascivious* elevates Hamlet's crudeness; performing the speech as a lecture, Branagh in effect makes a speech, forcing the words – whatever we take them to be – to do their work on Gertrude. Branagh's production is rich in visual imagery contextualizing and specifying the action of the play: Fortinbras' army, Horatio's dandyish costuming, the love scenes between Ophelia and Hamlet. But here, the *agency* of the words is foregrounded as verbal, the work they do in the scene is, in this sense, "Shakespeare's." (As an aside, it might be noted that the screenplay has a misprint here; while Hamlet delivers the usual lines onscreen, in the text he says "Nay, but to live / In the sweat of an enseamèd bed," an error that seems to have intruded between the shooting script – in which the line was correct, as it is in the film – and the published text. *Hamlet*'s performance of these lines is more faithful to the book than the book).[31]

The construction of the text as performance operates in a "life-support system" that, while metaphorically textualizable, is not fully textual. Of course the prim sexuality of Olivier has given way to more direct performances of Hamlet's sexual aggression against Gertrude. In the *BBC TV Shakespeare Plays* version directed by Rodney Bennett, Derek Jacobi impels Gertrude's "shame" by throwing her on the bed, forcing her down, pinning her arms, straddling her and – "simulating sex" would be the polite phrase for it. Claire Bloom's dress rises up, and we see, *avant la lettre* of the new Globe Theatre, authentic bloomers. Jacobi then rolls off her, allowing the camera to take in her "tinct" speech, but on the words *enseamed bed*, Hamlet's arm disappears out of the frame, reaching down below Gertrude's waist where he again thrashes her vigorously up and down.

While Olivier translates *enseamed* to *lascivious* as a way to displace and elevate the word that filmgoers might otherwise hear, Jacobi assimilates the word to the gross sexuality of the nasty sty, a sexuality he grotesquely reenacts. In Peter Brook's more intimate, more conversational production, much of Hamlet's preceding speech is cut, as it was in the Olivier film, but like Olivier and Jacobi, Adrian Lester moves to the bed on "O shame." Yet while Branagh's Hamlet depends on the rhetorical force of the words to do their dagger-like work, Lester's

Hamlet seems less confident in the power of language alone; though the camera is behind him for the *enseamed* line, its significance is immediately literalized as he makes an obscene gesture (the fig) with his fingers, then humps the air on "making love over the nasty sty," much as he had earlier done to depict "country matters" to Ophelia. Olivier replaces the word to avoid a distracting echo; Branagh absorbs it to the pedagogical force of his lecture; Jacobi enacts it; and Lester illustrates it, suggesting not so much that the text is a "stable signifier" as an empty one, requiring the supplementary work of pictorializing performance.

In many respects, the Almereyda *Hamlet* is tonally at the opposite remove from Brook's, and here it's Ethan Hawke who occupies the bed. While Gertrude cowers covering her ears, Hamlet attacks the bed – "*In a rage, he starts tearing the sheets from the bed*" according to the screenplay (Almereyda 81) – ripping those sweaty, greasy coverings and holding them close. On the line *enseamed* bed, pronounced en-*seem'd*, Hamlet glances at the blanket he's holding in his hands. This is difficult to read, but I think the word that Hawke's Hamlet speaks is sartorial rather than seminal; the sheets have seams. Hawke's pronunciation creates another "very Shakespeare" word, one that distances the word we would otherwise hear, with a similarly invented one.

In a sense, Hawke's explosive Hamlet is less erotically involved with Gertrude; his sheets have seams but are not ensemened. But Mel Gibson's are. By "O shame where is thy blush," in Franco Zeffirelli's film, both Hamlet and Gertrude are on the bed. Hamlet brutally flips Gertrude onto her back and pinions her; at this moment the camera angle changes, and rather than seeing Hamlet ride Gertrude, we see the Prince from something closer to the Queen's perspective. On "stewed in corruption," though, Gibson illustrates *enseamed* much as Jacobi had, Gertrude crying out on each jolt. And, again like Jacobi, he collapses on her breast on "O speak to me no more," the scene culminating in a violently erotic kiss. Olivier protects his audience from their ranker thoughts; Branagh subdues graphic language to the rhetorical gesture of pedagogical instruction; Lester deploys the language of gesture to illustrate his meaning; and Hawke resignifies the word by identifying with a handy prop. Zeffirelli's film, aiming neither toward Branagh's "definitive" nor Olivier's "experimental" status, takes a relatively popular approach to the play's "Freudian" dimension, staging Oedipal relations in a way that Olivier could only point to, perhaps

because, as Lisa Starks suggests, Olivier followed Ernst Jones's more
properly psychoanalytic account, in which Hamlet's "incestuous long-
ings reside in the unconscious and therefore can only be manifested in
a distorted manner" (Starks 166). Olivier's indirection is transformed
into Zeffirelli's literalism, and one index of this transformation is that
Mel puts the word we have – for sixty years, at least – heard, or feared
to hear, into Hamlet's mouth. Mel's Prince says, "rank sweat of an
ensemened bed."

It's a tiny moment in any production, yet, like Hamlet's play with
the book, we can use this performative crux to locate how writing
works in performance, not as a guide, instruction, paradigm, or template for "the play" to follow, illustrate, reproduce, but instead as
means to an action, action that will be constituted anew in every production because the technologies of the stage require its tools to do new
work. From Austin's sense of the theatre as *"parasitic"* on the "normal
use" of language to Derrida's and Butler's emphasis on the essential
reiterability, theatricality, of any *performative* (verbal or behavioral), the
theory of dramatic performance has struggled to redefine the New
Critics' settled priority of text to performance. This tension persists
nowhere so clearly as at the extremes, in fields where the "text" is taken
to motivate the purpose and value of performance (Shakespeare
studies) or is seen as the site of an intransigent will to cultural dominion over the repertoires of performance (performance studies).
Although this example may appear to license a kind of performative
liberty, in each case the work of performance attempts to accommodate
the word – actually, something like a symbol or abstraction of the
word, an empty phoneme standing in for "Shakespearean" language
– to the process of significant action.

The work of these productions may also seem to be urgently archival, the repertoire of performance struggling only to make sense of the
words on the page. Instead, the actor's use of the behavioral comple-
ment of performance action provides a means of grounding the word,
lending it a local habitation in the contemporary armature of active
signification. As a paradigm of performance, Hamlet's *enseamed* suggests that performance always – in Burke's terms – conceives of the
text as a means of parrying the thrust made to the play by the circumstances of contemporary performance. Far from merely illustrating the
meanings of a textualized *archive,* dramatic performance frames a
constant revision of the *archive,* indeed frames the *archive* in the

process of its materialization. Considering theatrical performance as a social technology implies that the performative "properties" of the text emerge when it is conceived as an *agency* within a particular *scene* of doing. That is, we can speak of the film or of any performance not as offering an interpretation of the text, but making the text do work, constitute an action through performative means. As Hamlet's scene with Polonius suggests, the point of acting is to get off book, to use the "words, words, words" as agency, parrying the thrust of performance. It's the parry, not the word, which scores a "palpable hit."

iii. "OK, we can skip to the book": The Wooster Group *Hamlet*

> *OK, we can skip to the book*
>   *Scott Shepherd/Hamlet, the Wooster Group* Hamlet[32]

To consider the uses of writing in live performance through the rewriting of the text for film should give us pause. Indeed, it may raise a provocative alternative question, not of how writing relates to embodied performance, but whether in the digital era the theatre's specific means of deception have not themselves been rendered residual by new technologies. Yet as Matthew Causey argues, "the immediacy of performance and the digital alterability of time and space through technology," far from being either essentially or culturally opposed, "converge" in the onstage and offstage landscapes of contemporary performance (Causey 6). Whether it's Peter Sellars's *Merchant of Venice* (1994), Frank Castorf's *Master and Margarita* (2002), Kristian Smeds's *Three Sisters* (2004), or Ivo van Hove's brilliant *Misanthrope* (2007), the past decade of performance has been preoccupied with the interplay between live and live-recorded performance, projecting live-feed video of events taking place onstage (some visible to the audience, some not), offstage, backstage, or outside the theater as part of the play.[33] The interplay with recorded media is widened in scope if we remember the longstanding use of still and motion-picture projections as scenography, a tradition originating in the 1920s, constellated in Erwin Piscator's *Hoppla, Wir Leben!* of 1927, extending notably through the work of Joseph Svoboda's Laterna Magika in Prague, and still visible in Mikhail

Baryshnikov's pas de deux with a Soviet-era film of a young Baryshnikov dancing in Benjamin Millepied's *Years Later* (2006).[34] Russell Jackson's image of Kenneth Branagh rehearsing his filmed *Hamlet* concisely images the dialogue between the live and live-feed as the condition of drama across the media of contemporary performance: "Ken stands alone in the hall to rehearse, the complete post-modern prince with a dagger in one hand and the tiny remote monitor to watch himself with in the other. ('I could be watching the football now')" (Jackson, "Film Diary" 198).

Here, I want to bring to bear a performance that rehearses the question, not only of the transformation of cultural traditions – the rituals of dramatic theatre – by digital technologies, but also of the ways we currently model the uses of writing in the practices of performance: the 2007 Wooster Group *Hamlet*. Developed over the course of 2006 and 2007, the performance is animated by a richly generative gesture.[35] The play opens with Scott Shepherd taking the stage and casually speaking *Hamlet's* famous first line – "OK, you can play the tape." An edited version of the 1964 film of John Gielgud's theatrical *Hamlet* starring Richard Burton begins to run on a large upstage screen, as well as on a number of smaller television monitors facing into the playing area. As the rest of the small Wooster Group ensemble (nine actors) enter, they gradually, sometimes ironically, begin a performance of *Hamlet* by imitating the movements, gestures, and vocal intonations of the Burton film. The film has been both digitized and edited – individual figures on the screen frequently fade out, partly or entirely disappearing; on a few occasions the screen goes blue and the word "unrendered" appears. Although the Wooster actors sometimes turn to the back of the house and tell the technicians to skip over a scene, the Wooster *Hamlet* is a complete performance, staging a live *Hamlet* in dialogue with the Burton film from beginning to end.

Perhaps the most prominent avant-garde theatre company working in the United States today, the Wooster Group has long explored the interface between theatrical presence and technological virtuality, its "dancing with technology" (qtd. Causey 43) providing the means of a searching interrogation of the ongoing vitality of classic drama. The company's initial work on *Three Places in Rhode Island* in the late 1970s (*Sakonnet Point*, 1975; *Rumstick Road*, 1977; *Nyatt School*, 1978) staged memory performance through a host of hands-on instruments manipulated by the cast: tape recorders, slide projectors, record players, a sound board, a conference-table with microphones. *Route 1 & 9* (1981) – in which video of Thornton Wilder's *Our Town* was placed in dialogue with a live blackface performance in part reviving Pigmeat Markham's vaudeville routines – constellated one of the Group's characteristic tactics, using a range of theatrical genres (blackface minstrelsy here, later Asian theatre forms) and its "dancing with technology" to intervene in the dramatic tradition: *L.S.D. (... Just the High Points ...)* (1984), notoriously taking on Arthur Miller's *The Crucible*; *The Emperor Jones* (1993); *The Hairy Ape* (1995), *Brace Up!*, "from Chekhov's *Three Sisters*" (1991); *To You, The Birdie! (Phèdre)* (2002).[36]

In its 2007 *Hamlet*, however, the Wooster Group uses the technologies of live and recorded performance to engage the reciprocity of *archive* and *repertoire*, in part by exercising one of the foundational notions of contemporary performance theory, *restored behavior* – "living behavior treated as a film director treats a strip of film" (Schechner, "Restoration of Behavior" 35) – and applying it to the interrogation of dramatic performance in information culture. Unlike *The Real Live Brady Bunch* stage show of the early 1990s, in which the cast of Chicago's Annoyance Theatre reenacted oft-rerun episodes of the 1970s TV show, or Jean-Claude van Itallie's *The Serpent* (Open Theater, 1968), in which actors mimed the gestures of the Kennedys and the Connollys in the Zapruder film of JFK's assassination, breaking it into segments and gestures that were, as we might say now, *shuffled*, the Wooster Group *Hamlet* replays a deliquescent film "original," dramatizing the work of performance in instrumentalizing and so remaking the "text" at the moment of its restoration. More to the point, the Wooster Group *Hamlet* stages the ongoing subversion of the *archive* by the *repertoire*, suggesting that a dichotomy between writing and performing, the recorded and the live, is inadequate to the critical assessment of performance today, if it ever was really adequate at all.

The Wooster Group undertakes a dialogic *Hamlet*, as the actors at first hesitantly, and then more assertively, reenact the voicing, gesture, and movement of a film "original" projected behind them upstage: the 1964 Richard Burton *Hamlet*, a minimally edited live film of the John Gielgud modern-dress "rehearsal" production. As the program notes suggest, the Wooster Group production "attempts to reverse the process" of filmed theatre, "reconstructing a theatre piece from the fragmentary evidence of the edited film, like an archaeologist inferring a temple from a collection of ruins." In this sense, the Wooster Group participates in our wider awareness of *Hamlet* as a document in the genealogy of remediation ("the representation of one medium in another"), recalling not only the Michael Almereyda film, saturated by recording technologies – films of live theatre (Gielgud's wartime *Hamlet*), silent films, talkies (James Dean), television, and Pixelvision, all subjected to digital recomposition – but also the sense of *Hamlet* as a meditation on Shakespeare's changing technologies of writing and performing.[37] As Margreta de Grazia points out, *Hamlet* was both "a recycling of an earlier play" and a remediation of a range of narrative sources, locating the play in a reflective history of dynastic transformation (*Hamlet without Hamlet* 7); the "problems of repetition and tradition that afflict *Hamlet* production" traced by Richard Halpern might also be seen to arise from the play's anxious regard for the interplay between writing and acting (268). Hamlet's book, Ophelia's book, Hamlet's "tables" and Polonius' "desk or table book," the treaties with Norway, Hamlet's letters to Claudius and Horatio, his poem, the "dozen lines, or sixteen lines" he writes, the Pyrrhus "speech," *The Murder of Gonzago*: *Hamlet* interrogates the uses of writing in a theatre itself being remade by the surging pressure of print, its preservation and simultaneous devaluation of what Hamlet calls ("*reading on a book*" in the Folio), "words, words, words." Though much of the reading and writing is cut from the Wooster Group *Hamlet*, traces remain. Scott Shepherd, apparently bored by the "fishmonger" episode, orders the technicians to fast-forward to something more engaging: "OK, we can skip to the book."

The Wooster Group *Hamlet* reconsiders the work of dramatic performance: its technology situates the question both synchronically (in relation to the impact of information technologies and virtual performances on "the text," "drama," "theatrical performance") and diachronically, in the extended encounter between writing and performing animating Western theatre. *Hamlet* critically distinguishes acting – the Player's monstrous weeping for Hecuba – from other modes of performing writing, Hamlet declaiming the Pyrrhus speech, Polonius reading his poem to Ophelia, Claudius reading his letter. The Wooster Group situates acting in a critical relation to recorded performance, more precisely with the moment that the stage, far from embedding recorded performance, seemed once more on the brink of being finally erased by it. That moment and its technology had a name: Theatrofilm by Electronovision.

Theatrofilm by Electronovision

The Electronovision film of Burton's *Hamlet* was predicated on the extraordinary success of John Gielgud's 1964 production at the Lunt-Fontanne Theatre in New York (the Group's Scott Shepherd wryly observes that the theatre is now host to *The Little Mermaid*). On 30 June and 1 July 1964, Alexander H. Cohen and Warner Brothers bought out the orchestra for three performances (Zolotow); audiences seated in the balcony and mezzanine watched as the live performance was recorded by seven small cameras (Crowther), the feed sent just outside the theatre to be recorded to film. The "Electronovision" process at once enabled the theatre to use normal lighting, and allowed Warner Brothers to strike prints from the film negatives "almost immediately" (Weiler). The experiment was expensive, an investment in potentially transformative new media. Figuring the purchase of seats, added salary to the actors, production and advertising costs, Warner Brothers spent about $700,000 on the project, but it was rumored that Burton alone – a stockholder in the Electronovision corporation – could reap "as much as $1 million" if the project were successful (Bart, "Filmed 'Hamlet'"). Central to the conceptual and economic design of the Theatrofilm *Hamlet* was its replication of the evanescent "liveness" of theatre, and the reproduction of that "live" experience on a national scale, an event perhaps recalling the Federal Theatre Project's production of *It Can't Happen Here* at twenty-two theatres in 1936. *Hamlet* was scheduled to be shown for four performances only, on 23 and 24 September 1964, at 976 theatres around the United States, and then destroyed (two copies survived, one that Burton donated to the British Film Institute, and one found by his widow Sally in 1988).[38] If successful, Burton's *Hamlet* would prove the vanguard of a new genre of moviehouse entertainment. Olivier's stage *Othello* was seen as a possible successor (Bart, "Stage-Film Group"), and *The T.A.M.I. Show* (*Teen-Age Awards Music International*) was recorded and shown in January 1965, a film including Chuck Berry, Marvin Gaye, Gerry and the Pacemakers, Smokey Robinson and the Miracles, the Supremes, the Beach Boys, the Rolling Stones ("a Beatles-like quintet from England, with mossy hair-dos"), and James Brown, "emptying his musical soul like a scalded cat" (Howard Thompson).[39]

Of course, it wasn't the technology that was seductive, it was the virtualization of liveness, itself a category of experience produced by recording technology.[40] Hoping to "draw people from their homes" (Bart, "Filmed 'Hamlet' "), *Hamlet* clearly responded to the widespread anxiety that television would prove the demise of both theatre and film. At the same time, the film was promoted in terms that underlined its complicity with the televisual, not only television's claim to bring distant spectacles into virtual proximity ("spanning the globe to bring you the constant variety of sport" is how ABC's *Wide World of Sports* put it, first broadcast in 1961), but to do so in ways emphasizing the ephemeral, "live" quality of mediated experience (even if that experience was both recorded and fictionalized, as in the famous *You Are There* series of the 1950s). What Susan Sontag has called the "vanished rituals – erotic, ruminative – of the darkened [movie] theatre" would be inflected by *Hamlet*'s stage-like occasionality, as Burton suggested in the promotional trailer: "This has never happened before. The immediacy, the sense of being there is unlike any experience you have ever known. This is the theatre of the future, taking shape before your eyes today."[41] As Burton noted in an interview now included on the DVD (and available on *YouTube*), responding to the sense that "movies are something you see on the screen and plays are something you see live on the stage," the performance was not redesigned for Theatrofilm, nor did the actors "make any concession to this new process" for the benefit of the camera: "there's no cheating of any kind."[42]

Today, the Metropolitan Opera transmits across the US, live and in high-def, and if we miss the live pay-per-view in the movie theatre, we can subscribe to the on-demand service; many TV programs are available online within hours of broadcast.[43] But in 1964 TV didn't have to cheat much: the evanescent experience of television was considerably more like the temporality of theatre than it is today. Like the Rockettes at Radio City, popular but seasonal programs like the stop-action animation *Rudolph the Red-Nosed Reindeer* (1964) had more of the occasional quality of theatrical revivals. At the same time, *Hamlet*'s impact was dependent on the theatrical origin encoded as its predominant aesthetic. Opening the month following the play's close on Broadway, the film articulated a complex, intense-yet-somehow-etiolated sense of "being there": the "sense of being there is unlike any experience you have ever known" ("Trailer"). In the 1950s and 1960s, television was indeed widely understood as replicating and so replacing theatre, and to this sense Theatrofilm added the experience of public occasion, a sense of being there destined to replace being there altogether, as

Burton intoned in the trailer: "This is the theatre of the future."[44] In the end, though, the Theatrofilm *Hamlet* was paradoxically not virtual enough to capture the peculiar *thereness* either of the stage or of film. For Gielgud, it could not "be very cinematic and it is not the theater," a judgment with which film critics largely concurred (Bart, "Filmed 'Hamlet'").

But the film's promotion had another resonance, poised as it was amid an American enthusiasm for all things futuristic (Tomorrowland had been open at Disneyland since 1955, *Lost in Space* aired the year after *Hamlet*, in September 1965, and *Star Trek* in 1966), a future that seemed to betoken the inevitable demise of old technologies of entertainment (we've heard that song, too, "Bye Bye Books"), but that was also perched on the fault line of a pervasive fear that the gadgetry of nuclear holocaust might extinguish tomorrowland altogether. "*Hamlet* bursts upon the twentieth century through the miracle of Electronovision," Burton purred in the theatrical trailer, and its explosion shared the screen with other films bursting with atomic particles, instantaneous communications, and sexy British masculinity. Stanley Kubrick's *Dr. Strangelove; Or, How I Learned to Stop Worrying and Love the Bomb*, Sidney Lumet's *Fail-Safe*, and *Goldfinger* (the third of Sean Connery's 007 films, but the first real blockbuster) all appeared in 1964, irradiating a media landscape aglow with televisual spies and space: *The Outer Limits* (1963), *The Man from U.N.C.L.E.* (1964), *I Spy* (1965), *Get Smart* (1965), *Mission: Impossible* (1966), *The Girl from U.N.C.L.E.* (1966), *The Prisoner* (1967), and of course *My Favorite Martian* (1963). While the Cold War was playing out on television, it hardly displaced "the big one," which continued (alongside Westerns) to dominate the small screen with comforting images of Allied (American) moral and technological superiority: in 1964–5, the ground war (*Combat!*), the air war (*Twelve O'Clock High*, a television series based on the 1949 film), and the comic war (*McHale's Navy*, *No Time for Sergeants*) were still being fought, alongside vignettes of contemporary life in the Marines, *Gomer Pyle – U.S.M.C. Hogan's Heroes*, that celebration of prisoner-of-war ingenuity marking the controversial sublimation of another monument of technological modernity – the concentration camps – as the subject of comedy, was first broadcast the following season.

The sense of an "epoch-making" moment informs the promotional interview with Burton that now accompanies the DVD, "Richard Burton Discusses 'Electronovision.'" As the unidentified interviewer notes, "The gentleman at my side is about to have an experience that no other actor ever had before: he's going to have a chance to see himself perform on the Broadway stage." It's not Burton's experience that draws us to the movie theatre, though, it's what will happen to us when *Hamlet* ignites. The interviewer asks Burton about the details of the film's two-day showing, a question more resonant against the background of Kubrick, Connery, and Illya Kuryakin: "What is the flight plan of this – and you've used a very good phrase – when *Hamlet* bursts upon the twentieth century, now with Electronovision, *Hamlet* can burst in over a thousand places at once. Are you going to synchronize it so that in every town in America, people go in the same day, buy their ticket, report to the theatre, and enjoy the play live but not quite live?" Imagined in the language of command and control, the Theatrofilm with Electronovision *Hamlet*'s "flight plan" takes it out over the country for a synchronized detonation, and in every town in America we'll be glad we *reported* to the theatre on time, where we can "live but not quite live," preserving an inaccessible culture and its simulation ("unlike any experience you have ever known"), until the fallout settles, perhaps. The interview concludes, "Richard Burton, the actor, at ground zero, when *Hamlet* exploded into the twentieth century."

The fact that Theatrofilm never really caught on is hardly the point: neither theatre nor film were killed by television, though both have clearly been inflected by televisual rhythms, aesthetics, ideologies. Indeed, embedded as we are in its networks, television's penchant for capturing, replaying, and thereby becoming the real seems to be what is at stake for us now, in the theatre as much as on *YouTube*. Summoning the Burton *Hamlet*, the Wooster Group use its now familiar aesthetic of remediation to forge a dialogue with a specific avatar, one already enwrapped in the questions of technology, of the assimilation of performance to the archive.[45]

(Re)playing Burton, performing Hamlet

The Wooster Group *Hamlet* functions as both an allegory and a critique of conventional notions of dramatic performance as the mere repetition of writing, of the text as an epistemologically imperial, "stable signifer" unchanged by its use in and dominion over performance. In one sense, replaying the film, the Wooster Group appears to enact what many theatregoers (and theorists, truth be told) take to be the purpose of the stage: to reproduce "the play" in the medium of live acting. Ben Brantley, for instance, wants a good Shakespeare production to make "me hear familiar language through virgin ears" ("Looks It Not Like the King?"), and he calibrates the Wooster *Hamlet* to the successful surrogation of Burton and company. The performance offers "a very sophisticated form of karaoke":

> The live cast members are hemmed in by their roles as replicants. Since their first duty is to present only the shells of the performances they are imitating, they are only rarely able to fill those exteriors with a transforming interpretive force.

Recalling two centuries of theatre criticism damning actors for their hollow incapacity, their inability "to fill those exteriors" with the

Photo 1 Scott Shepherd replicating Richard Burton as Hamlet; note that Shepherd watches a small monitor facing into the stage space to gauge his performance. Shepherd's hand appears on the moveable video screen in the lower left of the photo, recorded live by the camera downstage. (Photo: © Paula Court, used by permission)

"transforming interpretive force" of Shakespeare's great roles, Brantley at once praises the Wooster *Hamlet* as a "sometimes ravishing, often numbing homage to a fabled theatrical event" and as a finally doomed effort "to give flesh to the fading phantoms behind them."

Although Brantley models the Wooster Group's performance on the paradigm of theatrical fidelity to the text, incorporating the film-as-text seems not to be the Burkean *purpose* of the Wooster *Hamlet* but merely its means, its *agency*. He notes that the Wooster ensemble does render "to its best ability the exact stance and tone of the filmed actors," even striking different attitudes to reflect changing camera angles, and rushing downstage for "closeups." But the effect of this restoration is precisely to foreground the actors' physical virtuosity and technical skill, forcing the film "original" farther into the background, so to speak. For much of the performance, the live actors displace or even erase their avatars, as in the "rogue and peasant slave" soliloquy in 2.2, where Burton gradually disappears from the screen at "O vengeance," only his upraised hand visibly counterpointing Scott Shepherd's precise enactment. As in Samuel Beckett's *Play* or *Not I*, where the equipment of the stage – the spotlight – governs the actors' performance, here the bodies onstage are visibly possessed less by the phantoms on the screen than by the technological demands of the live remediation of film, which dictate much of the physical armature of their work, the stuttering gestures they use to reify the decaying film's jumpiness, the sudden shifts in posture or position to vivify the camera's changing perspective. Mere mimicry is hardly the production's definitive act, as though the restorative dimension of theatre were captive to the intention of offering us a copy, a new edition, a faithful version.[46] Although the Wooster Group *Hamlet* attributes a generative role to the Burton film, which surrogates the function attributed to "Shakespeare's text" in more conventional productions, the performance actually dramatizes the hollowness of that citation: what we see is that the Burton film – like the text of *Hamlet* – is an instrument, a means, an agency for making new work in a new scene of production.[47]

Indeed, the production marks its distance from a sense of dramatic performance as the "declamation and illustration of written drama" in a number of ways (Lehmann 21). In place of Burton's wide and empty stage, our space is foreshortened by the large projection screen upstage, decorated with monitors on vertical tracks and rolling stands, scaffolded by light and sound rigging, traced by wires, leads, feeds. A

Photo 2   Kate Valk as Gertrude and Ari Fliakos as Claudius; the pattern and color of Valk's blouse are restored to Eileen Herlie in the upstage film. (Photo: © Paula Court, used by permission)

microphone downstage center provides the focus of much of the action, and a video camera alongside it frequently records the events onstage, sometimes projecting them on one or more of the smaller screens. Several television monitors face into the acting area, playing what seems to be an unedited version of the projection on the large screen, so that the actors can keep an eye on the film actors' work without turning upstage. By recording the performance, simultaneously rendering it as digitized information, the live action can be blended into and alter the archival *Hamlet*: Kate Valk's costume as Gertrude appears – in color – on Eileen Herlie's Gertrude just after the closet scene; Rosencrantz's costume in the film is frequently "colorized" red, to match the coat worn by the live Rosencrantz; Judson Williams's (Horatio) hands appear on the upstage screen during the "heart's core" dialogue with Hamlet in 3.2.

The *archive* is remade by its performance; the interface between information and platform, recorded and live, text and performance is a dynamic exchange. Naturally, the actors are miked (body as

instrument of output) and wearing earbuds (body as receiver of input).
Like Stelarc, whose performance sometimes involves live digital video
of his inner organs, the actors stage the body as accessible to information, absorbed into its flow. Receivers and transmitters, their enactment
briefly transduces the datastream.[48] As a result, while the actors sometimes emphasize the performance-of-mimicry, speaking in audible
unison with the recorded voices from the screen (i.e., Shepherd and
Burton sometimes speak together; sometimes they begin together, then
Burton's voice fades out), the microphone enables other critical effects.
Kate Valk's Ophelia is echoed by a second, high-pitched voice; though
this voice "stands in" for Linda Marsh's in the film – whose voice was
sparingly used – it is in fact a distortion of Valk's voice; Ari Fliakos's
Claudius almost entirely displaces Alfred Drake's voice and – sitting
visibly just offstage in the wings – Fliakos redubs Gielgud's voice-over
of the Ghost as well.[49] More intriguing, the actor's live-but-digitally-
encoded voice can be subjected to immediate transformation. At several
points in the play, Burton's voice fades behind Shepherd's, but
Shepherd's live voice no longer sounds "live." Instead, it is given a
slightly tinny, flat "recorded" sound as it is processed through the
sound system. Kate Valk's blouse as Gertrude replaces Eileen Herlie's
on the screen; as Ophelia, her voice redoubles and displaces Linda
Marsh's. Shepherd's "recorded" voice, though, seems to arise at once
from the image and from the actor, in the past and in the moment of
its materialization. *His master's voice*: recording traditionally asserts a
(high) fidelity to the presence its mimicry at once encodes, preserves,
and displaces. Onstage, the voice indexes the theatre's dialectics of
presence: troped by writing, the voice is the sign of an external authority remaking the body; recoding writing in the grain of a specific body,
the voice simultaneously enacts the theatre's essential infidelity, writing
palpably transformed by the accents of its use. Placing the live voice
on the edge of the echo chamber, the Wooster Group *Hamlet* stages
living speech not as a dependent accessory to the *archive*, but as an
instrument for rewriting the *archive* in its restoration to performance.[50]

Theatrofilm differentiates theatre (what we see) from film (what we
see it on or through); the Wooster Group stages a more convergent,
perhaps conflictual relationship between origin and reproduction, liveness and its remediation, what Matthew Causey has called the *embedding* of the "real" in the "virtual" as a paradoxical means of guaranteeing
its plausibility or effectiveness (Causey 4).[51] Rather than illustrating the

theatre as a failed effort to recover or imitate the original, this conver-
gence implies a broader critique of dramatic performance understood
as the mere "declamation and illustration" of the text, that "stable
signifier." Reenacting Burton's film, the Wooster Group *Hamlet* foregrounds the film as its text, stressing less the authorizing stability of
this "writing" than its instrumentality in their performance. The
Wooster Group *Hamlet* treats the Burton film – like the Shakespearean
text – as a script in play. Throughout the evening, Scott Shepherd (and
occasionally other actors) directs the video operator to stop or skip
ahead. Like a script, the film has been edited, both shortened and engi-
neered to seem distant, "a collection of ruins" according to the program
note. The film actors are indeed like phantoms, appearing and disappearing from the screen as they are digitally erased, sometimes leaving
only hands or feet, sometimes nothing at all (in the duel scene, the
actors entirely disappear, replaced by empty white rectangles that
trace their now-invisible movements). The film we see is jumpy, incomplete, a fragment of an unseen architecture, a bad quarto or memorial
reconstruction, constantly held apart from the live performance itself.
Indeed, like a text, the film has its own materiality that doesn't so much
"limit" what can be done as provide – as Katherine Hayles argues –
the conditions of use, the "physical properties and historical usages"
confronted by the complex of contemporary practices of theatrical
embodiment (Hayles, *Writing Machines* 22). For the upstage film is
itself performed by its operator, changing from night to night as it
is edited live. While the Group actors watch unedited film on the
small monitors (some of which are visible to the audience), the video
operator introduces a range of technological distortions to the film we
see, editing it live: even Burton's film is performed.[52] Like writing,
repurposed by the practice of its materialization, the Wooster Group
Hamlet stages the play repurposed by its practices of performance,
those practices themselves inflected by the changing shape of the
archive they enact.

   The Burton film functions textually in another sense: it is both rewritten by and incapable of determining its performance. Not only do
figures in the Burton film disappear from the screen, but the film has
several unexplained lacunae, when the screen suddenly goes blue and
the word "unrendered" appears: the actors onstage are released from
impersonation, or more accurately released into another performance,
the performance of actors on "Pause." They take a break, make a phone

call, read a magazine. But these moments also dramatize the force of performance history in our imagining of dramatic potentiality. The actors summon other films to fill the "textual" gap. Bill Murray's "advice to Laertes" from the Almereyda *Hamlet* is shown on two of the small monitors the actors use to guide their mimicry, and briefly on the large screen. More strikingly, when the Players arrive onstage, they're costumed in clothes quite different from the rest of the cast, odd coats and hats, odd that is until the "unrendered" screen is filled by a Quicktime digital file ripped from the Kenneth Branagh *Hamlet*: "C.Heston.mov." The onstage Players' costumes echo those in the Branagh film, and Shepherd and his Polonius Bill Raymond briefly cover Branagh's and Richard Briers's backchat ("mobled queen," etc.). Yet Heston's performance as the Player stands alone, Shepherd desultorily tracing only a few forlorn gestures. Instead, during Heston's speech, Shepherd/Hamlet forces Kate Valk (here, one of the Players) downstage to the video camera, where she simulates not Heston's performance but the silent vignette of Judi Dench's Hecuba that illustrates it in the Branagh film, her final gesture – head back, mouth open – captured in a still frozen on a small video screen (Valk is also costumed with a head-wrap, resembling Dench's). Freeze-frame capture is used throughout the Wooster *Hamlet*, often to image death: Polonius' and Ophelia's bodies are both replaced by freeze-frame video images, and Scott Shepherd's "death" as Hamlet is simultaneously captured as well (as is the moment when he briefly opens his eyes). Here, Valk/Dench provides the spur to Hamlet's ensuing soliloquy, prompting him to reprise Burton while Burton fades from view, leaving only his upraised hand behind. Distancing its aims from Branagh's "complete" *Hamlet*, the Wooster Group uses that film to urge a sense that our access to *Hamlet* remakes the play through the history of its doing.

Despite its digital-culture texture, the Wooster Group *Hamlet* finally refuses to locate dramatic performance as the recovery of lost "information": the originals can be found, but they cannot be played, or at least they cannot be played as themselves. Even the digital inscription projected as Burton's film is itself a restoration and remediation of that nearly-lost original, made from two known surviving copies, recalling the two remaining, unidentical copies of that other *Hamlet*, the 1603 first quarto. The platform remakes the data. But does the production engage the history encoded in that "stable signifier," the strangely dysphoric elation of mutually assured destruction: "Richard Burton,

Photo 3   "O vengeance!" Although this photograph captures Scott Shepherd performing before a fully visible Burton, when I saw the performance on 7 and 8 November 2007, Burton's body then faded from the upstage screen, leaving only the upraised hand visible. The video operator "edits" the film live during each performance. (Photo: © Paula Court, used by permission)

the actor, at ground zero, when *Hamlet* exploded into the twentieth century"? We can hear the accents echoing from Suzan-Lori Parks's Great Hole of History (*The America Play*), we remember the words and even still use many of them, but – like *presently*, or *zounds* – they have a different agency for us, materialize a different world for us, here and now, down the street from another ground zero, not the one mortalized by the Bhagavad Gita at the Trinity test site in 1945 ("I am become death," Oppenheimer said), but where the involvement of the digital and corporeal, high-tech communications and low-tech commitment, the pervasive complicity of the electronic and the embodied trans-formed an everyday event into something "unlike any experience you have ever known," not the stratospheric missile squadron expected in 1964 but a flight of low-flying passenger planes strapped to suicide bombers. *Ground zero*: a text, a haunting trace in the *archive* refashioned by the *repertoire* of technology, culture, performance. Technologies of performance change, and as they change, their means of restoring the *archive* as enactment, and so the *archive* they restore, change as well. The Wooster *Hamlet* is neither degraded echo nor soulless pastiche of an earlier, heroic moment in the history of representation.[53] It measures, instead, the reciprocating fantasies of the inviolable script and the unscripted body, the fallacy of an unmediated, essentially authoritarian *archive*, of words, writing, and the history they encode unchanged by their use, their performance in history.

The Wooster Group performs the essentially Pirandellian vision of theatre as a waste of time, a waste, that is, only if we believe the Actors should inhabit the virtual corporeality of the strangely "real," outsized Characters, whose ambiguous presence relentlessly mocks, and is mocked by, their efforts. Much as Shepherd never "becomes" Burton, so too the live actors' imitation also lends a certain risibility to the filmed performance. While the stage can restore an effigy of the past, the instrument of that surrogation – the dramatic script, the Burton film – continually marks the past's continuity with and inaccessibility to performance, here and now, when even the words burst with unanticipated, unforeseeable force, force displacing or resignifying textual and gestural identities: "ground zero," "O vengeance," *Hamlet*. Doing *Hamlet*, the Wooster Group lays claim to a specific vision of dramatic performance. Far from staging the death-grip of the dramatic *archive*, the oppressive authority of writing over the bodily discourse of living action, this *Hamlet* urges a counterperspective, wearing its words and its wires with a difference. The book, *archive*, its "information," is always there, but as we transduce it through our bodies – as speech, as acting, as motion and soundwave, signals recoded to digital pulses amplified and distorted and stored – its gaps and stutterings are refashioned as the *repertoire* of our remaking.

Chapter 3

Embodying Writing:
Ibsen and Parks

I do not think it is difficult to penetrate into Rebecca's character and understand it.

But there are difficulties in rendering and representing this character because it is so concentrated.

Henrik Ibsen to Sofie Reimers, 25 March 1887
(Letters and Speeches 266)

One challenge posed by reading drama is the form in which we encounter the play, as book or as performance. But while we can take Hamlet's byplay with the book as an allegory of one of the disjunctions of the theatre – writing cannot contain the play, the play arises from how the words, words, words are used – it hardly exhausts the intricate interplay between writing and performing. But how, if the book neither contains nor prescribes the play, can it relate to embodiment at all?

Dramatic writing cannot determine its performance. At the same time, it frequently images the terms of an engagement with embodiment, representing, even allegorizing a vision of language as an instrument of enactment. As we saw in the first chapter, *Rosmersholm* has proven at least as challenging for critics as it has for actors, largely because of what we might take to be Ibsen's intrinsically theatrical challenge to the work that writing can do in performance, as speech and action. I would like to return to this recognition, and reframe it more carefully here: Ibsen's densely *scripted* drama tends to assert that its final, most significant moments of meaning cannot be captured by language, by the text. His verbal poetry is a means to another, unwritten meaning, that arises through performance, that *must* arise or the play will fail to play. This challenge to performance is not unique to Ibsen, of course. Even in as "trivial" a play as *The Importance of Being Earnest*, how Algy and Jack eat the muffins, how Cicely and Gwendolyn duel with their diaries, locates the salient aggression, the bite and articulation of the drama. While Wilde's comedy might be said to be "about" the trivial tribulations of originating in a terminus, it's the savage commitment to the trivialities that define and contour the practice of social life – the life it represents and that it demands from its performers – that the play must *play* in the theatre.

Our fixation on the text of the plays as *representing* the drama rather than *instigating* it, in this sense, draws our attention away from the text's *agency*. One of the reasons that a play like *Rosmersholm* has proven difficult to read derives from a cultural transformation of the relationship between dramatic writing and the stage, between the institutions of literature and theatre, the reconceptualization of *plays* as *books*. Plays had been published as printed books for some time, but as Ibsen, Shaw, and other playwrights recognized, *print* provided distinctive means for inscribing performance into the experience of reading the play. This "novelistic" aspect of modern dramatic writing – the extensive scenic descriptions, emotive stage directions, the audible voice of Shaw, O'Neill, or Stoppard alongside the dialogue – appears to encode or assert the *book* not only as the origin and agency of the playing, but as its container as well. Ibsen, in fact, often spoke of his plays as books, implying an organic integrity that may appear to render the performance nearly secondary.[1] From the specification of the decor (*"Around the walls hang portraits, both old and more recent, of clergymen, military officers and public officials in uniform. The window is open …"*) to the direction of gesture and intonation (*"Every now and then she glances expectantly out the window through the flowers"*), the text of *Rosmersholm* seems – like many plays of its era and beyond – to work to contain the play, to specify the performance as already pre-directed by the text.[2]

And yet Ibsen was deeply, reflectively engaged by the performance of his plays, and – as his letter to the actress Sofie Reimers about Rebecca implies – recognized the difficulties of playing them. Rather than encouraging Reimers to "suit the action to the word, the word to the action," Ibsen encourages the actress to subject the role to a wider conception of the play, to observe "what the other persons say about Rebecca" and so to gain a sense of "the character's position in and connection with the whole work." More to the point, perhaps, Ibsen notes, "you should bring to your assistance your studies and observations of real life":

> No declamation! No theatrical emphasis! No pomposity at all! Give each mood credible, true-to-life expression. Do not ever think of this or that actress you may have seen. But stick to the life that is going on around you, and give us a true, living character. (*Letters and Speeches* 265–6)

The actress does not reproduce a *character* inscribed in the text: she assembles a *role*, a series of actions, attentive to her interactions with other actors, to the "mood" of the developing event, and from this process of working with, through, and against the text a "true, living character" – a character-effect – might emerge.

Ibsen's letter and the critics' bafflement suggest a second way to consider the work of drama between poetry and performance. Critics like Brooks and Heilman mistake the play's "novelistic" appearance on the page for its essence, taking Ibsen's task as narrative, descriptive, as though he were offering actors a poem to paraphrase in performance. In this view, dramatic writing, like *Emma* or *Bleak House*, should represent, with whatever fascinating ambiguities, a "character" to its readers. To consider dramatic writing as *agency* in the two *scenes* of reading and performing, though, is to invite a different perspective on the writing, to consider *character* as an effect of the *role* – and role-playing – producing it. Like many of Ibsen's plays, *Rosmersholm* is deeply involved in the question of the limits of theatrical representation, training a skeptical attention to the uses of writing in performance, a problem directly confronted by actors: how, or whether, scripted language specifies the meaning of the acts it enables to be performed. *Rosmersholm* traces the problematic of language – words, speech, writing – as *agency* in performance. Is the writing able to describe the things we can make it do?

We might ask a similar question of Suzan-Lori Parks's work, which insistently locates a differential interface between writing and embodying, in part by inviting us to see the writerly conventions of plays on the page as a kind of performance. Troubling the grain of the voice by writing her plays in a kind of dialect, inventing a range of innovative designs for the layout of the play on the page, and locating dramatic performance in a contestatory relation to narrative history, Parks's drama rehearses the challenges of taking the stage, of finding a place

in performance for bodies that have, in the history of dominant representation, always already been misremembered.

i. Can We Act What We Say?: *Rosmersholm*

> ... *this iron time*
> *Of doubts, disputes, distractions, fears.*
>
> Matthew Arnold, "Memorial Verses"

From the late 1880s onward, drama increasingly came to use the page
as a site of performance alternative to, or perhaps anticipatory of, the
stage. In one sense, the new realism replicated the overstuffed environment on the stage in an apparently overstuffed printed page, full of
scenic description and stage direction. The authority of the book
seemed to "direct" the action of the performance from the page, an
apparent predetermination of performance that we – actors, directors,
playwrights, critics, and readers – have struggled to understand (and
undo) ever since. Yet much as Una Chaudhuri sees this drama to stage
a domestic environment that can never be, as Master Builder Solness
put it, a home for human beings, and much, too, as Georg Lukács saw
the drama of the environment rendering the drama of "individualism
truly problematic," so too the text of modern realism both materializes
its protagonists – describing their clothes, their actions, intonations,
intentions – and fails to enunciate them: realism locates the protagonist
as a problem, an absence, in the objective, objectified clutter of the
stage.[3] The general's portrait, the circulating pistols, the poetic innu-
endo ("vine leaves"), and even the climactic run on the piano all circumscribe Hedda Gabler's crisis, but Hedda neither tells us who she is
("I am Oedipus") nor implies that she might ("O, I could tell you – But
let it be," *Hamlet* 5.2.321–2). This sense that the scripted drama avoids
defining *character* in words is the frustrating problem that Brooks and
Heilman identified in their reading of *Rosmersholm*, concluding that
Ibsen grants the actor an unseemly "responsibility" for deciding the
significance of his actions onstage. But it is also cognate with the dominant approach to modern acting, the Stanislavskian notion that the
actor find, or invent, the often contradictory "subtext" of meaning and
value that will animate and transform the language of the page into a
living event.

Can we mean what we say? Can we act what we say? We might rephrase Stanley Cavell's question here, not asking how Ibsen fails to represent "character" or "motive" in the language that the actor speaks, but asking instead what kind of instrument Ibsen's drama provides the actor, how words become an instrument for *making* an action that may well stand apart from, contradict, or transcend what the words seem to say.[4] Despite its descriptive density, Ibsen's writing must also enable *agency*, providing an instrument for use first designed to engage and enrich the densely materialistic environment of the late-nineteenth-century stage. Much as *Hamlet* provides an implicit interrogation of the uses of writing in the process of theatrical performance generally, we might ask how Ibsen's drama – rooted in a sense of character cognate with the influence of the novel in the period, with the distinctive complication of identity inherited from Romanticism, and with the exploration of incipient psychoanalysis – tracks the uses of language, and so implicitly of writing, in the process of embodiment.

Toril Moi locates Ibsen's drama at the tipping point between a late Romantic nostalgia for an integrated identity and a modernist sense of loss and fragmentation. In this context, *Rosmersholm* enacts an essentially skeptical vision of language in action, framed in what Moi characterizes as the play's "unlivable, destructive, and death-dealing" central fantasy (291), the "fantasy of perfect communication between two souls," a fantasy that at once "devalues the body" and skeptically "devalues language, too, for it deprives words of all value: human speech can only ever be second best in relation to the true, wordless communion of souls" (276). Ibsen is well aware of the "power of language to define, describe, to make us self-conscious, to give us knowledge," but this power "comes at the price of separation and loss" (284), a separation brilliantly reified not only in the play's obsession with theatricality – Brendel redressed as Rosmer, Rebecca lurking behind the curtain – but also by its eventness *as* theatre. Moi suggests that the play forces its audience into "accepting our separation from these characters, by acknowledging their plight, we do what they cannot do for each other," namely accept, provisionally, their groping efforts to make sense to one another when meaning-making – in language, in action – has proven, like Rosmer and Rebecca themselves, finally faithless (270).

This reading of *Rosmersholm* thematizes the play at the fulcrum between the longing for a lost Romantic idealism and a modernist chagrin at the inability of language to articulate it, to make our world, our highest values, and ourselves cohere (see 272). Shifting our perspective slightly, though, we might ask how the play represents the incapacity of words to realize this fantasy, and at the same time requires its language to function as *agency*, as an instrument of *poiesis*, of making, as the vehicle for constructing an active *role* in the *scene* of action. Does the text both provide its actors with something to do, and provide an image, a critique of the theatrical uses of that instrument, of embodied language as the vehicle of action, and of the "character" it seems to create? For while the play indeed weighs an enormously skeptical pressure on the protagonists' rather abstract rhetoric of identity (*innocence, joy, happiness, belief, faith*), acting, especially acting in the cognate Stanislavskian mode, also conceives the linguistic surface as a means to creating an alternate process, the "subtext" and its elusive referent, what we might call the "depth effect." But this kind of acting demands a tactical renunciation of skepticism, a renunciation paralleled by Rosmer and Rebecca as they proceed to the mill-race ("We'll never sift to the bottom of that," Rosmer says). Although the play is about the failure of language, it requires a commitment to using language to embody action – to *mean* something in/through action – that Ibsen's skeptical dramaturgy finally refuses to specify in words.

Ibsen is the master of the apparently nugatory, prosaic language of everyday life, but his dramatic strategy often depends on spoken language meaning more or other than it can say, a tendency foregrounded and parodied in *The Wild Duck*. When Gregers solipsistically identifies with the "really fantastic, clever dog, the kind that goes to the bottom after wild ducks when they dive under and bite fast into the weeds down in the mire" (428), he's almost entirely opaque to his audience onstage. Hjalmar, mistaken for a poet only by himself and Gregers, is mystified by metaphor, and "can't follow a word" of it, though Hedvig notes, "I'll tell you something, Mother – it seemed to me he meant something by that" (429). But in *Rosmersholm*, it's not the language of passion (Nora's betrayed "miracle") nor of an unavailable Romantic ideal (Hedda's "vine leaves in his hair") that we struggle with, though the play's idealizing cadence of *freedom, innocence, joy, gladly* raises similar problems. In *Rosmersholm*, even descriptive language appears to be compromised, the vehicle for something else, the pulse of an unstated, perhaps unspeakable reality.

(MRS. HELSETH *goes over and shuts the doors to the hall, then crosses to the window.*)

MRS. HELSETH (*looking out before closing it*). But isn't that the pastor coming now?

REBECCA (*quickly*). Where? (*Rises.*) Yes, that's him. (*Behind the curtain.*) Stand back. Don't let him see us.

MRS. HELSETH (*stepping back into the room*). Look at that, miss – he's beginning to use the old mill-path again.

REBECCA. He took the mill-path the day before yesterday, too. (*Peering out between the curtain and the window sash.*) But now let's see –

MRS. HELSETH. Will he dare go over the footbridge?

REBECCA. That's what I want to see. (*Pause.*) No, he's turning back. Taking the upper path again today. (*Leaves the window.*) The long way round.

MRS. HELSETH. But, my heavens, it must be hard for the pastor to set foot on that bridge. Not *there*, after what happened –

REBECCA (*gathers up her crocheting*). At Rosmersholm they cling to their dead.

MRS. HELSETH. To my mind, miss, it's the dead that cling to Rosmersholm.

REBECCA (*looking at her*). The dead?

MRS. HELSETH. Yes, it's, so to say, as if they couldn't quite tear themselves free from the ones that stay on.

REBECCA. Where did you get that notion?

MRS. HELSETH. Well, I mean, otherwise you wouldn't have this white horse that comes.

REBECCA. Mrs. Helseth, what exactly is all this about a white horse?

MRS. HELSETH. Oh, why talk about it? Anyway, you don't believe in such things.

REBECCA. Do *you* believe in it?

MRS. HELSETH (*goes over and shuts the window*). Oh, I'm not going to make a fool of myself, miss. (*Looks out.*) Wait – isn't that the pastor down on the mill-path again?

REBECCA (*looking out*). Down there? (*Goes to the window.*) No, that's Dr. Kroll! (498–9)

In the opening scene of the play, conversation begins prosaically, descriptively, words comfortably assimilated to the naturalistic environment: only *dare* and the *white horse* trouble the linguistic surface. And yet the dialogue seems to signify more or other than it says. The women's language gains a haunted quality, as their words don't fail to measure what they describe, but seem simultaneously to be pointing to something else, an alternative, impalpable, nonetheless present reality. The invisible scene of Rosmer's journey toward and away from the bridge, his detour "the long way round" is what they see, but not what they account for to one another. What they describe is evidently unseemly, forcing the two women into concealment, spying on Rosmer's unwitting disclosure. It's a bit tawdry, but nothing new: Rebecca has been watching the open secret of Rosmer's return for some time. The women use their words to describe Rosmer in a suggestively theatrical perspective, and we learn that in the theatre, words – even the most banal description – are used to do something other than what they say. Fittingly enough, just as the account of Rosmer's approach appears to signal something else, the language swerves toward mystery, evoking the white horse and the clinging dead, evanescent spirits in the material stage world. Mrs. Helseth's words at once engender an immaterial reality and lend a different complexion to the signal decoration of Rosmersholm, the gazing portraits of the dead.

As the play proceeds we do, of course, learn about the bridge and the mill-race, about the deeper structure of Rosmer's habitual avoidance, and about the ghosts that cling to Rosmersholm. Émile Zola urged playwrights to sense "that poetry is everywhere, in everything" (363), but Ibsen's poetry of everyday language falls unexpectedly athwart its material world. Late-nineteenth-century naturalistic drama is often melodramatic in structure, and Ibsen is well known for adapting the conventional crises of melodramatic action and character to other purposes. So, too, he deftly complicates the typical assimilation of the impassioned melodramatic body to its setting (Nora's desperate dance of death, Hedda's pistols in the suffocating parlor, Oswald's infected sunrise all come to mind).[5] In *Rosmersholm*, though, language and the "character" it enables us to divine is first shown less to reflect the surfaces of the material world it inhabits than to project something else, something undefined or represented only in metaphor. Mrs. Helseth and Rebecca (and the actresses who play them) use language here to bring something they don't quite say into being, the meaning of Rosmer's perpetual avoidance. To this extent, their use of language complicates the insistent materiality of Ibsen's stage. It immediately speaks otherwise, a tendency reinforced by the ease with which it slides beyond or beneath the world of things, to the signs of Rosmer's unspoken motives, to the clinging dead and their emissaries, the ghostly white horses.

The challenge *Rosmersholm* poses to readers is a precisely dramatic problem: how to correlate the meanings we might attribute to the text and its language with the meanings that the text might instrumentalize, bring about. Ibsen's writing is urgently committed to what Elizabeth Grosz calls "surface effects," not only to staging the material world of provincial Norway – here reduced to Rosmer's *holme*, a "tiny island or large rock surrounded by water" (Moi 290) – but also the surfaces of behavior, bodily gesture and movement, opening a window, knitting a shawl, speaking. But Ibsen's words also become the means to some- thing beyond the "surface effects": "They are not merely superficial, for they generate, they produce, all the effects of a psychical interior, and underlying depth, individuality, or consciousness, much as the Möbius strip creates both an inside and an outside" (Grosz 116). Ibsen shows language at once projecting a world and rendering its surface doubtful; the use of language in the *role* opens and complicates dra- matic *character*.

Inscribing character

The play inflects this problem at the interface of the body, where the dense, contradictory mystery of motive meets the world of public action. Commentaries have long noticed the vague, aspirational quality of politics in *Rosmersholm*, mirroring, perhaps, Ibsen's own assertions of a "nobility of character, of a nobility of will and spirit" in political venues.[6] The generalized discourse of liberation vs. conservatism, of freedom vs. constricting morality, finds its cognate in powerfully unstable tokens used to account for inner vitality and desire, *innocence*, *joy*, *happiness*. Notably, these are Rosmer's words; other roles enable a precise and consequential adjustment between interiority and expres- sion in the world of action. The complexity posed by the play's central roles is measured in relation to the secondary parts, Kroll, Beata, and Brendel.

Dr. Kroll is a startlingly aggressive figure in the play. Since Beata's death, Kroll has also been a kind of ghost, absent from Rosmersholm, in the meantime becoming an "agitator"; smeared by his rivals he "bit back pretty sharply" (501), and now that he's "tasted blood" his oppo- nents should beware. His paper, *The County Herald*, indeed calls for "blood" (537) once Rosmer's political realignment is suspected. Kroll's language, as Rosmer points out, is nearly "fanatical" (533), and this violence is eventually turned on Rosmer, too: Rosmer's apostasy will mark his entry into "the battle of life," a "fight to the finish with all your friends." Yet Kroll's violence is precisely located in the temporal and material dimension of the play, his animus arising from his personal and professional displacement, the infection of his home, what might even be called its haunting by a foreign, uncanny spirit. As he notes to Rosmer, "that revolutionary spirit has insinuated itself even into the school" (505), and "dissent and rebellion has infiltrated my own house. My own peaceful life," even his wife and daughter going over to the other side (an embarrassing secret Kroll discloses only after checking that no one is listening at the door). Kroll's raging enmity, in other words, is carefully prepared, and the language he uses upon learning of Rosmer's apostasy, his "brutal speeches" and "vicious attacks" (519), stands apart from Rosmer's vocabulary of "peace and joy and reconciliation" (520). While it seems to defile the ennobling cause of liberation, though, Kroll's rage directly evokes his embarrassing marginalization, as he battles back to regain authority as teacher, father, and husband.[7]

Kroll's language of passionate disclosure actually works to disclose. His speech is the vehicle for animating personal history, personal relations, and situates the "interiority" of character in the paradigmatic terms of modern realism, connecting exterior action to internalized history, Stanislavski's "unbroken lifeline" (*Actor's* 288) revealing the impact of a delicately detailed *past* in the *present* of the scene.[8] In most of Ibsen's plays, language has a dense historicity, often a material history – think of Nora's forgery, of Løvborg's murdered history of the future, even of the promise that Solness makes to return to Hilde in distant Lysanger – and as a *role*, Kroll models the structure of character in modern realistic drama. Yet Ibsen's dramaturgy is also preoccupied by the performative problem of dramatic writing, the slippage between what words can say, and what we can make them do. *Rosmersholm* precisely allegorizes this problem, as the play's haunted plot circumscribes an ongoing, perhaps misprized, effort to use language anew, as one means to chart a new life for Rebecca and Rosmer.

More so than Kroll, Beata is a mystery in the play, but as the play proceeds she becomes considerably less mysterious. Rosmer and Rebecca evoke Beata as a figure of essential instability, voracious and threatening in her desire, and driven to suicide by her (in the end, entirely justified) fear of dishonor and displacement. But to her brother

Dr. Kroll, to the local firebrand Peter Mortensgaard, to the housemaid Mrs. Helseth, Beata's writings and behavior staged a different person, whose claims seemed incredible, but whose judgment seemed sound. Indeed, throughout the play, Beata's sacrifice is incarnated through the much less ghostly reiteration of her words, the words she used to imagine the play's driving crisis. In Act 1, Rosmer's confession, "I'm not so completely alone, you know. There are two of us to bear the solitude," prompts Kroll's "That, too. Beata's words," leading him to dismiss an "indecent" unspoken surmise as "inconceivable" (520–1). Throughout the play, Beata is projected as unreliable, Rosmer and Rebecca harping on the "wild sensual passion she couldn't control" (528), her "sick brain" (542), her "warped view of life" (583), even Kroll noting her "desperate infatuation" with Rebecca, verging on "idolatry – blind worship" (558). Stepping into the turbulent mill-race seems to reify that illegible interior vortex of guilt, sensuality, passion, and fear.

And yet, this vision of an unknowably irrational Beata is increasingly marked as a convenient fiction, a necessary "life lie" sustaining Rosmer's (and possibly Rebecca's) fantasies of romantic and sensual innocence. For as the play proceeds, Beata's motives become more and more clearly inscribed in her actions, actions that ultimately reveal them. Suspecting that one of Dr. West's freethinking books on marriage had made its way to his delicate and childless sister, Kroll reports two visitations. On the first Beata revealed Rosmer's incredible apostasy, which served at the time only to confirm "that she was mentally ill" (529). On her second visit, she told Kroll, "They can look for the white horse soon now at Rosmersholm," because "now John has to marry Rebecca at once" (528–9): two days later she was dead. Kroll's ferocious language of political retribution instrumentalizes the expression of a fully grounded and materialized psychobiography; so, too, Beata's apparently "insane" (542) claims – that Rosmer has become his demonic opposite, that Rebecca bears his child, that a ghostly equine visitation is in the offing – enable us, as they enable her survivors, to read her shocking suicide back to its invisible, nonetheless palpable cause.

Beata, of course, is hardly a *role* in the play: she is solely inscribed in the play's narrative, a figure created in and by words, a *character*. Fittingly, then, Beata is also projected by her own words, spoken and written. Dr. West's marriage manuals provide one cause of Beata's distress, but her motives are also traced in the curious letter Mortensgaard received at the hands of Mrs. Helseth beseeching him to ignore rumors of "anything disreputable," any "illicit relationship" at Rosmersholm (539). The letter declares what it would deny: Rosmer's and Rebecca's passionate involvement, and Beata's belief that Rebecca is pregnant (as Mrs. Helseth notes, "it was something awful they went and got that poor sick woman to believe" 550). Again, "Beata's words" return to relate motive and action. Mortensgaard found "no sign" (538) of derangement in her letter, and even Mrs. Helseth didn't "think she was that far gone" (551). Beata's words undermine the consensual reality, pointing to something unspeakable, incredible, invisible, but – like Beata's fear, and the attraction driving Rosmer and Rebecca together – nonetheless "there," unequivocally expressed by the words and deeds logically part of the play's material world.

Acting the role

At the center of *Rosmersholm's* modeling of embodiment stands the disembodied Beata. And yet Beata is legible as only a character in narrative fiction can be. The torment driving her last days is finally disclosed, her spoken and written words tracing the pulse of purpose through her then-misrecognized actions. But however paradigmatic Kroll and Beata may be of the terms of realistic characterization, they are hardly characteristic of the play's attentive troubling of the *agency* of performing words; if they were, the play's elusive finale would hardly be so transfixing. Ulrik Brendel is a kind of intermediate figure in this regard. From the outset, Brendel seems to shadow and parody Rosmer's idealism. Arriving under an assumed name, perhaps fresh from touring with a theatrical company, Brendel's declarations of political liberation are deeply ironized. He's eager for a drink until Rebecca offers him tea instead of alcohol, he unscrupulously cadges money from Rosmer, regards himself as innately superior to the lowly plebians he would liberate, and departs for his mission wearing Rosmer's old clothes. Yet while the play ironizes Brendel's mission, showing him to be deceived about himself, it nonetheless represents his language as adequate to declaring his intentions, even the "embarrassing discovery that I'm bankrupt," that the storehouse of ideals he had kept private, waiting for a transforming moment of public revelation, had in the meantime turned to "dust" (578).

But Brendel's confession of inner devastation, the declaration that there is, Beckett-like, nothing to express, is not his final word. Instead, warning Rosmer to "Erase everything," he avers that Rosmer's victory "is assured" only "on one immutable condition."

> That the woman who loves him will gladly go out in the kitchen and lop off her delicate, pink-and-white little finger – *here* – right at the middle joint. Moreover, that the aforesaid loving lady, just as gladly, cuts off her incomparably formed left ear. (579–80)

What work do these words, might these words, do? How do they engage with the play's foregrounding of the uses of dramatic language in performance? Unlike Kroll's rage, Beata's fear, or even his own earlier condescending idealism, Brendel's language is subjunctive, expressing not a reaction to the state of affairs, nor a description of the material world, nor even a suspicion that the material world is actually other than it appears, as in Rebecca and Mrs. Helseth's opening dialogue. Addressing "my seductive mermaid" (*min tiltraekkende havfrue* 10: 433), Brendel's language is neither narrative nor descriptive, nor is it terribly lucid as expression; it markedly swerves away from the material environment (the "mermaid"), and so strikes a different relation to the uses of a dramatic *role* to imply dramatic *character*. Its strange, disorienting weirdness seems to demand both actors and audiences to do something with and through the language, to create a verbal/performative event whose meaning is not in the end expressed by the words themselves. Brendel's vision is readily translated to Rosmer's call for Rebecca's self-mutilating sacrifice, presumably opening the way for her journey to the mill-race. At the same time, as Cleanth Brooks might have noted, such thematic paraphrase entirely bypasses the uncanny pleasure of Brendel's figurative words. Like Gregers, Brendel speaks in metaphor, but unlike Gregers's flat-footed image of the "little dog," Brendel's words here do the work of poetry: they enable an event to happen in both *scenes* of performance (we perhaps feel the clammy chill of the words even more than the characters do), an event whose significance extends beyond the words alone. Though it confuses the Ekdals, Gregers's metaphor expresses his own desire to act the humble savior clearly enough. Brendel's speech not only forces actors and audiences to decide its meaning; it unfixes the play's paradigmatic use of words – locating an explanatory motive for action – in fashioning a dramatic *role*. Just at the moment Brendel declares his bankruptcy, his inner emptiness, he gives voice to the play's most bewitching speech. Brendel provides an exquisite description of an act that will never happen, can never happen in the world of *Rosmersholm*. Recalling Rebecca's charms, it fascinates, but more than merely providing an index to the theme of "sacrifice" (which Brendel gets wrong; Rebecca's sacrifice won't save Rosmer, as they eventually recognize), these words, when put into action, do something else. They prompt the alluring, disturbing, vivifying pleasure that governs the play's final events.[9]

Confession, disclosure, detour

Rosmersholm foregrounds words as an instrument for exposing motive, character, interiority, for reading beneath the texture of behavior, physicality, embodiment. And yet the play's action directly challenges this use of words, proceeding through a series of confessions, which paradoxically dramatize the extent to which interiority can and cannot be signified in words. Rosmer's avoidance of the footbridge is a kind of confession, but few plays so relentlessly expose confession as self-deception. In the opening scene, Kroll immediately confesses to feeling ill at ease visiting as a "living reminder" of Beata's tragedy, though his reason for visiting has nothing to do with Beata. Rosmer, for his part, remarks, "I don't find it painful at all to think about Beata. We talk of her every day. To us it's as if she's still part of the house. [...] We've nothing to reproach ourselves for," blithely folding the ironies of his desire to escape Beata into her ongoing presence. But Kroll has not come to mend fences. Disillusioned at home and at school, Kroll visits Rosmersholm to win Rosmer's support against Mortensgaard. Yet the more Kroll opens his bitter, wounded anger, the more deflected Rosmer becomes. Rebecca urges Rosmer to "Tell him"; "Not tonight," he replies (506). When Kroll presses him to ally himself with the conservatives, Rosmer at first hedges ("I'm just not up to it" 508), and when Kroll wants to use Rosmer's name, it's Rebecca who seems on the point of outing him – "I'll tell you exactly why" – when Brendel arrives (509). Only on Brendel's departure does Rosmer circuitously reveal that his views differ from Kroll's, that he stands "There, where your children stand" (517), that "It's the forces of liberation I want to give myself to" (518), the question of how he will rouse the populace leading eventually to the main revelation, "I am no longer a man of God" (519). For a play built on confession, it's notable how indirect, and difficult, and finally unreliable these disclosures are, the declaration of liberation predicated on Rosmer's initial detour-as-disclosure: "We've nothing to reproach ourselves for." It's also notable how often Rosmer's confessions "misfire," fail to perform *confession*, as though revealing a concise, reliable motive were not, in the end, really the point of the playing. Kroll is actually baffled by Rosmer's confession here – "But why are you confessing your secret? Why now, of all times" (519) – and several of the play's most consequential confessions are, like Beata's report of Rosmer's apostasy, simply "inconceivable." The climax of Act 2, Rosmer's proposal of marriage, produces one of the most resonant, and typical, moments of the play: Rosmer proposes, Rebecca confesses that she can never marry Rosmer, and he remains mystified: "But I don't – understand – " (547).

"Tell him!" (506); "Because now I'll tell you exactly why – " (509); "Somehow or other, I must have revealed my feelings" (542); "Then I'll tell you everything" (563): confession is the principal motif of the play's action, what Francis Fergusson might have called its defining "analogy." Michael Goldman notes the close approximation of this aspect of Ibsen's dramaturgy to the practice of modern realistic acting, the discovery of "layer after layer of motivation, memory and hidden feeling – exactly the elements that any actor of these roles would have to call upon, to work back to, to prepare the past" (*Freedom* 135). Yet while "the actor or actress must possess and assemble clues from a character's life that are scattered throughout the text," in Ibsen's major roles the language used to register these motives in performance strategically refuses to locate and define them. The writing of the major roles refuses the illusion that either actors or characters can "possess and project the forces that drive them" in words. Instead, this powerful, suspect, almost broken language is transformed into action, an act that can only point toward an absent, mysterious cause, what Goldman describes as alienated drives, "buried, removed, unpossessed, oblique to the text – though they may finally break through in geyserlike eruptions like Hedda's burning of Løvborg's manuscript" (*Ibsen* 20).

Goldman's remarks here identify the challenges of acting Ibsen, and reorient our attention to Ibsen's allegorization of the uses of writing in performance. Kroll and Beata, alongside Mortensgaard and even Mrs. Helseth, confess effectively: their language describes a narrative that motivates and provides the conditions for interpreting their behavior.

But Kroll and Beata are not the center of the play's preoccupations, they provide a conventional dramatic ground against which to measure the complexity of the play's major roles:

ROSMER (*after a pause*). Have you confessed everything now, Rebecca?
REBECCA. Yes.
KROLL. Not quite. (566)

What do Rebecca and Rosmer have to disclose? Ibsen's use of language to structure the practice of a dramatic *role* sharply distinguishes Rosmer and Rebecca from Kroll and Beata. Kroll and Beata disclose themselves: Kroll's anger at discovering his students' and family's political betrayal; his plan to manipulate Rebecca through her relation to Dr. West; Beata's urging of Mortensgaard not to believe what he might hear. But Rosmer and Rebecca confess differently, marking Ibsen's sense of the variable agency of writing in the embodiment of performance.

KROLL. Didn't you finally suggest to Beata that it was necessary – not just best, but necessary – for your sake and Rosmer's, that you should go away somewhere – as soon as possible? Well?
REBECCA (*in an undertone, indistinctly*). Maybe I said something like that. (566)

Beata's confession, "Beata's words," echo through the play, but Rebecca recalls only "something like" her own words. Her confession begins equivocally – "She could have understood me that way, I guess" – and insistently frames her disclosures as detours:

You think I went through all this with ice in my veins? That I calculated every move! I was a different woman then than I am now, standing here, telling about it. Anyway, I think a person can be of two wills about something. I wanted Beata out of here, one way or another. But even so, I never dreamed it could happen. With every step ahead that I gambled on, it was as if something inside me cried out: "No further! Not one step further!" And yet I *couldn't* stop. I *had* to try for a tiny bit more. Just the least little bit. And then again – and always again – until it happened. That's the way these things *do* happen. (567)

The roles of Kroll and Beata model language as a means to disclosing motive that eventuates in action; Rebecca's language points to a rupture between motive and act. The past Rebecca is not continuous with the present woman. Moreover, she describes a harrowing self-division, a kind of possession by fantasy that renders her own motives alien. Like Mouth in Beckett's *Not I*, Rebecca cannot inhabit the first-person of her own desire, become the agent of the acts "she" has performed: "it happened."[10] Perhaps this "vehement refusal to relinquish third person" (*Not I* 375) is simply another avoidance; we'll never know. For dramatic language can bring us no farther. The "source" – whether in trauma, desire, or something else – of this kind of human action cannot be seized with words, all efforts to specify it will fail, disclosure will always be a detour. Perhaps not surprisingly, moments later she will make an analogous confession to Mrs. Helseth, deploying the play's master image of compacted guilt, passion, and retribution: "I thought I saw something like a glimpse of white horses" (568).

Rebecca does, eventually, confess "the crux of everything" (572), how her "fearless free will" was crushed by "a wretched fear" (573), how her "wild, uncontrollable desire" ("I thought it was the meaning of 'to love' – then. I did think that that was love") came over her "like a storm at sea" and "swept poor Beata into the mill-race." For a moment, clarity. And yet, this Rebecca is the stereotypical *femme de trente ans* Kroll creates, the scheming interloper caught up in a sexual triangle of conventional melodrama. But insofar as *Rosmersholm* has transformed Rebecca, confession complicates rather than merely revealing the subject: she has been at once "ennobled" and "infected" by "The Rosmer way of life" (575), enslaved by – by what, exactly? By Rosmer's lassitude and inactivity? By his desire for a peace and innocence that choke off sexuality, allowing joy and happiness to leach away, draining "the power to act" altogether? By the happiness-killing moral probity and solemnity of the house, an island tomb silently watched by the grim dead, where the children neither weep nor laugh? What is extraordinary about this confession – anticipating Brendel's confession of emptiness – is its inability to specify what drives Rebecca. The play's principal values (*joy, freedom, innocence*) are sustained by a disacknowledged sensual desire, the pulsing undercurrent of the work of ennoblement finally killed by the torpid, depersonalizing "Rosmer way of life," a fantasy of sensual denial that is, as the play shows, finally indistinguishable from death. And yet, recalling T. S. Eliot's remarks on poetry as renunciation, as an escape from emotion and personality, "only those who have personality and emotions know what it means to want to escape from these things" ("Tradition" 43).

In J. L. Austin's terms, where Rebecca and Rosmer are concerned, "I confess" is a *performative* doomed to misfire.[11] Rosmer is the play's most challenging role in this regard, for while Rebecca's disclosures are evasive, Rosmer's are even more deeply deflected – he barely confesses anything at all. Rosmer's idealistic language frames his social project in the discourse of desire: "liberating their minds and tempering their wills" (518) is fully cognate with the "full freedom of action" he wants to share with Rebecca (541), the "joy that ennobles the mind" (543), even "the calm joy of innocence" that "makes it so marvellously sweet to be alive" (544). Rosmer and Rebecca struggle to fashion joy with one another, a joy Rebecca vows to restore (563), and that tolls through their final dialogue in the repeated word, *gladly* (584). Rosmer's assertions of a purely intellectual relationship with Rebecca confess a state of mind that is, the play suggests, false, a detour away from a guilty desire for her complicit in his rejection of Beata, the understanding that "Somehow or other, I must have revealed my feelings. She must have noticed how much happier I was after *you* came here to live. [...] When I look back on it, I don't think, to save my life, I could have done more to shield her from our involvement" (542). The more aware we become of a deeper, more sensual connection between them, a connection that Rosmer's compulsive "Rebecc – Miss West" at once signals and denies (replicating, in a sense, Beata's note to Mortensgaard), the more Rosmer's confessions come to feel peculiarly "hollow or void," not because he intends to deceive but because these utterances have a deftly theatrical quality, as utterance that at once realizes the performative agency of a speech act while masking, deflecting, and evoking an alternative, ulterior agent, an agent unknown to or denied by the speaker (see Austin 22).

Ibsen sets Rosmer's first invocation of "innocence" – *skyldfrihed*; literally, being free from guilt (10: 395) – in a rich context of self-revelation, his proposal of marriage at the end of Act 2. Rosmer regrets never again being "able to relish the one thing that makes it so marvellously sweet to be alive," and Rebecca leans over the back of his chair, asking "And what's that, John?" At his answer – "The calm joy of innocence" – she "*steps back*," one of several retreats she will make from Rosmer in this scene (she refuses his offer of marriage, to become his "second wife" – *min anden hustru* 10: 39 – moments later).[12] Rosmer's insistence on his innocence of sexual passion, of Beata's suspicions, of complicity in her death, of desire for Rebecca, has rightly drawn censure; Freud may have thought him impotent, but even the most sympathetic critics find his assertive desexualization "suspect" (Goldman, *Ibsen* 112).[13] Here, at the midpoint of the play, the deeply Romantic language of interiority joins the public language of politics to the protagonists' emotional life: it's "joy that ennobles the mind" (543), a *"joy"* (*glaede* 10: 397) that Rebecca *"cries out"* at Rosmer's offer of marriage (545). Rebecca's heart leaps up, disclosing a kind of Wordsworthian *joy*, but Romantic joy is often laminated to a harrowing, alienating terror. For Rosmer, her joy prompts an apprehensive detour, back to Beata, the "corpse" he fears to bear on his back forever: "let's drown all these memories in joy [*fryd*], in freedom, in passion" (546). Rosmer seems to echo Rebecca's outcry of *joy, glaede*, but uses a different word here, *fryd*, perhaps something more like giddy *glee* (10: 397). Swerving away from *joy*, Rosmer casts the most intimate moments of inspired passion as the uncanny reenactment of the repressed crime, hoping to drown their memories as they fear to have drowned Beata.

Beata is very much on Rosmer's mind: the word for "passion" he uses here – *lidenskab* – is the same word he uses earlier to describe Beata's distasteful sensuality; as Janet Garton points out, "Rebecca, being more direct," describes her own passion for Rosmer as " 'begœr' (sexual desire)" (110). *Rosmersholm* is nothing if not "uncanny." The play's most urgent moments – Rebecca's refusal here, Brendel's weird image, the finale – create and instigate a kind of fascinating "fear and dread" (Freud, " 'Uncanny' " 123), the nearly indescribable, unpredictable, yet palpable sensation arising from feeling possessed, from being drawn into an apparently ineluctable cycle of repetition, from confronting one's double, from seeing one's thoughts realized in action, from being unable to resist going, wanting to go, the way Beata went. Yet for all its quirky power, the language of interiority here – in contrast to the language of action, "I'll never be your wife" (546) – relates in a peculiar way to the work of acting. In his elation, Rosmer proposes to discover joy, freedom, passion as the reflex of denial, as a moment of deep self-erasure. What will that joy be like? Neither Rosmer nor the performer can say, for the rich language of Romantic interiority points toward an imagined experience, one grasped only in the most general terms. In later plays, Ibsen lends a cognate desire more verbal specificity, providing actors and audiences an instrumentalizing image to constellate the longing for this apparently impossible, evanescent desire for joy: Hedda's "vine leaves" or Solness's "castles in the air," while no more revealing about the content of this yearning, provide a more textured instrument for working that desire into the fabric of action and so into the experience of the dramatic event. Ibsen's dramaturgy demands commitment to these terms, as compromised as they may be, for it is clear that disavowing joy, freedom, passion must drive Rebecca's renunciation, even though her motives cannot be spoken.

What can be spoken is what will destroy joy and destroy any performance of *Rosmersholm*, too, the opposite of commitment, "doubt": about Beata's insanity (542), but also about the authority of one's own expression, the extent to which any declaration of motive may merely enact disacknowledged detour away from an inexpressible truth. Unlike the language of Romantic identity, the language of doubt is richly detailed:

> ROSMER. […] Oh, all these wild speculations! I'll never be rid of them. I can feel that. I just know it. All of a sudden, they'll swarm in on me, reminding me of the dead.
> REBECCA. Like the white horse of Rosmersholm.
> ROSMER. Yes. Rushing out of the darkness. Out of the silence. (544)

Joy is luminous but indescribable; doubt, on the other hand, swarms out of the silent darkness, galloping from the frontier of conscience. While Brendel speaks his inner bankruptcy, his emptiness, Rebecca and Rosmer have something less clear to disclose, something that, as the play demonstrates, can only be disclosed through action, as embodiment, using words to promote a deed not enclosed by the language it uses. From the outset of the play, even descriptive language has been shown to point elsewhere, an agency for hollowing out the solid, material world it evokes and setting an alternative, shimmering, almost inconceivable life inside. Brendel describes his inner void, but his final speech nonetheless suggests a strange awareness of the emotional tension sustaining Rosmer and Rebecca. Disclosure, even the Beckett-like disclosure that there is nothing to disclose, feels like a detour, a gesture to something that language cannot seize but nonetheless enables to take place.

Doing (unspeakable) things with words

The general contours of the play's brilliant, mysterious final scene are clear. Rosmer and Rebecca take one another as man and wife, in effect admitting and enacting their attachment, and its relation to the past. In so doing, however, they move toward a zone where deeds redefine language, meaning.

> ROSMER. I said, I'll go with you.
> REBECCA. Out to the bridge, yes. You never set foot on it, I know.
> ROSMER. You've noticed that? (583)

Rebecca's recognition articulates one final assertion, though it, too, remains unspoken: no more detours. But despite the fact that Rosmer and Rebecca renounce disclosure, even the possibility that disclosure can disclose, the actors must nonetheless act, using words even if "We'll never sift to the bottom" of the actions they sustain (584). The only bottom they can reach is the mill-race.

The act is not described in its language; language can only be a vehicle for doing, creating an act that the play's principal explanatory categories gesture toward but fail to describe. The fitness of this perspective is measured by an act which, as is often the case in Ibsen (Nora slamming the door offstage, Hedvig and Hedda's unseen suicide, Rubek in the avalanche), takes place out of the proscenium frame, as though beyond the limits of material representation onstage, amid the slapdash poetry of everyday life. Mrs. Helseth describes their "sinful" embrace, watches as they fall into the water, and concludes: "No. No help now – the dead wife – she's taken them" (585). Representing the offstage scene in language returns us to the opening moments of the play, where an action offstage seemed to enact something else. This time, though, Mrs. Helseth at once describes and moralizes what she sees, the enactment of their sinful passion and Beata's final vengeance. But the poetic dimension of dramatic language is not confined to what the words say. In the theatre, poetry arises from what we do with words, and throughout the play, much as here, Ibsen alerts us to the degree to which identifying the meaning of words with the meaning of deeds is to risk misapprehending the work of dramatic writing. Much as we might think that Mrs. Helseth's account fails to take into account what we have seen, what Rosmer and Rebecca attempt to achieve at the mill-race, so too Ibsen's allegory of language and action in the play suggests that words promote acts they cannot themselves contain, acts that neither simply illustrate nor oppose the meaning of words, but are richly engaged yet incommensurable with them, a poetry of action.

The finale of *Rosmersholm* is a parable of the drama's challenge to poetry and performance, one reason, perhaps, for the extraordinary range of opinion about the force of this final scene, about what it is that Rosmer and Rebecca *do*. Even bearing Ibsen's distasteful reputation among many of his contemporary critics in mind, reviews of English productions in the 1890s obsessively point to the play's "enigmatical personages": "Impossible people do wild things for no apparent reason"; they are "vile unlovable, unnatural, morbid monsters"; "*Rosmersholm* is not very dramatic. It is hardly at all literary" (qtd. in McFarlane, ed. and trans., *Rosmersholm* 449–50). While the play's reputation has improved, the sense of its ending remains enigmatic, duplicitous. Joan Templeton likens the final dialogue between Rosmer and Rebecca to Wagner's "Liebestod litany" in *Tristan and Isolde*. Here, though, Ibsen seems to train a skeptical eye on the Liebestod, for while Wagner's lovers "die for a fatal but triumphant passion, eros has been banished from Rosmersholm. The couple's embrace on the bridge is the first their bodies have shared" (193). Toril Moi finds "something tragic about the end," but refuses "to idealize the kind of love that Rosmer and Rebecca reach at the end: their relationship, after all, has been based on Rebecca's explicit lies and Rosmer's failure to acknowledge her difference from himself. Their fantasies of merger and union are unlivable, destructive, and death-dealing, for they are built on a vision of the body as an obstacle to the merger of souls" (291). Goldman stresses the play's "thrust toward *lykke* and gladness" as a means to recoloring the ironic, compromised quality of the finale: "Their desire for each other, their desire to have pleasure, to be capable of pleasure, to overcome the blockage that makes pleasure impossible, keeps them shifting, attacking, touching, fleeing; it makes every moment between them *konsekvent*. Ghosts and gusts of fulfillment drive them on" (*Ibsen* 140). Rather than valorizing a skeptical regard toward Rosmer and Rebecca's idealizing suicide, or affirming the longing for a possibly inaccessible pleasure, *Rosmersholm* seems to hold these alternatives in suspension. Death may well be "the other side of sex" (Moi 289), and yet entirely renouncing the drive toward joy and happiness (*glaede* and *lykke*) in our dubious regard for the lovers' endless self-deception may also deny our participation in the experience Rosmer and Rebecca enact, an experience the actors perhaps also engage in transforming Ibsen's words into action, an experience – unlike Mrs. Helseth's rigid dichotomies – which cannot finally resolve the ironic interlacing of doubt and joy.

Any performance will necessarily decide, manifestly or ambiguously, this balance: Brooks and Heilman were right to sense the actors' "responsibility" in shaping the significance of the events onstage. But *Rosmersholm* is paradigmatic rather than exceptional in this regard. In its final moments, *Rosmersholm* refuses to ground dramatic meaning in the words on the page, much as the play repeatedly highlights the distinction between what words say and what they might be used to do, in description, in fashioning the template of a *role*, in modeling the detours of *character*. Rather than marking Ibsen's failure to inscribe the play's action and significance in a sufficiently "poetic" language, the finale of *Rosmersholm* – like much else in the play – foregrounds Ibsen's defining modern achievement with regard to poetry and performance. The final moments of *Rosmersholm* stage a scene of undeniable fascination, of moral and psychological complexity. But while the actors, much like the characters they evoke, use Ibsen's words to shape the play's climactic event, its defining act, the words do not ground the action in a single referent, a defining motive. In Burke's terms, while the words provide the *agency* for action, they are not the privileged means of insight into the *agent*: the *agent's purpose* is not privileged as defining the meaning of the *act* (this is what distinguishes Rosmer and Rebecca from the paradigm of Kroll and Beata). For all that the words afford action, what they do not do is specify its meaning. The incipient poetry of *Rosmersholm* allegorizes a resistance to a literary sense of theatre, of "text-based" performance, of dramatic performance as the declamation and illustration of writing, however "responsible" it might or might not be. Instead, Ibsen shapes an urgently dramatic perspective here, valuing words as instruments of action, affording the ungovernable apparition of meaning elsewhere, the evanescent return of the white horses to the stage.

ii. Footnoting Performance: *The America Play* and *Venus*

> *Footnotes, and the habit of turning back in order to check a point, need to be introduced into play-writing too.*
>
> > Bertolt Brecht, *"The Literarization of the Theatre"*
> >
> > (Brecht on Theatre 44)

The Negro Resurrectionist
Footnote #8
Definition: Medical: Maceration:
(Rest)
"*A process performed on the subject after the subjects death. The sub-
jects body parts are soaked in a chemical solution to separate the flesh
from the bones so that the bones may be measured with greater
accuracy.*"
(Rest)

(Parks, Venus 120)

Rosmersholm foregrounds the indeterminacy of writing in the representation of *character* in the theatre: however we may, as readers, attempt
to plot dramatic character to the paradigm of causal narrative, and
however much actors trained in a Stanislavskian tradition may find the
location of an historical cause of the events of the stage in a moment
of past psychology, Ibsen's masterpiece foregrounds a different sense
of poetry and performance, one in which performance finally points to
a zone of enactment that the poetry names, but cannot disclose.

It is tempting, though, to take Ibsen as a special case, working within
a form of theatre so deeply inscribed by the culture of print that writing
occupies a distinctively overdetermining, *archival* authority. In one perspective, the rise of the psychologically consistent and coherent individual – a subject who behaves as a *character* – is a distinctively modern
invention, arising with and through a series of Western technologies:
print, Enlightenment philosophy, mercantile capitalism, evolutionary
biology, the novel. We might take Ibsen's drama to locate a fulcrum of
change, contesting the theatre's ways of representing and problematiz-
ing this individual at the moment of its achievement. Ibsen distinguishes the logic of narrative *character* – Beata – from the elusive subject
of performance, a "character-effect" emerging from the committed use
of writing to perform a *role*, to create an event whose significance
exceeds what the words alone can say. Ibsen's drama accomplishes this
inquiry through a mastery of the formal and practical conventions of
stage naturalism, a genre notably resistant to the foregrounding of
"language," poetry. But while naturalism subordinates its language to
the visible rhetoric of the *scene*, other modes of theatre position words
differently, suggest a different *agency* for writing in the fashioning of
dramatic embodiment. In their complex representation of the past,

Suzan-Lori Parks's plays interrogate not only history but also how we have access to it, engage it, understand it. Spatializing the past, the (in)determinacies of the printed texts of her plays vie with the embodied (in)determinacies of performance. Parks's theatre self-consciously underscores the *performative*, the citational dimension of the ritualized events taking place onstage. Parks foregrounds the materiality of dramatic writing on the page and its complex *agency* in the *scene* of theatre as part of a wider interrogation of the documentary character of history. The close attention to staging writing in her drama – the many footnotes, extracts, and lectures performed in her plays – foregrounds the involvement of writing in dramatic embodiment.

In all of Parks's plays, the performance of the past appears as a multiplex replaying, as events staged and restaged: the reenactment of the Lincoln assassination in *The America Play*, the repeated efforts of Black Man With Watermelon to move his hands in *The Death of the Last Black Man in the Whole Entire World*, the patterns of verbal and gestural echo that run throughout *Venus*. "Repetition and Revision" is "integral to the Jazz esthetic in which the composer or performer will write or play a musical phrase once and again and again; etc. – with each revisit the phrase is slightly revised" ("from Elements" 8–9), and Parks's plays stage the recovery and interpretation of the past, Rep & Rev, at the reciprocal interface between writing and performance, words and things, the linearity of language and the spatiality of embodied performance. Texts and performances are counterpointed in a variety of ways in Parks's plays. Characters are presented onstage as slide images while the actors speak from offstage in *Imperceptible Mutabilities in the Third Kingdom* and *Betting on the Dust Commander*; history is staged as creative reenactment, onstage in the "Lincoln Scene" of *The America Play* and offstage in *Topdog/Underdog*; brief plays-within-the-play ramify the relationship between "original" events and their insertion into representation, such as *Our American Cousin* in *The America Play* and *For the Love of the Venus* in *Venus*; various instructors, lecturers, demonstrators frame the action of several plays, The Naturalist, The Foundling Father, The Baron Docteur, and The Negro Resurrectionist.

This emphasis on the structuring event of performance is not opposed to writing, but demands an innovative attention to its affordance, how writing might be used in/as action. The pages of Parks's plays urgently defamiliarize the conventions of printed drama, and so the conventional expectations of the *agency* of words in performance. The striking formal appearance of Parks's page – the unusual speech prefixes (BLACK MAN WITH WATERMELON), the repetition of speech prefixes without dialogue ("spells"), the idiosyncratic spelling (*thuh*) and punctuation – urges a rethinking of the relation between writing and performance, especially with regard to the modern, American realistic tradition and its rhetoric of character. Innovative writing demands innovative technologies of embodiment.

The dialectic of dramatic writing – representation or instrumentality – informs Parks's critical prose as well, taking shape as two finally irresolvable impulses, a desire to use writing both as the means toward new performance events, an instrument performers will have to learn to play, and as a means of encoding, even determining, that performance: "I'm working to create a dramatic text that departs from the traditional linear narrative style to look and sound more like a musical score" ("from Elements" 9). In "Possession," Parks describes the play as "a blueprint of an event: a way of creating and rewriting history through the medium of literature" ("Possession" 4). As we have seen, the score and the blueprint are useful yet distracting metaphors for the work of poetry in performance. Although both suggest that the final performance exceeds the script, as metaphors, the blueprint and the score figure the determinative force of writing in the design and execution of the events on the stage. Yet dramatic performance uses its writing differently than a symphony or a skyscraper does: even the most densely textured play – an Ibsen or a Shaw play, Beckett's *Not I* or a videoscript like … *but the clouds* … – conveys considerably less information about the shape, tempo, flavor, material embodiment of the final performance than either the score or the blueprint, even while appearing to bear greater semantic weight, to convey more insistently what the performance means.

Although Parks's writing is designed to provide the *agency* for new embodiment, the critical account of her work often struggles with a familiar tension between the text as a representation of a fictive event and the text as an instrument for creating an actual event involving fictive means. Rep & Rev, for instance, displaces the traditional revelatory climax of modern realistic drama, the *scène à faire* and its programmatic disclosure of the long-buried causal narrative behind the events of the stage, with an incremental, accreting composition, in which "the 'climax' could be the accumulated weight of the repetition" of events onstage ("from Elements" 10). As Parks suggests, this structure creates "a real challenge for the actor and director as they create a physical life appropriate to that text" ("from Elements" 9), or, more precisely, as they use the text to create a physical life outside it. This rhythmic element "is an integral part of the African and African-American literary *and* oral tradition" (my emphasis), a means of using, resignifying writing. And while Rep & Rev evokes the improvisatory aesthetic of jazz, a *repertoire* of performance practice remaking the music, Parks's critical account is haunted by a sense of the *archive*, the *score*, writing imaged in a more determining, prescriptive role in performance. Does the script provide the instrument for a revisionary, improvisational, unanticipated embodiment, or does it score its performers by representing the dramatic world and their appropriate embodiment in it?

This tension animates many of Parks's formal innovations as a playwright. For instance, Parks typically devises an original orthography, "foreign words & phrases" – *thuh, iduhnt, heud, k* ("from Elements" 17). Sometimes, the writing seems designed to shape pace and pronunciation – "There wont b inny show tonite" (*Venus* 3); in *Fucking A*, characters speak a private language, mainly shared by women, TALK, which requires an appendix of translated passages (*Fucking A* 223–5). Appearing to inscribe pronunciation into the performance, Parks's orthography points to an effort to resituate writing in the physical production, alienating (making *foreign*) familiar words and their position in reproducing (Rep & Rev) American language, culture, and history. Parks is often said to write in dialect, and there is a sense in which dialect incarnates the representational aspect of dramatic writing at the level of the word. And yet, as Bernard Shaw recognized, directing the sound and rhythm of spoken English from the page (Eliza Doolittle's or Bill Walker's Cockney, perhaps Hector Malone's American), scripted dialect also provides the means for the performer to physicalize the role, spoken words reifying the struggle of social class, executive and intellectual power at stake in any Shaw play: in *Major Barbara*, Undershaft's Nietzschean dialect of moral transvaluation, Stephen's common-sense dialect of impoverished moral judgment, Rummy Mitchens's cringing parody of the Salvation Army's lingo of bootstraps self-improvement.

The sense that writing might govern this aspect of verbal performance extends to Shaw's work as a director, famously scoring his actors, annotating their scripts with musical notation to dictate the rhythm, pace, tone, and volume of their work. Parks shares something of this impulse:

> Language is a physical act. It's something which involves your entire body – not just your head. Words are spells which an actor consumes and digests – and through digesting creates a performance on stage. Each word is configured to give the actor a clue to their physical life. Look at the difference between "the" and "thuh." The "uh" requires the actor to employ a different physical, emotional, vocal attack. ("from Elements" 11–12)

On the page, Parks's orthography is sometimes mistaken – as it often is with Shaw – as a merely literary means of representing the fictive world, but she also implies a more complex sense of the uses of orthography, not merely to dictate aspects of character, but to provide the actor with a rhetorical instrument for inventing and inhabiting the *role* as an action. Although it's commonplace to refer to what actors do as making speeches, what they do is in fact something closer to digestion: the language is taken into the body, expressed through and by the body, gaining specificity and performative force through the way the actor's body sustains and shapes it into action, reciprocally identifying the actor's body – and the character's – in specific ways as well. *Heud* implies a distinct social world, situating the use of English speech in a cultural and linguistic environment; it also demands, perhaps, a different address to embodied, spoken action than *He'd* or *He would*.

"Language is a physical act – something that / involves yr whole bod" ("from Elements" 18), resting on the interface of *agency* and *scene*, an instrument for doing, and always already part of a larger world hedging what words can – or can appear to – do. Different orthography, different words, different pronunciations both enable and represent different acts:

> Sometimes people say, "o.k." Sometimes people say, "k." And it's fun to write. So, I just was trying to get more specific because, if someone says, "I'm going with you, 'k?" that's different from "I'm going with you, o.k?" [*sic*] It's different, it's a different thing going on. It's "the" sometimes, and sometimes it's "thee." It's a recording of, not only the way words sound, but what that means. The difference between "k" and "o.k." is not just what one might call black English versus standard English, for example. Or black English versus mid-Atlantic English. It's not that, so

much as it's an attempt: I am trying to be very specific in what's going on emotionally with the character. Because if you just try out, "I'm going with you, O.K.," "I'm going with you 'K,'" it's a different thing going on. If you jump to that word faster, if you put your words together in a different order, you're feeling something differently, and it's just an attempt to try to be more specific so that I don't have to write in all these parenthetical things. It's a Shakespearean thing, and it's a Greek thing. (Jiggetts 311)

Here, Parks defines writing – the choice of *k* or *o.k.* – less as an instrument for working the *role* than as a decisive element of the representation of a specific *character*, a kind of "recording" of the interior life ("feeling something differently") that enables her to avoid describing that attitude in stage directions, "all these parenthetical things." Parks's sense of poetry and performance here is deeply dyed in the culture of print, which stabilizes orthography, grammar, syntax, and allows typographic distinctions like *k* and *o.k.* to emerge as potentially significant, and so to mark a potentially different visual-and-physical incorporation by actors.

In other words, while her dramatic writing often demands an imaginative, innovative sense of its possible *agency*, an attention to how it might afford behavior and action, Parks often describes her plays as determining performance: "*How* the line should be delivered is contained in the line itself," dispensing with the need for "a pissy set of parentheses" altogether ("from Elements" 15–16, 18). Of course, Parks sometimes uses stage directions more or less conventionally, to direct the quality of action from the page:

> After a moment Monster comes by.
> He looks her over surreptitiously
> then sits and watches the sea.
> She notices him and composes herself.
> (*Fucking A* 154)

> She gets up and puts on her apron,
> then wearily sits back down.
> (*Fucking A* 221)

Parks is deeply committed to the "craft of writing," and to the use of writing to change theatre, "the marvel of live bodies on stage" ("from Elements" 6). At the same time, what enables writing to do this work is its uptake by performance practice, practice that must discover how to use it. In this sense, dialect spelling provides an emblem of the dialectical character of dramatic writing. The *thuh* both represents a form of speech and provides an instrument for an actor to create it, play it, pointing to strategies of embodiment that cannot reside in the text alone, but in the shifting uses of language on and off stage.[14] The cultural conventions of embodiment, including the embodiment of speech, are invoked by *thuh*, perhaps, but they are as outside the text as the discourse of Osric's hat lies outside the text of *Hamlet*.

Parks straddles a familiar dilemma: the playwright's desire to inscribe the play in the writing, and the knowledge that the performance will inevitably remake the poetry. This instability also lies behind Parks's notion that she does not write plays with *characters* but with *figures*: "They are not *characters*. To call them so could be an injustice. They are *figures, figments, ghosts, roles, lovers* maybe, *speakers* maybe, *shadows, slips, players* maybe, maybe *someone else's pulse*" ("from Elements" 12). We should resist being distracted by the distinction Parks seems to make here, between the inhabitants of other plays and the inhabitants of hers. For the sense that Parks's writing is writing for use, a means for inhabitation, returns us to the notion of the *role*: not a prescribed thing, but a process of doing that involves the text in a practice of embodiment external to it, reciprocally shaping and being shaped by the writing.

In this sense, the distinction between Parks's *roles* and, say, Ibsen's has more to do with ways of conceiving the script as the means of performance. Conventionally, modern *character* is understood as driven by the subtext, an unspoken (sometimes unspeakable) through-line of inner action, the referential ground invented by Stanislavski to organize the apparently undramatic eccentricities of Chekhovian playwriting into a consistent performance. The director devised a practice that could instrumentalize Chekhov's indirections, lend them a relatively familiar shape as theatrical event: a progressive, consequential through-line bringing the playing to its climactic objective. Stanislavski – and, following him, a dominant line of English-language actor training – sometimes appears to locate the subtext *in* the writing; in this sense, the subtext can also be "found" in Shakespeare, Sophocles, or other premodern playwrights, whose available conventions of writing and performance, and notions of human being and action, may well not have had much in common with those of the 1890s. But the subtext is not found, it's made, made as part of the transformation of writing into a specific genre of theatrical performance, one that produces the drama as the consequence of coherent inner, psychological drives finding expression in a densely material environment determined by a cognate sense of historical causality. I don't think we can distinguish Parks's *figures* from *characters* merely in terms of what they represent, as though *characters* must represent self-present psychological beings, while *figures* "lack a subtext, but may be motivated instead by historical necessity or by happenstance" (Haring-Smith 47). Parks's roles are difficult to assimilate to Stanislavskian acting, but perhaps no more so than Sophocles' or Shakespeare's. As Shawn-Marie Garrett puts it, "Parks's use of the term *figures* emphasizes that her *dramatis personae* are only words, words words" (8): but that's all that *dramatis personae* can ever be, verbal instruments for articulating the duplicitous agency of dramatic performance.

Parks's writing appears to demand an alternate conception and practice of embodiment, best captured by asking not *who* Parks represents but *what* instrument she provides for inhabiting action onstage. It's "an old idea. The Greeks did it and Shakespeare too" ("from Elements" 16): though the text may represent a fictive action, its theatrical purpose is to instigate a present event, here and now. Parks visibly brings the apparatus of writing into performance in ways that refocus our attention to the duality of poetry and performance. Her plays often stage a manifest critique of the various structures of empowerment represented by writing, bringing the concealed power of the *archive* – such as the "Footnotes" spoken onstage in *Venus* – into the *repertoire* of performance.[15]

One convention of dramatic writing is the speech prefix, an openly instrumental device for assigning parts of the text to individual actors. There's no reason to understand the prefix as a "name," and in the history of Western scripted drama, this device has appeared in various forms. Early published versions of Shakespeare's *Romeo and Juliet*, for example, have the "character" of Lady Capulet appearing under several different prefixes – *Wife*, *Old La.* (*Old Lady*), *Mo.* (*Mother*); in *Much Ado About Nothing*, some speech prefixes occasionally – and quite logically – refer to the actors playing the role. In Javier Malpica's recent play, *Our Dad is in Atlantis*, the text is divided into thematic sections, not "scenes" ("Stuff about the Countryside," "Stuff about Terror"), the "Characters" are listed as "Big Brother: an Eleven-year-old boy" and

"Little Brother: an eight-year-old boy," and the speeches are prefixed with the greater-than/less-than symbols, followed by a colon (>: <:); < indicates the first speech – is < = "Little Brother"? The speech prefix is an invisible, unheard, yet crucial element in distributing the *role*, a way to mark the *agency* of the text for performance. Parks often attempts to work this fact suggestively into performance, by having the performers announce themselves at the opening of the play, as "The Figures" do in *The Death of the Last Black Man in the Whole Entire World*:

OVERTURE

BLACK MAN WITH WATERMELON: The black man moves his hands.
  (*A bell sounds twice*)
LOTS OF GREASE AND LOTS OF PORK: Lots of Grease and Lots of Pork.
QUEEN-THEN-PHARAOH HATSHEPSUT: Queen-then-Pharaoh Hatshepsut.
AND BIGGER AND BIGGER AND BIGGER: And Bigger and Bigger and Bigger.
PRUNES AND PRISMS: Prunes and Prisms.
HAM: Ham.
VOICE ON THUH TEE V: Voice on thuh Tee V.
OLD MAN RIVER JORDAN: Old Man River Jordan.
YES AND GREENS BLACK-EYED PEAS CORNBREAD: Yes and Greens Black-
  Eyed Peas Cornbread.
BEFORE COLUMBUS: Before Columbus.
  (*A bell sounds once*)   (101)

In *Venus*, **The Man, later The Baron Docteur** introduces "The Man, later / The Baron Docteur!" (1), and the *dramatis personae* cunningly differentiates between "The Roles" – Miss Saartjie Baartman, a.k.a., The Girl, and later The Venus Hottentot; The Man, later The Baron Docteur; The Players of *"For the Love of the Venus"* – and "The Characters" performing in *For the Love of the Venus*: The Father, The Mother, The Young Man, and so on.

While the instrumental *role* is often misconceived as a fixed *character*, Parks tactically resists this slippage, identifying the prefix not as an individual "name," but as a transient label for an ongoing process of historical subjection (BLACK MAN WITH WATERMELON), and of historical oppression (**The Mans Brother, later The Mother-Showman, later The Grade-School Chum**), grasped by a single actor in the cognate process of theatrical embodiment. In *The Death of the Last Black Man in the Whole Entire World*, the prefixes gather a range of historical and cultural associations into a given series of actions in play, much as the role of Willy

Loman might do if he were prefixed THE SALESMAN THE FATHER THE
CHEATER THE DREAMER. In *The America Play*, the principal role, prefixed
THE FOUNDLING FATHER AS ABRAHAM LINCOLN or THE FOUNDLING
FATHER, is never identified by that "name" in performance. The actor
speaks of himself in the third person, as "The Lesser Known" (distinct
from "The Great Man" he plays), though his son Brazil makes a slant
association, referring to his "foe-father" and "faux-father" (178, 184).
The prefix known to readers – and, perhaps usefully, read by actors
when preparing to play – is part of theatrical play only as an instrument
for distributing the text in a particular way, and, perhaps, providing
an enabling perspective on ways of conceptualizing the role.

Perhaps the most notable features of Parks's inscription of dramatic
action – the *rests* and *spells* – are also more readily understood in terms
of *role* than *character*. The *rests* suggest tempo, directly addressing the
practice of performance: "Take a little time, a pause, a breather; make
a transition." The *spells* are more complex, denoting a slippage between
page and stage: "An elongated and heightened (rest). Denoted by repetition of figures' names with no dialogue. Has sort of an architectural
look" ("from Elements" 16). Parks uses *spells* throughout her work,
perhaps most notoriously in Scene 19 of *Venus*:

Scene 19: A Scene of Love (?)

The Venus
The Baron Docteur
The Venus
The Baron Docteur
The Venus
The Baron Docteur
The Venus
The Baron Docteur
The Venus
(*Venus* 80)[16]

Much as actors and directors initially took the ellipses and *Pause*s of
Harold Pinter's plays as moments to be "filled in," given an enriching
and eliding subtext of desire, Parks also seems to assimilate the *spell* to
the traditions of realistic characterization:

This is a place where the figures experience their pure true simple state.
While no "action" or "stage business" is necessary, directors should fill
this moment as they best see fit.

The feeling: look at a daguerreotype; or: the planets are aligning and as
they move we hear the music of their spheres. A spell is a place of great
(unspoken) emotion. It's also a place for an emotional transition. ("from
Elements" 17)

Amplifying this way of reading the page through familiar stage practice, Joseph Roach suggests that the *spells* are "what actors and directors
in the American theater call a 'beat'" ("Great Hole" 314), and they
certainly can be made to function that way, as a transition between the
fulfillment of one impulse of intention, an objective (beat), and the
beginning of another. At the same time, much like her remarks on
dialect, Parks's remarks on *spells* tend to domesticate the estranging
power of this invention, which retains an alien quality, pointing toward
other perhaps as yet unrecognized uses. Jennifer Johung suggests that
the *spells* work to locate an event absent and unknowable in words and
not specified in practice, an evasion perhaps akin to Rosmer and
Rebecca's *joy*: "Parks's spells also metonymically mark a continual
passage back and forth between the page and the stage. The spells are,
thus, an index on the page and of the stage. They do not, however, exist
between the page and the stage, but are, in my mind, both the page
and the stage" (47). Both page and stage, the *spell* refuses to govern the
passage between them; the *spell* provides no instruction, no implicit
stage *direction* – it is writing that resists stage practice, but must nonetheless be performed.

A wink to Mr. Lincolns pasteboard cutout

Language is a physical act, and a radically ambiguous one in the two
material scenes of writing, page and stage. Much like Gertrude Stein,
Parks tactically toys with the conventions of print: putting prefixes
into the action of performance, showing the imprinted backstage, the
writerly support of the drama, inscribing moments of action where
neither the deed nor its meaning is specified in words. Although Parks's
account of her work sometimes stresses the literary determination of
writing in performance, her plays articulate a more challenging, and
more fully dramatic sense of the work of poetry in the embodiment of
performance.

   Parks's plays interrogate the work of writing in making "history";
they locate this inquiry at the interface of dramatic writing and

dramatic performance. In performance, dramatic writing is prosthetic, one of several instruments enabling the playing to do the work of embodiment, play. *The America Play* is richly attentive to this prosthetic dimension of performance, performance as a means to inspecting a finally inaccessible historical past through the "properties" – actors, words, costumes, objects – of the stage. The play considers the role of performance in re-embodying historical narrative by taking the historical museum, the theme park, as its presiding, spatializing metaphor. The play opens in *"A great hole. In the middle of nowhere. The hole is an exact replica of the Great Hole of History"* (159), a theme park in the eastern US. The main performer, THE FOUNDLING FATHER AS ABRAHAM LINCOLN, a former gravedigger, describes how he (the "Lesser Known") traveled west, and built this replica of "the Great Hole": "The Hole and its Historicity and the part he played in it all gave a shape to the life and posterity of the Lesser Known that he could never shake" (162). The original Great Hole replayed "all thuh greats," not only "Amerigo Vespucci hisself," but "Marcus Garvey. Ferdinand and Isabella. Mary Queen of thuh Scots! Tarzan King of thuh Apes! Washington Jefferson Harding and Millard Fillmore. Mistufer Columbus even" (180). Journeying west, the Lesser Known (played by an African American actor, though this is not formally stated anywhere in the text) brought the mythology of America with him. Capitalizing on his "strong resemblance to Abraham Lincoln" ("He was tall and thinly built just like the Great Man. His legs were the longer part just like the Great Mans legs" 159), he devised a kind of "Great Man" living-history performance.

The play's engagement with the problem of embodying writing is advanced at the beginning, with a series of lines – according to the footnotes – mainly exemplifying *chiasmus*.

THE FOUNDLING FATHER AS ABRAHAM LINCOLN: "To stop too fearful and too faint to go."
(*Rest*)
"He digged the hole and the whole held him."
(*Rest*)
"I cannot dig, to beg I am ashamed."
(*Rest*)
"He went to the theatre but home went she."
(*Rest*)

Goatee. Goatee. What he sported when he died. Its not my favorite.
(*Rest*)
"He digged the hole and the whole held him." Huh. (159)

In performance, *The America Play* opens with an intriguing, disorienting act, an African American man dressed as Lincoln delivering a series of illustrative quotations. This event is difficult to describe in terms of a fictive subtext, as though each line evoked a distinctive *beat* of intention or desire. Taking shape as an act of quotation, THE FOUNDLING FATHER's performance enacts two principles of writing in performance: its properties as formal rhetoric (*chiasmus*, for example) and its rhetorical use to shape a specific relationship with an audience. For the list of examples of *chiasmus* is interrupted by a different kind of address to the audience: "Goatee. Goatee. What he sported when he died. Its not my favorite."

Brecht had his actors speak the stage directions while rehearsing: dramatic acting occupies the interface between the third and first person, telling and doing, narrating and impersonating. THE FOUNDLING FATHER narrates, telling the story of the Lesser Known's marriage to Lucy, the impact of the "Big Hole. A theme park. With historical parades" (162) and his decision to leave the east and forge westward, eventually digging "his own Big Hole" and, after a day of digging, reciting the Great Man's speeches (163–4). But as it turned out, "None of those who spoke of his virtual twinship with greatness would actually pay money to watch him be that greatness"; indeed, "when someone remarked that he played Lincoln so well that he ought to be shot, it was as if the Great Mans footsteps had been suddenly revealed" (164). Choosing a beard from his extensive collection – "as authentic as he was, so to speak" (160) – the Lesser Known devised a new act, one involving him more fully in embodied performance, and more fully in relation to his public. He sat in "a single chair, a rocker, in a dark box. The public was invited to pay a penny, choose from the selection of provided pistols, enter the darkened box and 'Shoot Mr. Lincoln.' The Lesser Known became famous overnight" (164).

Speaking and acting: two ways of conceptualizing the text-in-performance are displayed and distinguished by THE FOUNDLING FATHER. Onstage, the Lesser Known's performance history is dramatized through narration, and this image of drama as the reproduction of literary "character" is literalized onstage by two of THE FOUNDLING

FATHER's most distinctive repeated gestures, gestures notably narrated at the moment he makes them:

> A wink to Mr. Lincolns pasteboard cutout. (*Winks at Lincoln's pasteboard cutout*) (160)

> A nod to Mr. Lincolns bust. (*Nods to Lincoln's bust*) (166)

Narration provides one image of the process of engaging the textuality of theatre, staging dramatic performance as the reiteration and recovery of writing. But the pasteboard cutout no longer winks back, the bust of Lincoln never nods. Reciting words – as the Lesser Known learned in his unsuccessful effort to reprise the Great Man's speeches – is merely the lifeless effigy of performance. Instead, dramatic performance requires the transformation of writing through enactment, the use of the script – the script of the Lincoln assassination in this case – to frame a new event. The Lesser Known simultaneously enacts the defining moment of the President's martyrdom, the subsequent history of African American oppression, and the moment of his own racist dismissal (he should be shot for impersonating Lincoln) in the first-person scene of present performance.[17]

The America Play alternates narration with impersonation, those moments in which THE FOUNDLING FATHER steps away from narrating the Lesser Known's history and steps into performance itself. At some moments, like "Its not my favorite," he speaks directly to the audience, usually about the material prosthetics of performance, the shoes and especially the beards, considering their propriety as instruments of impersonation: "This is my fancy beard. Yellow. Mr. Lincolns hair was dark so I dont wear it much. If you deviate too much they wont get their pleasure. Thats my experience. Some inconsistencies are perpetuatable because theyre good for business" (163). *Character* is unrecoverable as performance: playing the role, using the business of the stage to perform "the Great Man," the Lesser Known invariably produces something else, not a narrative summary of who the Great Man *was* but an instance of who he – the Lesser Known as the Great Man – *is*, what Richard Schechner might call *restored behavior* or Joseph Roach *surrogation*, an image that produces the past in the material of the present, yellow beard and all.

More to the point, in the structure of *The America Play*, performance constantly interrupts narration, as customers arrive in this replica of

the Great Hole of History to pay up, shoot "Lincoln," and shout various
slogans in emulation of John Wilkes Booth. The first customer shouts
" 'Thus to the tyrants!' " or " 'Sic semper tyrannis.' Purportedly, Booth's
words after he slew Lincoln and leapt from the presidential box to the
stage of Ford's Theatre in Washington, D.C. on 14 April 1865" (165, 165
n.8). Although THE FOUNDLING FATHER suggestively quotes Lincoln's
gesture ("*Booth shoots. Lincoln 'slumps in his chair.' Booth jumps*,"
the stage direction informs readers), in the Rep & Rev of THE FOUND-
LING FATHER's performances, the customers pay to revise history,
not merely repeat it. A WOMAN, playing Booth's role, shouts " 'Strike
the tent,' " the "last words of General Robert E. Lee, Commander of
the Confederate Army" (167, 167 n.10); another shouts "LIES!,"
then "LIIIIIIIIIIIIIIIIIIIIIARRRRRRRRRRRRRRRRRS!" B MAN plays the
assassination not as an act of Southern heroism, but to emphasize
Lincoln's martyrdom, quoting Secretary of War Edwin Stanton, " 'Now
he belongs to the ages' " (169), and a newlywed couple play Booth
ensemble, C WOMAN shouting Mary Todd Lincoln's "Theyve killed
the president!" (170). Replaying the Lincoln act not only rewrites the
text of history; the assassination becomes a means of recoding and
resisting the work of race in the fashioning of the dominant narratives
of America, creating the murder of Lincoln and the oppression
of African Americans as, in effect, one act.[18] Citation differentiates
while it authorizes; THE FOUNDLING FATHER's prefix orphans the role
in the act of claiming its descent from an unnamed namesake, the
Founding Father. The Lincoln Act defines dramatic performance as an
act of difference – from history, from writing – that creates revision,
change.

Unlike THE FOUNDLING FATHER's third-person narration, these
scenes take place in the performance present, the here and now
shared between us.

> Comes once a week that one. Always chooses the Derringer although
> we've got several styles he always chooses the Derringer. Always "The
> tyrants" and then "The South avenged." The ones who choose the
> Derringer are the ones for History. He's one for History. As it Used to
> Be. Never wavers. No frills. By the book. Nothing excessive.
> (*Rest*)
> A nod to Mr. Lincolns bust. (*Nods to Lincoln's bust*)
> I'll wear this one. He sported this style in the early war years. (166)

Performance uses writing in a range of ways, to accomplish acts that the writing itself cannot prefigure. *The America Play* implies that narrative, the effort to grasp events as a sequence of verbal events, cannot reframe the temporality of history: "the Greater Man had such a lead although of course somehow still 'back there.' If the Lesser Known had slowed down stopped moving completely gone in reverse died maybe the Greater Man could have caught up" (172). In one sense, the temporal logic of narrative prevents historical revision. The confrontation between past and present, between the Greater Man and the Lesser Known requires the undoing of narrative, of history. Only then might the Greater Man "have sneaked up behind the Lesser Known unbeknownst and wrestled him to the ground. Stabbed him in the back. In revenge. 'Thus to the tyrants!' Shot him maybe. The Lesser Known forgets who he is and just crumples. His bones cannot be found. The Greater Man continues on" (172–3). And yet, this fantasy seems to illustrate what has in fact happened, the temporality of narrative history obscuring its consequences in the present: the Lesser Known buried in obscurity, while the Greater Man (and the dominant history he represents) "continues on." *Chiasmus* depends on a *caesura*, the still point between two phrases, the second reversing the order (subject–verb; verb–subject) of the first. Yet while *chiasmus*, so to speak, reverses the order of narrative history without altering its syntax, its underlying logic, performance occupies the *caesura*, a moment between going forward and going back, or perhaps simultaneously going both forward and back, when the text of history can be explored and altered by embodiment.

As Pirandello's Father might put it, narrative *character* cannot be displaced by the actor's discandying body. And yet, performance in the first person incarnates a different perspective, sensing that the event shaped *now*, here and now, the event that *you* and *I* invent, might use its language, text, as a prosthetic for something else, as the *agency* of an act that exceeds recuperation to what has been written: "Whatdoyou say I wear the blonde" (173). Performance and historiography, acting and writing, are always distinct. In the second half of the play Lucy and Brazil listen for echoes (the gunshot) and dig up the materials of American history – Washington's nibblers, and a long list of documents and medals ("For makin do," "For bowin and scrapin" 186). In the Great Hole of History, or its replica, words and things aspire to the condition of history, a history variably grasped through the rhetoric of narrative and the rhetoric of performance. Acting and writing: as Lucy puts it, "Fakin was your Daddys callin but diggin was his livelihood" (181). The Great Hole is a replica both of the fullness (whole) of history and of its undoing, its absence (hole) in representation; materializing the past as object and as echo, it enacts the anxious citationality of performing history, and of playing drama.

Dramatic performance is evanescent, however durable the text: we share the Lincoln Act with THE FOUNDLING FATHER in the opening act of *The America Play*, but once it passes from the stage the performance is lost among the echoes and wonders, as lost to us as it is lost to Lucy and Brazil. The Hall of Wonders threatens to transform the process of performance into the recovery of portentous objects ("Uh glass trading bead – one of the first. Here are thuh lick-ed boots. Here, uh dried scrap of whales blubber") and influential documents ("peace pacts, writs, bills of sale, treaties, notices, handbills and circulars, freein papers, summonses, declarations of war, addresses, title deeds, obits, long lists of dids" 186). But while the Hole of History – I'm tempted to say, the hole of the proscenium – reanimates the script of history, the Hall of Wonders petrifies it.

> To my right: our newest Wonder: One of thuh greats Hisself! Note: thuh body sitting propped upright in our great Hole. Note the large mouth opened wide. Note the top hat and frock coat, just like the greats. Note the death wound: thuh great black hole – the great black hole in thuh great head. – And how this great head is bleedin. – Note: thuh last words. – And thuh last breaths. – And how thuh nation mourns – (199)

Performance rewrites its script, winks at the effigies of history, insists on the separability of specific bodies – raced bodies in this case – from the mythic drama they resignify. Unlike the stage, the museum can display the wondrous writs, and prop its effigies before us, effigies that – like *characters* – will never change. More important, they can never change us.

Diggidy-diggidy-diggidy-dawg

> *… I profess to be a scientific man, and was exceedingly anxious to obtain accurate measurement of her shape; but there was a difficulty in doing this. I did not know a word of Hottentot, and could never therefore have explained to the lady what the object of my foot-rule could be; and I*

*really dared not ask my worthy missionary host to interpret for me. I
therefore felt in a dilemma as I gazed at her form, that gift of a bounteous
nature to this favoured race, which no mantua-maker, with all her
crinoline and stuffing, can do otherwise than humbly imitate. The object
of my admiration stood under a tree, and was turning herself about to
all points of the compass, as ladies who want to be admired usually do.
Of a sudden, my eye fell upon my sextant; the bright thought struck me,
and I took a series of observations upon her figure in every direction, up
and down, crossways, diagonally, and so forth, and I registered them
carefully upon an outline drawing for fear of any mistake; this being
done, I boldly pulled out my measuring-tape, and measured the distance
from where I was to the place she stood, and having thus obtained both
base and angles, I worked out the results by trigonometry and
logarithms.*

Francis Galton, Narrative of an Explorer in
Tropical South Africa *(Fabian 46–7)*[19]

Embodying writing is the central problematic of *Venus*, a play that
kaleidoscopically refracts an ethical encounter between bodies and
texts through the lenses of racial, social, scientific, and theatrical performance. If the theme park is the organizing image of *The America Play*,
the presiding spatialities of *Venus* – the anatomy theatre, the freakshow
stage, the bed – transform the spectator from amused observer of historical reconstruction to a culpable participant, a voyeur: "Diggidy-
diggidy-diggidy-dawg" indeed. Of course, restoring Saartjie Baartman,
the famous Hottentot Venus, to the stage, Parks risks replaying
Baartman's spectacular abjection. Does the spectacle of The Venus in
Parks's play merely duplicate Baartman's historical oppression, or does
the play's voyeuristic intricacy – figuring the theatrical audience in the
onstage Chorus of the Spectators, The Chorus of the Court, The Chorus
of the 8 Anatomists, The Baron Docteur – alienate the politics of visibility or its specific ways of framing race in the trigonometry of theatrical
representation?[20] And, more to the point here, how does the play's
placement of **The Venus** at the intersection of writing and performance
allegorize dramatic embodiment as a site of racial and political
critique?

Baartman is in one sense an extraordinary index of the fracture of
text and performance. While parts of her body – her genitals, skeleton,

and a plaster cast – were preserved in the Musée de l'Homme in Paris, little of her own voice has survived. The "texts" that preserve her are court proceedings, newspaper accounts, advertisements, political cartoons, memoirs, and Georges Cuvier's anatomical treatises. In print, as in her life, Baartman remains an extraordinarily public property, part of an extensive genre of performance. As Richard D. Altick's *The Shows of London* amply demonstrates, the Hottentot Venus was only one of many human spectacles populating early-nineteenth-century stages and museums. She was succeeded by "Tonio Maria, 'the Venus of South America'" in 1822 (Altick 272–3), but William Bullock (who declined to exhibit Baartman in his London Museum, generally known as the Egyptian Hall) drew 58,000 spectators to his "Exhibition of Laplanders" in 1822, and in the 1840s the painter George Caitlin booked the Egyptian Hall for an exhibition including his paintings of American Indians, artifacts, and "Tableaux Vivants Indiennes" (acted first by English impersonators, and eventually by Ojibbeway performers) (see Altick 273–7).[21] Baartman was brought to London by Hendrick Cezar and Alexander Dunlop and exhibited in Piccadilly in 1810; in November the attorney-general, on behalf of the "African Association for Promoting the Discovery of the Interior of Africa," appealed to the Court of King's Bench to discontinue the exhibition, on the grounds that she had been both brought to England and exhibited without her consent, and was being mistreated.[22] The court had Baartman examined in Dutch, and determined that "This woman was plainly not under restraint, and the only effect of taking her from her keepers would be to let her loose to go back again." Noting that "If there be any offence to decency in the exhibition, that comes on in another way: – that may be the ground of a prosecution," the case was dismissed on November 28 ("Law Report").[23] She continued to be shown in Piccadilly and on an extensive tour of the provinces before being taken to Paris in 1814 by an animal trainer, who displayed her from eleven in the morning until ten in the evening for fifteen months. A sensation in the press, Baartman was examined by Georges Cuvier in 1815, who commissioned two "scientific" nude paintings at the Jardin du Roi before she died in December. Cuvier obtained the body, conducted measurements before and after maceration, and used them to confirm his general thesis of the racial inferiority of African races.[24]

Understood as alienated commodity in her own day, "the figure of Sarah Bartmann" was, as Sander Gilman remarks, reduced to "her sexual parts" in ways that made the analogy between freakshow stage, anatomy theatre, and museum explicit: "The audience which had paid to see her buttocks and had fantasized about the uniqueness of her genitalia when she was alive could, after her death and dissection, examine both" not only in Cuvier's presentations, but indeed on the shelves of the Musée de l'Homme (232).[25] Baartman is a figure almost uniquely captive to spectacle, or, more accurately, to the narrative accounts of the spectacle of her performance as the object of the specta- tors', the court's, the anatomists', and the museumgoers' gaze. There can be few figures of comparable importance whose history today is so reliant on Altick's *The Shows of London* and the Toole-Stott bibliog- raphy of *Circus and Allied Arts*.

The "whole" of Baartman's history has a "hole" at its center, obscured by the prefix that labels it: **The Venus**. *Venus* is merely the latest effort to restore that spectacle to view. "As a playwright I try to do many things: explore the form, ask questions, make a good show, tell a good story, ask more questions, take nothing for granted" (Parks, "from Elements" 6). How does one go about making a "good show" about Saartjie Baartman, and how might we read that show to stage the ques- tion of embodying writing? This problem animates *Venus* from its opening moments. For after the principal characters all introduce them- selves, we are told by **The Negro Resurrectionist**, "I regret to inform you that thuh Venus Hottentot iz dead. … There wont b inny show tonite" (3). It may well be an "Outrage!" (4), but the play announces at once its citational logic: staging The Venus may "cite" an historical *character*, the Venus Hottentot, but Saartjie Baartman cannot be re- membered onstage or in print, for in an important sense she never appeared in either medium. As Sara L. Warner suggests, the play dis- rupts the sense of represented *character* as commodity: "Baartman does not belong to all of us, [Parks] seems to say – she belongs to none of us" (197).

In formal terms, the play contests our ability to know Baartman as a *character*, by resisting the "retrospective method" of realistic drama- turgy, showing the cause of present events in the logic of their historical development. The play's reverse sequence of scenes works differently from plays like Pinter's *Betrayal*, in which the "final" scene of an affair appears first in sequence, and the play traces events back to their origi- nal cause. In *Venus*, scenes are numbered in reverse order and announced by **The Negro Resurrectionist** (*"Scene 31: May I Present to*

You '*The African Dancing Princess*'/*She'd Make a Splendid Freak*" 11), but
the action develops chronologically from The Venus's contracting
in South Africa to her death in Paris. "*Counting Down*" the scenes –
"31, 30, 29, 28, 27, 26, 25, 24" (41) – **The Negro Resurrectionist** complicates the sense of a determining origin and of its accessibility to the
theatre audience. For the "origin" we discover in Scenes 2 and 1 is
not an instigating event, like Mary Tyrone's entrance with her
wedding dress in the finale of *Long Day's Journey into Night,* or Willy
Loman's infidelity in Boston. *Scene 1: Final Chorus* begins by reminding
us that "thuh Venus Hottentot iz dead. ... There wont be inny show
tuhnite," and then proceeds to quote various lines, gestures, and scenes
from the play we have seen: **The Baron Docteur** excusing himself from
guilt ("I say she died of drink"), the **Chorus of Spectators** ("Diggidy-
diggidy-diggidy-dawg"), the voice of **The Mother Showman** ("Hur-ry
Hur-ry Step in Step in") (160–1). *Venus* ends where it begins, in the
spectacularizing of The Venus. Indeed, in the play's final moments,
having told us that "There wont be inny show tuhnite," **The Venus**
solicits us

The Venus
... Love's corpse stands on show in a museum. Please visit.

All
Diggidy-diggidy-diggidy
Diggidy-diggidy-diggidy-dawg!

The Negro Resurrectionist
A Scene of Love:

The Venus
Kiss me *Kiss* me *Kiss* me *Kiss* (161–2)

Much like the padding that sometimes signifies The Venus's nude body
in performance but conceals the actress's, *Venus* stages the "singular
anatomy" (5) of Baartman through prostheses, stand-ins, surrogates.[26]
What remains of Saartjie Baartman is the dismembered corpse of
La Vénus Hottentote, connected to the present by the dynamics of
visibility that the contemporary theatre audience shares with its
nineteenth-century progenitors, a dialectic in which desire ("Diggidy-
diggidy") sustains history, science, and theatre in erasing Baartman
from view.

Parks's writing provides the means to perform **The Venus**, but only under the sign of erasure, not a knowable *character* but merely the prefix to action. In its many surrogations of the act of looking, the writing also renders – and renders culpable – the embodied seeing of the audience. The inscription of vision sustains the work of the play-within-the-play in *Venus*, the inset *For the Love of the Venus*, Parks's allusion to a theatrical vogue inspired by Baartman, plays such as *The Hottentot Venus or the Hatred of French Women* performed in Paris in November 1814.[27] In the play, The Young Man is bored with his Bride-to-Be, and feels emasculated because he has not gone to Africa: "'The Man who has never been from his own home is no *Man'*" (26). Since his wedding is looming, he's in something of "uh pickle." If "A Man to be a Man must know Unknowns" (48), then he must conduct his exploration of the exotic closer to home. "I wanna love / something Wild," he says, and commands his Uncle to procure "something called 'The Hottentot Venus'" he read about in the paper (49). The Bride-to-Be is faced with a number of theatrical options – mainly suicide in the mode of Cleopatra, Phaedra, or Ophelia (122) – when The Mother hits on a plan: "We'll get you up, make you look wild / Get you up like a Hottentot" and so "Bring my Son to his knees" (122–3). In the final scene, The Young Man kneels to the Bride-disguised-as-The-Venus, promising fidelity. The Bride removes her disguise and he "*gives her a red heart box of chocolates. Love Tableau*" (154).

For the Love of The Venus structures *Venus* as a whole, and allegorizes its relation to the theatre audience.[28] The Bride/Venus gratifies The Young Man's desire for an exotic other, while at the same time staging that "other" as the marriageable, white Bride-to-Be at "thuh core" (154). Exoticizing Baartman in the fictive Venus, desire for the "other" reproduces and reinforces the privileges of white identity. Beyond that, *For the Love of the Venus* locates the work of vision, visibility, and voyeurism in constituting The Venus in history. In the first three scenes – Scenes 29, 26, and 23 – the play is watched by **The Baron Docteur** (who has yet to appear as a character in The Venus's life).

Scene 29: "For the Love of The Venus." Act I, Scene 3

A play on a stage. The Baron Docteur is the only
person in the audience. Perhaps he sits in a chair.
It's almost as if he's watching TV.
The Venus stands off to the side. She watches The Baron Docteur.

The Baron Docteur enacts a spectatorial relation to *For the Love of the Venus* that is duplicated in his (and our) relation to The Venus herself. Later, watching The Venus, *"He grows more and more interested and watches more and more intently"* (58), a specular relationship consummated, so to speak, in Scene 19, "A Scene of Love (?)," a scene of pure – or impure – *looking*.[29]

These performances are interrelated in other respects as well. *"The Baron Docteur applauds"* (27) the play, and then participates in a related performance in the following scene, in which **The Negro Resurrectionist** reads an extensive "Historical Extract. Category: Medical. Autopsy report" from doctor's notebook: "Her brain, immediately after removal, deprived of the greater part of its membranes, weighed 38 ounces" (28). Much as Baartman's "charming hands" (144) are dissected in The Baron Docteur's (and Cuvier's) anatomy – "In the left hand the tendon was also split, but the 2 divisions (*Rest*) passed through the same groove" (97) – so the spectator is, in *Venus*, always an "Anatomical Columbus" (131). The stage dismembers what it displays to the desiring, oppressive, spectatorial eye ("I").[30]

Citing Saartjie Baartman as **The Venus**, Parks's play rigorously performs the occlusion of "Saartjie Baartman"; The Venus emerges onstage as a label, a prefix for performance which we encounter as the signifier of an unavailable – perhaps unimaginable – history.[31] Although Saartjie Baartman appears, usually as the unnamed Hottentot Venus, in historical writings, in few of them does she speak. Onstage, the body "digests" and displaces writing, but the written record has fully consumed Baartman. For Cuvier, Baartman's body – her genitals – played a conclusive role in his demonstration of European racial superiority. Although he noted in his examination of Baartman in 1815 that "Her character was gay, her memory good, and she recognized, after several weeks, a person whom she had seen only once; she spoke tolerable Dutch, which she had learned at the Cape, knew also a bit of English, and was beginning to speak several words of French" (3), her complaisant willingness to "strip" – "having been led to the Jardin du Roi, she had the complaisance to strip (*se dépouiller*), and to let herself be painted in the nude" – extended only so far: "she kept her genitals carefully hidden" so that "it was only after her death that one knew what she possessed there" (Cuvier 3–4, my translation). It's a striking moment. Baartman's grace and modesty are recorded, though as ultimately ineffective obstacles to Cuvier's investigation. The term *se dépouiller* generally means "to strip off," and while the transitive usage of the verb *dépouiller* can also mean to strip ("the wind stripped the leaves from the tree"), its primary meaning is "to skin," offering a bitter fore-taste of the violence of the naturalist's need to possess the body, to subject it to his spectatorial seeing.

Though consigned to history, Ibsen's Beata can speak, her words recalled by Kroll, her writing remembered by Mortensgaard. Parks stages the limited agency of either narrative or dramatic writing to restore Baartman, her voice, as anything other than The Venus. Baartman's speech is recorded, however, in an extraordinary account of a visit by two actors – Charles Mathews and John Philip Kemble – to the exhibition in Piccadilly, as recalled by Mathews's widow:

I had observed that at the time Mr. Mathews entered and found her sur-rounded by some of our own barbarians, the countenance of the "Venus" exhibited the most sullen and occasionally ferocious expression; but the moment she looked in Mr. Kemble's face, her own became placid and mild, – nay, she was obviously pleased; and, patting her hands together, and holding them up in evident admiration, uttered the unintelligible words, "Oh, ma Babba! Oh, ma Babba!" gazing at the face of the trage-dian with unequivocal delight. "What does she say, sir?" asked Mr. Kemble gravely of the keeper, as the woman reiterated these strange words: "does she call me her *papa*?" "No, sir," answered the man: "she says, you are a very fine man." "Upon my word," said Kemble drily, with an inclination of his head, as he took a pinch of snuff for the first time since he entered, which he had held betwixt his finger and thumb, during his suspended admiration and surprise: "upon my word, the lady does me infinite honour!" Whether his fine face in reality struck the fancy of the lady, or whether Mr. Kemble's pitying tones and considerate for-bearance of the usual ceremonies, reached her heart, it is certain that she was much pleased with him. The keeper invited him once more to touch the poor woman, a privilege allowed on more liberal terms than in the case of Miss Crackham, as it was without additional fee. Mr. Kemble again declined the offer, retreating, and again exclaiming in tones of the most humane feeling, "No, no, poor creature, no!" – and the two actors went away together; Mr. Kemble observing, when they reached the street, "Now, Mathews, my good fellow, do you know this is a sight which makes me *melancholy*. I dare say, now, that they ill-use that poor creature! Good God! how very shocking!" – and away he stalked, as if musing, and totally forgetting his companion until the moment of sepa-ration recalled his recollection. (qtd. Altick 269–70)

Mathews's anecdote provides an extraordinary revision of the conventional portrait of the actor gazing into the mask of character. Rather than signifying the artistic mystery of the actor's transformation, the vignette signifies the actor's essential humanity, which distinguishes him from and elevates him above his barbarous countrymen through his consideration for the sullen, ferocious, degraded "Venus." Although the "Venus" speaks, she functions here as an instrument for fashioning European humanity; Baartman's behavior reflects more than it signifies, illuminating Kemble's "beautiful countenance" and sympathetic response. Much as she emerges as an example of the court's probity, and of Cuvier's perspicacity, so here, onstage and surrounded by actors, the "Venus" cannot evoke her own meanings, only the melancholy of the compassionate tragedian.[32]

The Venus is revealed only as the reflection of a specular desire, the desire to fashion the (civic, legal, professional, masculine, white, erotic) self through the projection of a fictive "other" – The Young Man's "something Wild" (48). And much as Baartman emerges only indirectly through the dense, conflicting testimony of the historical record, Parks vividly foregrounds the *agency* of writing in the making of this latest spectacle. Not only are most of the scenes announced by **The Negro Resurrectionist** – "Scene #30: She Looks Like Shes Fresh Off the Boat" (18) – in effect resurrecting writing as living enactment, but much of the source material is *performed* in the catalogue of footnotes, historical extracts, entries from diaries, advertisements, and anatomical readings that punctuate the play, indeed that *are* the play. **The Negro Resurrectionist**'s many footnotes, for example, bring the testimony of writing *as* writing into the play.

Scene 28: Footnote #2

> The Negro Resurrectionist holds fast to The Venus's arm. He reads through The Baron Docteur's notebook.

The Negro Resurrectionist
Footnote #2:
(*Rest*)
Historical Extract. Category: Medical. Autopsy report:
(*Rest*)
"Her brain, immediately after removal, deprived of the greater part of its membranes, weighed 38 ounces." (*Venus* 28)

Staging the fissure between writing and performing, the Footnote at once identifies and distinguishes The Venus from the textual subject, the fleshly and the macerated Venus held together in a duplicitous resurrection.

This reciprocity between print and performance is focused in the final scenes of the play, which repeatedly distinguish writing and performance as – failed – means to recover The Venus. Although **The Baron Docteur** delivers a long anatomical lecture during the play's intermission, his more critical discoveries as an "Anatomical Columbus" are delivered, as **The Negro Resurrectionist** announces, in "Scene #6: Several Years Later, at a Conference in Tübingen: The Dis(-re-)member-ment of the Venus Hottentot, Part II" (147). Taken in part from Cuvier's description of Baartman in the *Histoire Naturelle des Mammifères*, the lecture literalizes print's role in the spectacularization of The Venus: here, **The Baron Docteur** delivers a detailed anatomical account of an unnamed "Hottentot or Bushman" woman's genitalia. Despite its clini-cal vocabulary, the lecture is disturbingly graphic. Moreover, in theatri-cal terms, it offers a spectacle from which the contemporary audience cannot simply "Turn uhway / dont look / cover yr face / cover yr eyes" (161). Realizing the print-record as performance, *Venus* not only urges the complicity of that record in the transformation of the histori-cal woman Saartjie Baartman into the theatricalized Venus Hottentot, but makes that transformation part of the experience of the play's con-temporary audience: it is what the play has promised *us* all along, however unwilling we may be to recognize our likeness to the play's nineteenth-century theatrical/scientific voyeurs.

Embodying The Venus intensifies the problem of dramatic embodi-ment: embodying writing involves actors and audiences in a complex act of exposure, in which writing – at its best – provides no cover for the complex, ethically dubious seeing it often exacts. The closing minutes of *Venus* are preoccupied with the different kinds of disclosure embodied writing might enable. In Scene 3, **The Venus** has an extra-ordinary monologue, *A Brief History of Chocolate*, in which the role of chocolate in the economy of nineteenth-century colonial expansion, as well as its exotic, erotic, and emotionally satisfying qualities, explicitly parallel the ways in which Baartman herself was and continues to be exploited, a parallel reinforced by having **The Venus** perform this "history":

While chocolate was once used as a stimulant and source of nutrition
it is primarily today a great source of fat,
and, of course, pleasure.
(*Rest*) (156)

Yet, *A Brief History of Chocolate* is both metaphorical and metaphorizing:
it requires a *tour de force* performance from the actress yet is a markedly
"fictional" speech in the play, a moment where **The Venus**'s performance preempts the historical narrative. The moment of **The Venus**'s
most revealing, extroverted performance is the moment of her most
complete surrogation, her address across history to the present audience. It is also the moment when the actress fully spectacularizes The
Venus, rendering her – and herself – most vividly as performance com-
modities, for sale, to us, in the present tense. The actress's body plays
a crucial part here. When played in a padded costume, The Venus is
at once displayed and displaced: there won't be any show tonight, only
the openly constructed sign of that body's absence. Alternatively, when
the actress is not padded, there's also no show tonight, for to "see" The
Venus seen by the others onstage the audience must participate in its
ways of seeing, projecting The Venus on to the prosthetic body of the
performer.[33]

Any successful performance of *Venus* will depend on the force of
this scene, which counterpoints **The Venus**'s next narrative, moments
later in Scene 2, *The Venus Hottentot Tells the Story of Her Life*:

I was born near the coast, Watchman.
Journeyed some worked some
ended up here.
I would live here I thought but only for uh minute!
Make a mint.
Had plans to.
He had a beard.
Big bags of money!
Where wuz I?
Fell in love. Hhh.
Tried my hand at French.
Gave me a haircut
and the claps.
You get thuh picture, huh? (159)

If *A Brief History of Chocolate* cites and conceals Baartman behind the powerful rhetoricity of the actress's performance, this biography points in a different direction, to the poverty of the external details of Baartman's life, their inability to fill in a subject, an authoritative text of "Saartjie Baartman." Parks's characters are not only *"figures, figments, ghosts"* of the historical characters they invoke and displace ("from Elements" 12), but figments of the idea of dramatic *character* itself, of *character* as anything other than a rhetorical device for fashioning the appearance of identity in the citational performance of writing. While the metaphorical *Brief History of Chocolate* is the set-piece that enables the actress to perform, spectacularize The Venus, the biographical narrative frames the wages of voyeurism. The *Chocolate* speech calls for extroversion, but this abject narration demands that we avert our eyes: *"Dont look at me / dont look … (Rest) She dies"* (159).

Performance can surrogate history, metaphorize it, cite it, but not reclaim it, at least not *this* history: it is too closely bound to the rhetoric of performance itself ("dont look"), a rhetoric that has allowed Saartjie Baartman to enter European history and its dramatic traditions only as The Venus. Yet behind The Venus and Cuvier's unnamed subject, perhaps we can still discern a gesture, a trace of Baartman in the sidelong recollections of her temperament, facility with language, and her effect on the delicate temperaments of English actors. Parks invents The Negro Resurrectionist not so much to resurrect Baartman (Cuvier's essay claims that there was no need for an illicit "resurrection man" – "She died the 29th of December 1815; and the Chief of Police having permitted that her body be brought to the Jardin du Roi, there began a more detailed examination" 4), as to resurrect the ways in which she has been dis/re-membered, to articulate the history of missing history as part of our experience of the play.[34] Throughout *Venus*, **The Negro Resurrectionist** is master of ceremonies, articulating the play's progress, its relation to writing, and to the contemporary audience. Here, alongside **The Baron Docteur**'s lecture, the spectacular *Brief History of Chocolate*, and the relatively untheatrical *Story of Her Life*, **The Negro Resurrectionist** performs this history, evoking *as* performance the footnotes confined to the margins of Parks's other plays. Closing the play, **The Negro Resurrectionist** quotes from "Footnote #3: Historical Extract. Category: Literary. From Robert Chambers's *Book of Days*" (36):

"Early in the 19th century a poor wretched woman was exhibited in England under the appellation of *The Hottentot Venus*. With an intensely ugly figure, distorted beyond all European notions of beauty, she was said to possess precisely the kind of shape which is most admired among her countrymen, the Hottentots." (159)

Chambers's *Book of Days* provides a miscellany of *Popular Antiquities* along with *Oddities of Human Life and Character* (title page). Citing Chambers, **The Negro Resurrectionist** enacts Chambers's retrospective gesture, in which the sufferings of that "poor wretched woman" are located among the "curiosities" and "oddities" of a bygone era. Even in her own time, Baartman could only be represented as The Hottentot; complicit in the creation of The Hottentot, print has few resources to restore, to remember Saartjie Baartman. **The Negro Resurrectionist**'s final lines return us to the moment of Baartman's arrival in England, the moment in which Baartman disappeared into spectacle:

> The year was 1810, three years after the Bill for the Abolition of the Slave-Trade had been passed in Parliament, and among protests and denials, horror and fascination her show went on. She died in Paris 5 years later: A plaster cast of her body was once displayed, along with her skeleton, in the *Musee de l'Homme*. (159)

Speaking "footnotes" throughout the play, **The Negro Resurrectionist** performs both the citation and emulation of print. **The Negro Resurrectionist**'s performance is important in other ways, too, for while he reads "texts," this reading is also a transformation of print into something else, acting, performance. The performers of the three principal roles – **The Venus**, **The Baron Docteur**, **The Negro Resurrectionist** – are always visible to one another onstage, always "inside" and "outside" the action. Citing writing establishes a relation to the events onstage, but is also shaped as an event itself, inseparable from the performance it records, documents, and contextualizes. While **The Venus** withdraws herself from view – "dont look" – she is absorbed into the historical record, a record assimilating her to its own distorting canons of propriety, its own urgent strategies of dismemberment and remembering, strategies the stage can mark, distantiate, defamiliarize, repeat, replay, and revise, but not erase.

How do we embody writing on the stage? And how might that embodiment engage, for better or worse, with the oppressive uses of both writing and performance, the *archive* and *the repertoire*? In *Venus*, Parks locates a "figure" whose abjection in both spheres is so complete as fully to deny the notion of *character*. Like The Great Man, The Venus can only be played as prosthetic: the writing represents only her macerated remains, and performance involves us in the ethically rebarbative spectacle of their seductive, repellent reanimation. But *Venus* also enacts a shrewd analysis of the force of writing and its ongoing implication in performance now, even in the waning of print culture. In *Venus*, Parks stages a spatialized critique of the relationship between print, performance, and racist representation during the opening era of widespread literacy. Reconstructing that relationship in performance, the play suggests not merely that we are its inheritors, but that we continue to occupy that space as our own.

Chapter 4

Writing Space: Beckett and Brecht

> *Desert. Dazzling light.*
> *The man is flung backwards on stage from right wing. He falls, gets up immediately, dusts himself, turns aside, reflects.*
> *Whistle from right wing.*
> *He reflects, goes out right.*
> *Immediately flung back on stage he falls, gets up immediately, dusts himself, turns aside, reflects.*
>
> Samuel Beckett, Act Without Words I *(203)*[1]

Samuel Beckett's *Act Without Words I* provides an elegant opening to the agency of writing in the framing of theatrical space. The play impels a signal location, a place at once the material space of the stage – with its wings, sound effects, props and invisible, malevolent or indifferent propmasters – and a fictive locale, a "Desert." An epitome of modern, absurdist theatre, the play is nonetheless classical in its proportions, an Aristotelian evocation of the primacy of plot, explored in a single site of action, intensified through the manifest identification of dramatic time with the duration of performance. Here, "character" arises directly from the minimal events of the play, a body flung into place, whose compulsion to act exfoliates a paradigm of action itself.

Beckett's blending of the presentational space of the stage with the represented space of the drama is distinctive, but hardly new, nor is it quite captured by the ready tag of metadrama, "all the world's a stage." Instead, Beckett's play points to an apparently constitutive preoccupation of Western dramatic performance, the reciprocal mapping of the place of the play and the place of its playing. As Samuel Weber suggests, theatre "entails not just *space* but, more precisely, its disruption and rearrangement. In other words, *theatricality emerges where space and place can no longer be taken for granted or regarded as self-contained"* (300). One of the tendencies even of modern naturalistic theatre – a mode of production eagerly insistent on the erasure of its "theatricality" – has been to complicate its celebrated "objectivity" by foregrounding scenes of observation, *watching*, as a means to refract and complicate the silent, concealed audience's theatrical complicity with the action of the fictive play. Rebecca and Mrs. Helseth's secret spying, staging the unobserved Rosmer at the opening of *Rosmersholm*, reenacts the *agency* of our own theatrical participation – our action – in the scene of the drama. Many plays construct their fictive space, their castles in the air, so to speak, while simultaneously drawing our regard to their solid, earthbound, stagey foundations. For Pirandello's six characters, the theatre's conventional parlor furniture can never present Madame Pace's shop organically, coherently, accurately; yet in *Six Characters in Search of an Author*, the theatre's tattered instrument is the only means of the drama. Hamlet, of course, invites Rosencrantz and Guildenstern to contemplate "this goodly frame, the earth," openly laminating medieval Elsinore to its theatrical vehicle, the wood-framed Globe. The savage soldiers and forlorn shepherds populating the English Corpus Christi cycles anachronistically contour a distant, sacred place to the immediate landscape of contemporary civic life, to say nothing of Herod raging in the street he shares with the audience; Lysistrata and her women pour their libation to abstinence at the *thymelê* of the Athenian orchestra; Agamemnon treads the carpet of his degradation to his horrific death behind the *skene* doors.

Plays take *place* through the agency of the play, incorporating the *scene* of the theatre as the *scene* of the drama. Beckett's plays train a disciplined attention to the interplay between dramatic writing and the material stage, often by evoking a fictive elsewhere largely indistinguishable from the space of play. *"A country road. A tree.":* *Waiting for Godot* provides a kind of Cartesian center for the act of waiting for Godot's appearance, a character who will appear – much like the props in *Act Without Words I* – from the wings, where Didi disappears to relieve himself. The claustral box set of *Endgame* faces its audience, that "multitude … in transports … of joy" (106). Many of Beckett's most aggressive dramas seem to explore the use of theatre to constitute a represented space, as Lucky might put it, "outside time without extension" (42), space not actually inhabitable, imaginable as material space. In *Not I*, the stage directions call for Mouth to be isolated from a performing body and placed high in the air. How should we read the few metres separating Mouth and Auditor onstage: within the represented world of the play or as a sign of a much greater distance? In the darkness from which Mouth emerges, it's not possible to say what distances are, how far she is from the cowled Auditor, or whether he/she/it sees her, is her, is the body she has escaped, "the machine ... so disconnected ... never got the message ... or powerless to respond ... like numbed" (378). Beckett even came to resist the spatiality implied by this visual relationship onstage, removing the Auditor from the 1978 production he directed, much as had been the case for video versions of the play.[2] *Play* places three urns, cunningly constructed to seem nearly too small to conceal the bodies of the actors, adjacent onstage, yet M, W1, and W2 are apparently unable to hear one another in the represented space they share in the play. In the elegant design of *Footfalls*, May paces, wheels, and paces in a precisely delineated *"Strip: downstage, parallel with front, length nine steps, width one metre, a little off centre audience right"* (399). Yet while this place is inscribed in theatrical space, the dramatic coordinates of May's pacing are more challenging to locate, occupying several different temporalities in the various narratives of the play. May's steps are accompanied by a Voice, but the voice has an ambiguous relationship to the onstage figure, and to us. Sometimes it speaks to her, from within the dramatic space; sometimes it speaks to us about her – "But let us watch her move, in silence" (401) – locating the pacing we see in the narrative of May's pacing life. May, too, halts her footsteps to deliver a "Sequel," the tale of Amy, walking "up and down, up and down" in a little church, and of her mother Old Mrs. Winter, who resumes V's question, "Will you never have done ... revolving it all?" (402–3). Pacing here, now, before us in the theatre, May's drama is, in a sense, eternal, "outside time," much as Amy complains to Mrs. W of being outside space, of her inability to *take place*: "I was not there." Writing puts a world in motion, revolving it all, using theatrical space to motivate a drama of displacement, a drama that disorients the temporal and spatial coordinates of the event itself.

> *Fade up to even a little less still on strip.*
> *No trace of* MAY.
> *Hold ten seconds.*
> *Fade out.* (403)

Ibsen's onstage space is a place of disclosure, framed by a haunting, dangerous, destructive – and, in his dramaturgy, finally unknowable – offstage. Beckett's writing illuminates a space of play, a space of potential action, meaning ("We're not beginning to … to … mean something?" *Endgame* 108), dependent on an offstage world. This unseen scene is known by its signifiers: Godot, of course; the barren land and sea outside the windows in *Endgame*; the bell that opens Winnie's happy day; the inquisitorial spotlight of *Play* ("When you go out – and I go out. Some day you will tire of me and go out .. for good" 312); the offstage room where Bim, Bam, Bem, and Bom are all taken, all tortured (*What Where*); the *"Distant storm of applause"* summoned by the Director's "catastrophe," silenced when the Protagonist *"raises his head, fixes the audience,"* applause at once anticipating and ironizing our own (461). As in *Act Without Words I*, this offstage elsewhere is projected as capable of resolving our captivity, the mystery of our being here, in this place: "Tell him … [*He hesitates*] … tell him you saw me and that … [*He hesitates*] … that you saw me," Didi urges Godot's emissary (86). And yet, like Didi, we suspect that again tomorrow the boy will not recognize them when he announces that Godot will surely come the next day. Clov suggests, "Something is taking its course" (107), and in Beckett's dramaturgy the narrative logic defining this place and our experience of it is urgently predicated on a logic inaccessible to us, outside the space we share with the stage. This is, I think, Mouth's recognition toward the end of *Not I* as well:

> … what? .. not that? .. nothing to do with that? .. nothing she could tell? .. all right … nothing she could tell … try something else … think of something else … oh long after … sudden flash … not that either … all right … something else again … so on … hit on it in the end … think everything keep on long enough … then forgiven … back in the – … what? .. not that either? .. nothing to do with that either? .. nothing she could think? .. all right … nothing she could tell … nothing she could think … nothing she – … what? .. who? .. no! .. she! (382)

"Space in itself may be primordially given, but the organization, and meaning of space is a product of social translation, transformation, and experience" (Soja 79–80). Writing cannot create space, but it can be used to transform it, to lend the spatial configuration of a specific theatrical location significance, meaning, at its intersection with dramatic place. In his brief, suggestive essay "Of Other Spaces," Michel Foucault argues that "we do not live in a homogeneous and empty space, but on the contrary in a space thoroughly imbued with quantities and perhaps thoroughly fantasmatic as well" (23); he is particularly interested in what he calls "heterotopias," spaces that gather and concentrate a range of often contradictory social attitudes in a given place, typically a place that is outside the normative spatial terrain of everyday life, but – unlike utopias – a space that is "somewhere" and "nowhere" at once. Foucault characterizes boarding schools, the honeymoon, cemeteries, prisons, retirement homes as heterotopias, but his crucial observation is that such places contour a culture's ideological crises in space, by "juxtaposing in a single real place several spaces, several sites that are in themselves incompatible. Thus it is that the theater brings onto the rectangle of the stage, one after the other, a whole series of places that are foreign to one another" (25). Like the actors' bodies, the space of the stage is always outside dramatic writing. And yet dramatic performance uses the *agency* of writing to frame the significance of that space, to render it as at once real and fantasmatic, indeed to use the fictive *scene* of dramatic action to chart an inquiry of action, the specific action that *takes place* here and now. Beckett's drama traces an allegory of writing in the theatre, and so provides a way to reflect on the agency of dramatic writing in charting the space of performance.

i. *Quad*: Euclidean Dramaturgies

Beckett's writing is preoccupied with the production of place, places often ambiguously rooted in space. Much as Euripides' drama explores the ways the *orchestra* and *skene* might be thematized by dramatic writing, or Shakespeare the "sterile promontory" of the platform stage, Beckett's writing engages the frontality of the proscenium house. Whether in plays like *Endgame* or *Happy Days* or *Come and Go*, or in video works from *Eh Joe* to *...but the clouds ...*, Beckett's drama conceives the space of play perspectivally, located before an audience placed – as the notes to *Play* suggest – "outside the ideal space (stage) occupied by its victims" (318). Placed downstage center, toward the edge of this ideal space, the inquisitorial spotlight in *Play* articulates the activity of the play's audience, soliciting the characters from the darkness it shares with us. This sense of a playing space projected before the viewer informs much of Beckett's writing for video, too. In *Eh Joe*, the camera follows Joe's "opening movements [...] at constant remove," then establishes its position as "one yard from maximum closeup on face," closing in within this perspective in nine four-inch movements (361). The camera of *Ghost Trio* tracks into a rectangular playing area, following a path perpendicular to the door centered in the rear wall, transforming the virtual space of the tv box into a box set; while the voiceover describes what we see, each of the camera's movements (from point A to B to C on the track) and closeups maintain this alignment, taking us into and out of the space from a single viewing perspective. In ... *but the clouds* ... the camera is located at a fixed distance from the illuminated circular playing area, an area nearly contiguous with the camera's focal field. Beckett's writing constitutes a performing space in which the auditors face into the playing area, are shaped (whatever their actual seat in the house) within a single perspective (one sometimes articulated onstage, as by the spotlight in *Play*, or by precisely governed camera work in the videos) that reciprocally shapes the space of play and the space of our attention. In *Catastrophe*, Beckett's most overtly self-referential play, the Director poses the Protagonist on his plinth, then moves toward the back of the auditorium, at one point to "the front row of the stalls" to "see how it looks from the house" (459). Taking a position behind the audience, the Director frames both stage and audience within his constitutive perspective on the performance: "Good. There's our catastrophe. In the bag" (460).

Beckett's mobilization of the proscenium theatre at once enables his images to be "felt as a true dereliction," and, more urgently, as a means to extend what Daniel Albright calls the "incompetence of being" of his characters through the house (Albright 79, 135). The plays conceive dramatic writing as the agency for shaping a specific kind of space, using writing, in Stanton Garner's phrasing, to undertake "an essentially scenographic composition" (54).[3] Indeed, one of Beckett's most exiguous works for performance – *Quad* – provides a useful paradigm for questioning the agency of writing in the framing of dramatic place. Written for the Stuttgart Preparatory Ballet School (Brater 109), the text projects an essentially theatrical vision before the motionless camera eye, theatrical enough for director Alan Schneider to have asked Beckett's permission to experiment with the play for live performance (see Herren 127). The conceptual design of the play is straightforward:

each of four players enters in turn, and traces a geometrically precise path around what we learn is a square playing area. In the opening directions, Beckett depicts a square with each corner labeled, A, B, C, D; A–D and B–C are opposite corners. The first player enters at corner A: s/he ("Sex indifferent" 453) paces along one side of the square playing area toward corner C; at C, s/he turns left crossing the hypotenuse to the opposite corner B, turns left along the side of the square back to A, turns left crossing the hypotenuse to the opposite corner D, turns left along the side of the square B, turns left crossing the hypotenuse to the opposite corner C, turns left along the side of the square D, turns left crossing the hypotenuse to the opposite corner A, which completes the sequence. The player, then, has paced each side of the playing area once, and has crossed the hypotenuse from one corner to another four times, always revolving, like Dante's damned, to the left. Each player (1, 2, 3, 4) enters at a different corner (A, B, C, D) and follows the same pattern for the series, apparently entering for the subsequent series one corner to the left.

> 1 enters at A, completes his course and is joined by 3.
> Together they complete their courses and are joined by 4.
> Together all three complete their courses and are joined by 2.
> Together all four complete their courses. Exit 1. 2, 3 and 4 continue and complete their courses. Exit 3. 2 and 4 continue and complete their courses. Exit 4. End of 1st series. 2 continues, opening 2nd series, completes his course and is joined by 1. Etc. Unbroken movement.

1st series (as above):	1, 13, 134, 1342, 342, 42
2nd series:	2, 21, 214, 2143, 143, 43
3rd series:	3, 32, 321, 3214, 214, 14
4th series:	4, 43, 432, 4321, 321, 21

(451)

Each of the players paces to a distinctive percussion ("say drum, gong, triangle, woodblock" 452); while Beckett suggests that the percussionists may be "barely visible in shadow on raised platform at back of set" (452), productions have tended to keep the musicians out of the picture.

"What is there to keep me here?" Clov asks; "The dialogue" (*Endgame* 120–1). Identifying *Quad*'s genre has proven troubling; as Enoch Brater remarks, "there is no real script, only the *pretext* of one" (110).

In contrast to Beckett's other wordless plays, though, what seems to distinguish *Quad* is the texture of the writing, Beckett's decision not to adopt a novelistic, descriptive, narrative stance toward the action of the play ("The man is flung backwards on the stage from right wing. He falls, gets up immediately, dusts himself, turns aside, reflects" 203), but to *direct* the action, to use the conventional rhetoric of the *stage direction* as his principal textual means. In this regard, *Quad* extends one of the most innovative and troubling aspects of Beckett's framing of the work of drama. As the many controversies surrounding directors' departures from Beckett's stage directions imply, Beckett's writing claims to authorize the page of the play in distinctive ways, extending the claims of the "work of drama" from the dialogue to that other writing, hitherto understood as something else, a supporting texture with different, significantly weaker, claims to authority.[4] Conceptions of authority are conventionally – legally – enforced; the sense that Beckett's writing successfully incorporates a previously disregarded zone of the text into the contractual warrant of theatrical production gains some of its traction from the character of the directions themselves. The language of stage directions in modern drama is partly a function of the parallel expansion of the printed play as a readerly commodity and of the playwright as a writerly "author" in the late nineteenth century; Ibsen, Shaw, and others used stage directions to articulate dramatic setting to a reading audience, and to articulate it with the apparatus of the stage. And yet, while contextualizing the material framework of the action, the style of modern stage directions often stands apart from that of the dialogue. Ibsen's or Wilde's relatively flat description, Shaw's mildly ironic instruction of the reader's eye, or Stoppard's chatty commentaries maintain a stylistic as well as formal distinction from the play's dialogue.

In this sense, the propriety of the various legal challenges to unwarranted departures from "the text" in stage productions of Beckett's plays rests in part on Beckett's distinctive approach to writing stage directions and production notes. The parsing of place often anticipates, even intensifies, the arch, bitter bite of the dialogue:

> *The response to light is immediate.*
> *Faces impassive throughout. Voices toneless except where an expression is indicated.*
> *Rapid tempo throughout. (Play 307)*

While it has become conventional to take *Quad* as "really more a set of assembly instructions than a play proper" (Herren 124), or to note Beckett's characteristic attention to the medium of performance ("they were written specifically for television and are not stage plays" Kalb 95), Beckett's writing here extends one of the defining impulses of his dramaturgy from *Play* onward: to write the space of drama. Although *Quad* is a play without dialogue, it's hardly unwritten, no mere pretext. The language is embellished with Beckett's typically laconic ornament, and performs a rigorously Aristotelian purpose here, articulating the play's precisely drawn plot. More to the point, as an *agency* of the playing, writing suggests the construction of dramatic space by its performers: as each actor takes the stage, place is shaped, known, identified with how it is occupied. Each player enters to distinctive percussion (and, if possible, footfall, as "Each player has his particular sound" 452). The illuminated area is given its dimensions and shape by the trajectories of the players' journeys. The players are shrouded, faces concealed, "As alike in build as possible. Short and slight for preference"; "Some ballet training desirable," presumably to make their pacing (six per side) and deviation step as precise and identical as possible (453). The path demarcates the square, and as they bisect the hypotenuse, each swerves slightly but precisely to his/her right, opening another space, a gap at the center, point "E supposed a danger zone. Hence deviation. Manoeuvre established at outset by first solo at first diagonal (CB)" (453).

Dramatic writing, though never brought into the play as "speech," nonetheless claims a place in the spectacle. Beckett's plays often circumscribe the actors' means (jugging them in *Play*, reducing an actress to a mere Mouth), withdrawing the movement, gesture, and vocal emphases that might color the performance in the tones of the actor's personal style, charisma (recall Beckett's notorious remark to Deirdre Bair that the best play would have "no actors, only the text" 513). And yet, the rhythms of the writing – ".... out ... into this world ... this world ... tiny little thing ..." (*Not I* 376) – provide the instrument for embodiment. In *Quad*, Beckett's rhythmic, exhaustive, rather mechanical recitation of the patterns of movement, often in short phrases linked by sequence rather than syntax ("Raised frontal. Fixed. Both players and percussionists in frame" 453), lends a sense of urgency, dispensing with the stray gestures of unnecessary pronouns, articles, verbs: "All possible combinations given" (452). The language of *Quad* is, like all dramatic language, the language of *agency*: it provides a means for doing, and a specific texture of doing that will be granulated by the acts of performance.

The text of the play diagrams the "Area: square" of the play (451), but the place of the play is created by its performance, ordering the course of each actor's journey, and the sequence with which the actors enter and depart. The sequence is arithmetical, so that in the desired twenty-five minutes (453) – which turned out to be considerably shorter when Beckett came to direct the play (Brater 109) – all combinations of individual and group journeys are staged:

> Four possible solos all given.
> Six possible duos all given (two twice).
> Four possible trios all given twice.
> (451–2)

The event is rhythmic, each of its four sections beginning with a single journey, swelling to four simultaneous performances, and then receding to a single actor. In the systole and diastole of the performance, the actors, concealed in gowns, are not explicitly forbidden other movement or gesture, but the rigor of the design and its rigorous expression in Beckett's writing seem to exclude actions other than those explicitly stated.

Quad allegorizes the agency of dramatic writing as it engages the material space of the stage. As in many of his plays, Beckett's demarcation of space here is distinctive and relies principally on lighting. The playing area is initially defined as an illuminated zone shading off into blackness, the light "Dim on area from above fading out into dark" (452). The text projects space as limitless and unknown; until the players enter to give it scale, the zone of illumination is demarcated but without dimension. The writing projects place that is – unlike, say, the places of Brecht's theatre – ambiguously located in the apparatus (theatre or video) of its visibility, crepuscular, fading into darkness. Instigating theatrical space; occupying – *taking* – place; rendering it significant through a precisely calibrated sequence of events; instrumentalizing fictive "characters" at the interface of writing, body, movement, physicality; articulating space in time, with a beginning, middle, and end: *Quad* directs light, sound, and embodied movement, carving a signifying place out of nothing, nowhere, darkness. It shapes it literally (a square six by six paces), but also figures it as place *for*, place with a purpose, an *orchestra*, the dancing place of the classical *theatron*, seeing place, a place where the dialectic between the one and the many is at once the presiding subject of dramaturgy and a question animating the civic arena of the theatre.[5] The space is occupied and rendered significant through the means of the drama: explored in geometrical patterns governed by arithmetical sequence, space is mapped as points, lines, vectors, angles, a Euclidean space that represents the imposition of order, illumination, clarity stepping out from the unformed darkness. The space assumes these features, conforms to the mapping of its potentiality for the period of time that the actors perform. Once Player 1 departs (though it is not entirely clear from the text that he does depart – "Without interruption begin repeat and fade out on 1 pacing alone" 452), the space resumes its unformed undimensionality.

Quad rigorously subjects its space to the authority of writing, or seems to: writing directs how the space will be created, used, rendered meaningful, and abandoned. At the same time, as Beckett's own production makes clear, any production will *use* this writing to construct a specific place, a precise, focused, minimal moment of drama, the moment that erupts just as the shrouded figures appear about to meet one another, and take their step of deviation to the side. This moment of attention, climax emerges in performance but is signaled by the slightly heightened rhythm of the text as well: "Negotiation of E without rupture of rhythm when three or four players cross paths at this point. Or, if ruptures accepted, how best exploit?" (453). *Quad* establishes a movement plot: side, cross, side, cross, side, cross, side, cross to home, exit. The moment of drama is the moment of deviation from this emplotment, a moment that's noticeable with one player in motion, but that rises gradually to crisis when the four actors careen toward one another, and then precisely step to the right. Putting the playing into place, *Quad* suggests, realizes the rigorous execution of the necessary and probable consequences inherent in the drama. The consequences are – in *Quad*, as in any play – visible in the script, but their texture as event depends on the play's execution (no staggering, no stumbling), an act that becomes more arresting, perhaps even more necessary the more precisely it is performed.

"E supposed a danger zone. Hence deviation" (453): the climactic event of the play is sustained by its richest, most suggestive, minimally poetic phrase. To conceive this moment as "deviation" is to allude to a perfect geometry, a Platonic *Quad* that could not be realized in three dimensions, and so would not be *Quad* at all.[6] The deviation is a *deviation* because it deforms the perfect trajectories of the players, the pure arithmetic of movement, confirming their physicality as performers, who cannot pass simultaneously through the same point, occupy the same space at once. The writing directs the occupation of space, but it also directs the evacuation of space, a space that is avoided, unfilled, a small "hole" in the center of the play's endlessly repeating history. The point, that central node of avoidance, is never occupied, and remains unknown and unknowable; though square in shape in Beckett's diagram, even its precise frontiers emerge and vanish with the players' footsteps around it (453). Its center, point E, is "supposed a danger zone. Hence deviation," but the terms of the danger are unstated. Although the actors cannot occupy the space simultaneously, Beckett's word "deviation" suggests avoidance, perhaps recalling Mouth's "vehement" deviation from the first person in *Not I* (375). As an agency of the performance, writing creates place and evinces the design of its embodiment, a design that subjects its human occupants to a single space/time order of representation. At the same time, however, the performance also implies a fictive elsewhere mapped onto the concrete parameters of the stage. It's tempting, given Beckett's predilections, to see this central space created by writing but untouched by its performance as the space from which writing emanates, a space writing can create as part of the theatrical event, a space writing can locate but performance can never quite inhabit. Writing enables the occupation and even representation of the space of the stage, while at the same time also creating – here at the symbolic center of representation – a hole, an absence in the mapping at hand.

As a text, then, *Quad* undertakes a suggestive exploration of the agency of dramatic writing in constructing the space of the stage. At the same time, *Quad* is a somewhat eccentric example of dramatic writing, particularly in its relation to performance. Beginning in the mid-1960s, Beckett began to direct his own plays and teleplays, giving rise not only to an extraordinarily rich body of performance, but also bringing the question of the agency of writing in the performance into focus in a different way. How are we to treat Beckett's directorial revisions to the play at hand? As final revisions in the standing dramatic work? As emendations necessitated by the circumstances of a specific production, and confined in their purpose to that production? As one instance, or as the definitive instance, of the materializing of the *agency* of writing in the *scene* of performance?

Quad suggestively models the ways notions of authority mediate our access to and understanding of dramatic writing and its implication of dramatic space. Beckett directed *Quad* with his collaborator Walter Asmus in 1981; produced by Süddeutscher Rundfunk as *Quadrat I + II*, this version was broadcast on BBC 2 on 16 December 1982 (Ackerley and Gontarski 472). The production was at once challenging and instructive: the script's suggestion that the players' coloring be determined by lighting was ineffective, and they were clothed in colored gowns, and the alacrity of the pacing produced a performance significantly shorter than the estimated twenty-five minutes. Moreover, when the German technicians checked the film on a black-and-white monitor, Beckett was entranced, conceiving and producing a second version, "100,000 years later"; *Quadrat II* stages the first series only, much more slowly, the actors gowned in white, to the scraping sound of their sandals on the floor (see Brater 109). In *The Complete Dramatic Works*, this version of *Quad* is traced only in a series of notes:

1. This original scenario (*Quad I*) was followed in the Stuttgart production by a variation (*Quad II*). (5)
2. [*Light*] Abandoned as impracticable. Constant neutral light throughout.
3. [*Time*] Overestimated. *Quad I*, fast tempo. 15' approx. *Quad II*, slow tempo, series 1 only, 5' approx.
4. [*Problem*] E supposed a danger zone. Hence deviation. Manoeuvre established at outset by first solo at first diagonal (CB). [...]
5. [*Quad II*] No colour, all four in identical white gowns, no percussion, footsteps only sound, slow tempo, series 1 only. (453–4)

Beckett's direction produced revision, elaboration, cuts, and – in the case of *Quad II* – a performance that adapts the design of an existing script, leaving only the trace of another script, a lost quarto. Ackerley and Gontarski suggest that Beckett's "video-taped German production constitutes the only 'final' and accurate text" (472), and there's considerable sentiment along these lines, that the play is merely a kind of "pretext" rather than a "play proper." And yet, in an important sense, even in *Quadrat I*, Beckett seems less to "follow" the text than to map its potential agency in the physical space of play, executing the writing in specific ways – ways that need not be taken as final.

Quadrat I, for instance, delineates the "Area: square" visibly and distinctly: rather than understanding the paths of the players to describe a square, we see a sand-colored box painted on a darker background. Beckett's production projects the square as a preexisting place, one that captivates the players in their leftward orbits, rather than being a place shaped by their engagement with it. Similarly, though the text doesn't specify that the central point of the square be visible ("E supposed a danger zone"), in *Quadrat I* we see a dark central point, a hole, a *thymelê* perhaps, around which the players circle in deviation. Are these ways of instrumentalizing the play now essential to the play? Although Beckett eventually cooperated with the efforts of the editors of *The Theatrical Notebooks of Samuel Beckett* to print revised texts of the plays, he was finally undecided whether some of his directorial changes – cutting the Auditor from productions of *Not I* is the most dramatic example – should be retroactively inscribed in a refitted text. *Quad* was not included in the *Notebooks* series.

Beckett's wordless play presents a concise critique of the drama's writing of space, its ability to transform the nowhere of the stage into a specific location. More to the point, *Quad* allegorizes the sense in which this space arises in momentary and relational ways. Regardless of whether the stage is set with Roebuck Ramsden's Fabian study or Stanley Kowalski's ramshackle apartment, the significance of the space emerges through its playing: an empty set is just a set, gaining its performative force only as it is used. Like the absent square of Beckett's *Quad*, and even like the visible square of *Quadrat I*, the place of play can be pointed by the drama, but gains its significance as place, a place that emerges, is played, and then left behind, in the process of the playing itself.

ii. By Accepting This License

The problem of writing space stands at the center of one of the most remarkable controversies animating the theatre, a controversy that arises directly from the drama's dual identity between poetry and performance. The New Critics of the 1940s and 1950s located the fundamentally literary character – the poetry – of drama in the dialogue: the dialogue keeps Hamm and Clov on the stage, and locates work of dramatic writing in performance, as *"characters*, who make *speeches"*

(Ransom, *New* 169). But Beckett's texts – like those of Ibsen, Shaw, Stoppard, and others – clearly extend an authorial voice, presence, and propriety beyond the dialogue, into that zone of the text once considered merely instrumental to the play's staging, but peripheral to its claims as drama: the stage directions. The stage directions materialize the dual status of dramatic writing in the modern era. Since the rise of the director in the late nineteenth century, it has been conventional to see the dialogue as the playwright's property, but instrumentalizing the play in the three dimensions of the stage as the director's job. Insofar as "the text" is understood as *agency*, one element of the mutual construction of the *scene* of drama in the *scene* of theatre, it seems plausible to ask whether its potential *agency* might be represented differentially, different aspects of the poetry articulating with the work of performance in different ways.

One of the most celebrated playwrights of the twentieth century, initially controversial for his scrupulous inscrutability, became more controversial when his inscrutable plans were not followed scrupulously enough. The Beckett controversies of the 1980s and beyond bring this question into focus, in that they typically turn on the materialization of the spatial element of Beckett's writing. Several productions have, in fact, become both theatrical and legal landmarks in this regard: JoAnne Akalaitis's staging of *Endgame* at the American Repertory Theatre in 1984, in which Beckett's legal agents threatened to close the show for staging the "*Bare interior*" of the play in a derelict stretch of subway tunnel (they were satisfied when the show was characterized as an adaptation of the play in the program); Gildas Bourget's pink *Fin de partie* at the Comédie Française in 1988; an all-female *Waiting for Godot* by De Haarlemse Toneelschuur also in 1988; Deborah Warner and Fiona Shaw's *Footfalls* in 1994, which clothed May in a red wrap, illuminated her more brightly, and placed her pacing in two locations in the theatre, on the stage and on a platform above and behind the stalls; and a 2006 production in Pontedera, Italy, in which the casting of twin sisters to play Didi and Gogo was challenged by the Beckett estate, but upheld by the courts.[7] These productions and the controversies they generated foreground the *agential* character of dramatic writing in the theatre, the use of writing as part of the making of an event, an event that necessarily exceeds determination by writing, even in the case of such apparently overdetermined writing as Beckett's. After all, in these productions, the dialogue was relatively unchanged:

what was altered was either an element of physical embodiment (Beckett noted that "women don't have prostates," but the gender of characters in *Godot* is not otherwise specified; Ackerley and Gontarski 89), or a departure from Beckett's scenographic conception of the play, the text's inscription of theatrical space.

Although generally regarded as a contest of authorities – the author vs. the director – this controversy points more directly to the labile character of writing in the theatre: plays written to map a specific kind of stage space – the Athenian civic amphitheatre, the early modern platform stage – will necessarily map new or different spaces in different ways. The Athenian theatre materializes a sense of political democracy as contest, not only between the various *protagonists* playing in the *orchestra*, but also between the tribes, sponsoring competitive dithyrambic choruses, seated alongside but distinguished from one another, framed within the densely religious, ritual, civic, imperial event of the festival of Dionysus. To perform *The Bakkhai* in a modern proscenium theatre, where seating is a matter of price, not affiliation, the invisible audience of atomized consumers facing forward into the box, is necessarily to use the play to configure a different space as the place of dramatic action, memorably captured in Oliver Taplin's phrase, "round plays in square theatres" (172). The history of Shakespeare performance since the late nineteenth century is partly the history of efforts – from William Poel to the new Globe – to restore something akin to Shakespearean production practices to performance. And yet, even in the new Globe, the space of the drama's emplacement is altered, if not in size, shape, technology, and exposure to the elements, then in the cultural signification of the space that emerges in contemporary performance. For all its likeness to the new Globe on Bankside, Shakespeare's theatre was located very differently in relation to a potential tourist economy or long-range plans for urban development, and could not have been understood as part of an entertainment continuum that also takes in living history museums, theme parks, film, and television. Nor did it stage "classic" drama, plays whose identity as writing, as texts, had an independent, influential existence beyond their performance in the theatre.

The Beckett controversies are conceived around the interlocking, and somewhat misleading, questions of property and propriety: has the production mounted a "defensible scenic interpretation" of "the text," respecting both "the meaning of the dialogue" and the implied configuration of theatrical space (Gussow), or has Beckett's property been

damaged by its use onstage? Much as these controversies attend to
the management of space, they also witness the challenging double
agency of dramatic writing, its character as poetry in constructing
the double *scene* of performance, a dramatic place mapped onto the
landscape of an existing theatrical space. Beckett's writing cannot
govern this mapping; no writing can. And it's a mark of the situation
that the contracts to stage Beckett's plays through Samuel French typically contain a rider, writing meant to constrain the implementation
of dramatic writing already said fully to constrain its proper use in
the theatre:

> There shall be no additions, omissions, changes in the sex of the charac-
> ters as specified in the text, or alterations of any kind or nature in
> the manuscript or presentation of the Play as indicated in the acting
> edition supplied hereunder; without limiting the foregoing; all stage
> directions indicated therein shall be followed without any such addi-
> tions, omissions, or alterations. No music, special effects, or other sup-
> plements shall be added to the presentation of the Play without prior
> written consent. By accepting this license and rider, the licensee agrees
> that non-compliance with the terms will cause the Owners immediate
> irreparable damage for the which there is no adequate remedy at law
> and will entitle them, among other remedies, to immediate injunctive
> relief. (Performance License Rider)[8]

Though Beckett's plays appear to resolve these ambiguities, the need
for the rider suggests otherwise. On the one hand, in specifying place,
any performance will necessarily materialize the writing in specific
ways. How might the *"Bare interior"* of *Endgame* be identified with the
material theatrical *scene* of a small storefront theatre? With the theatrical *scene* of the Olivier Theatre? How will *Godot*'s *"country road"* be
imaged? In most productions, including those directed by Beckett, the
road is merely assumed, the stage itself. In *Quadrat I + II*, Beckett
depicts a square playing area, though whether a box is to be outlined on
the stage floor is perhaps ambiguous; the lighting, "Dim on area from
above fading out into dark" (452), perhaps implies an "area" marked by
the pacing alone. It might be recalled that the "circular, about 5 m.
diameter" set of ... *but the clouds* ..., "surrounded by deep shadow," is
created entirely by illumination (418), nor is the *"Strip: downstage, parallel with front, length nine steps"* of *Footfalls* actually marked by a line on
the floor, despite the diagram in the stage directions (399).

Quad argues that the space of the stage is rendered dramatic by how it is seized, occupied: writing provides an instrument for that activity, a means of taking and making place, but insofar as the theatre changes, the space that plays render dramatic changes, too. The rigorous frontality of Beckett's writing for the camera merely extends the frontality of his writing for the stage: Beckett's visual imagination charts the landscape of a proscenium theatre, a darkened audience looking furtively into a space of fitful illumination. And yet, while we continue to use proscenium theatres, as an instrument of the social technology of the theatre, even the proscenium stage gains new uses, the capability of figuring the *scene* of performance in unanticipated ways. Having become the dominant structure of Western theatre space by the nineteenth century, the proscenium theatre is now one of many technologies for emplacing performance; most university and civic performance complexes feature some combination of proscenium, thrust, and/or flexible-seating venues. More to the point, the boundary between the *scenes* of live and mediated performance is increasingly fluid. The contemporary theatre, proscenium or not, tends to be animated by a dynamic desire to amplify the human figure onstage, surround him or her with sound, oppose him or her with video.

Henri Lefebvre suggests that "(social) space is a (social) product," and while some space may seem – illusorily – to be given, the space of theatre is *representational space*, space that at once represents an ideology of space, and uses it to represent space itself (Lefebvre 27, 33).[9] The space of contemporary performance, at least in the Western metropolis, is one where the live and the mediated have been in dynamic interaction throughout the period of Beckett's writing career. The desire to reshape the scripted space of Beckett's plays, and the increasingly commonplace practice of staging Beckett's plays for radio and television as theatre, enforce an important recognition: the familiar spatial potentiality even of proscenium theatricality is, like all space, constantly under pressure, a tool capable of accomplishing different kinds of work as it is deployed through the changing social technologies – including those of writing, acting, directing, and design – of its use. Several recent productions of Beckett's work witness the ways in which a changing sense of the space of the stage asserts changing *agencies* of dramatic writing, not least because they might well have been refused a license not long ago. JoAnne Akalaitis's *Act Without Words I & II*, *Rough for Theater I*, and *Eh Joe* at the Theatre Workshop (December

2007) deployed Beckett's writing on a frontally oriented, digitally enhanced stage. *Act Without Words I* used video to amplify and distort the various objects tantalizing the anguished protagonist. *Eh Joe*, originally written for television, flanked Joe (Mikhail Baryshnikov) with large projection, magnifying his responses to the woman's voice he hears; rather than hearing a disembodied voice, in this production Joe faced his tormentor, a living actress onstage. Atom Egoyan's staging of *Eh Joe* for the Gate Theatre, which starred Michael Gambon in Dublin, and Liam Neeson in New York (July 2008), followed the scripted television protocol of staging the woman's voice only as voiceover, but similarly doubled the silent actor onstage with a large screen, registering his every minute response to the offstage voice.[10] And despite it's apparently prescriptive textuality, *Quad* has proven an extraordinarily rich inspiration for the stage, especially for choreograpers (see Protopapa, Carboni, and Katsura Kan).

From the moribund Krapp soliciting the palpable, lost vitality of his own extinguished past, the voice from "Box ... three ... spool ... five" (216), Beckett's writing has explored the interface between writing and the different media of dramatic performance; remediating television or radio for the stage, such productions at once rewrite the text in an alternate spatiality and subject the spatiality of the stage to new opportunities as well. Indeed, bringing Beckett's nontheatrical drama to the theatre elucidates the problems of writing space in a wider, and more consequential sense. We might, for instance, take David Wiles's comments on the space of classical Athenian drama as propositional: "The texts presuppose performance in a space that was not neutral or 'empty' but semantically laden. The theatrical space was not a mere context for the play; rather the play lent meaning to the space" (*Tragedy* 62). Dramatic writing presupposes space, imaging its fictive landscape on the groundplan of its contemporary theatre and the social environment it encapsulates and intensifies. Hamlet stands on a "sterile promontory" literalized by the Globe's thrust stage, its "goodly frame" absorbed into the play's presiding metaphor. And yet, thanks to writing and the social technologies of its use – papyri and pedagogy for much of Greek drama; the York Register; print, literacy, libraries, and "literature" – plays have long survived to inhabit unanticipated theatrical technologies, technologies they simultaneously shape and are shaped by. The National Theatre of Scotland's 2007 *Bacchae*, performed in English, on tour, and featuring Alan Cumming's rock-star Dionysus and a back-up bevy of black Bacchantes, shares, it might be fair to say, nothing of the social or aesthetic technologies of performance in the Athenian civic amphitheatre. In the theatre, architectural and scenic design – the construction of a permanent amphitheatre; moveable scenery; the proscenium; "modern dress"; live-feed video – is not the changing *scene* of an unchanging drama, fixed by "the text," but engages and defines the *agency* of drama, the kinds of work dramatic writing, one of the tools of performance, might seem to afford as performance.

Quad provides a dramatic allegory of a model of theatrical spatiality associated with Beckett, and even more so with Peter Brook: the empty space. When Brook declared in 1968, "I can take any empty space and call it a bare stage" (8), his manifesto laid claim to an essential theatricality, a space, like the unformed space of *Quad*, barely identifiable *as* theatre before its occupation and signification in play. Yet as the argument of *The Empty Space* makes clear, this space is never empty; it's defined both by what Brook urges us to cleanse away – all the boring, stultifying detritus of "deadly theatre" – and by the emerging practices, the social technologies that Brook summons to reanimate it: "rough theatre," "holy theatre," "immediate theatre." Brook's gesture is cognate with Beckett's, and cognate with many rather different gestures of new performance in the 1960s and 1970s: with the importation of Artaud's merciless assault on a theatre of "texts and *written* poetry" (78), with Grotowski's search for a "poor theatre" reduced to its essences, with participatory theatre's desire to undo the licensed boundaries between spectators and performers, with the environmental theatre's spatial redefinition of the theatrical box itself. While much of this revolution – the Performance Group's *Dionysus in 69*, for example – involved multiplying perspectives on and access to the performance, Beckett characteristically empties a proscenium-like space and restricts our perspective on it, approximating the audience to the camera's single, unblinking eye.

iii. What Where: Brechtian Technologies

The recent history of Beckett radio and television plays in the theatre, then, indexes the pressure of dramatic writing on the signifying capacity of theatrical space. Writing may help to shape new technologies of performance, to lend them specificity and meaning, but these technologies will continue to be forged by their use, and forge new uses for dramatic writing as well. As George Tabori's 2006 production of *Waiting for Godot* at the Berliner Ensemble perhaps suggests – the actors backchat with the prompter and the audience; the tree falls over; the actors playing Pozzo and Lucky get fed up and leave through the auditorium – the surprising emptiness of *Waiting for Godot* in the 1950s is no longer recoverable to us, any more than the bustle of Shakespeare's Globe or the civic/religious power of the chorus dancing in the Athenian orchestra. Beckett may have emptied the stage, but no one knew better than Bertolt Brecht that there is no empty space, that the theatre is always social space, framed within a given culture, projected as a spatial materialization of specific, often unstated, typically coercive meanings.

> Today we see the theatre apparatus's being given absolute priority over the actual plays. The theatre apparatus's priority is a priority of means of production. This apparatus resists all conversion to other purposes, by taking any play which it encounters and immediately changing it so that it no longer represents a foreign body within the apparatus – except at those points where it neutralizes itself. The necessity to stage the new drama correctly – which matters more for the theatre's sake than for the drama's – is modified by the fact that the theatre can stage anything: it theatres it all down. (*Brecht on Theatre* 43)

Here, in his notes to *Threepenny Opera*, Brecht complains that the theatre "apparatus" – the entire ensemble of artistic, mechanical, economic, cultural, and social practices producing the kinds of event we call "theatre" – is a deeply homogenizing one, absorbing the potentially innovative instruments of new dramatic writing and innovative production work and *theatring it all down*. It might be said that the theatre has, today, succeeded in theatring down Brecht, neutralizing the instruments with which Brecht sought to disrupt "theatre," transforming epic theatricality into mere decoration, one "aesthetic" or "look" among many, a stylistic commodity that rarely changes the work or function of dramatic performance. But underlying Brecht's complaint about the commodification of theatre is a deeper recognition. In the technology of theatre, the book and the play, character and actor, fictive place and theatrical space, poetry and performance dialectically define and reciprocally reshape one another.

Calling for a "radical *separation of the elements*" of theatrical production (37), Brecht summoned a technology of theatrical performance that
would at once reveal the mode of (theatrical) production and so potentially dramatize the implication of theatre – the images it constructs
and our consumption of them – in the reproduction of social reality. In
this sense, Brecht's dialectic works to restore essential elements of dramatic performance, a sense of theatre artificially obscured by the
hegemony of the dominant bourgeois entertainment theatre of his era,
and our own. Brecht asserts the independence of the various productive functions of performance. Writing need not be consumed and
erased from the stage, for "texts" can be displayed onstage to move the
narrative forward. Since acting is both being and showing, performing
"in character" is only one means of putting written dialogue into action.
Acting isn't one activity, but many, and when an actor changes modes
of performance – bursting into song, for instance – his/her means of
using the play to engage the audience changes as well. The relation
between actors and audience is always changing according to the ways
the text might be used. The stage need not be homogeneous, as actors
will use some instruments (Mother Courage's wagon) in different ways
than others. Film is not merely an innovative counterpoint to theatre,
but an "integral part of the settings" of modern theatricality. The spectator, "smoking-and-watching" (44), is always both inside and outside
the performance.

Many of the crucial innovations in modern dramatic performance
have arisen from efforts to restore "original" practices, or a modern
imagination of them, against the overwhelming dominion of the scenic
realism of the nineteenth-century stage: discovering the vitality of the
orchestra as a *dancing-place*, the cinematic flexibility of the Shakespearean
empty platform, and so on. But Brecht's work is critical in another
regard, asserting the theatre not as the site for the representation of a
fictive narrative, the recitation of *"characters*, who make *speeches"*
(Ransom, *New* 169), but a *scene* of action defined not in relation to the
text but as part of the larger world surrounding the stage. In this sense,
the various *agencies* of performance – acting, design, space – are not
subordinated to dramatic narrative, as though the act of theatre were
identified with the *purpose* of representing the dramatic fiction for
our consumption. Instead, insofar as Brecht claims a theatre not of
consumption but of production – changing the spectator's relation to
the event, making him/her an *agent* in the proper function of the *scene*

of theatre – he lends the various instruments of the stage different *purpose*, different *agency*. Rather than "serving the text," the arts of theatre and of the text are instruments for creating a specific event. While for Brecht that event is the alienation of the spectator from an unrecognized identification with the oppressive machinery of social life, what Brecht's sense of theatre brings to the foreground is this interplay between poetry and the agencies of performance in rendering the space of play.

Brecht's investment in the work of writing in the theatre is reciprocal with his overt concern for the deployment of space in performance. Whether it's Courage's wagon, pulled on a turntable on an otherwise bare stage, the Control Chorus of *The Measures Taken*, Azdak's bench, the exposed lighting, narrative placards, or illustrative films, Brecht's theatre resists the assimilation of theatrical space to a single perspective. As might be said of Shakespeare's use of *locus* and *platea*, Brecht maintains the visibility of the theatrical *scene*, keeps theatre a visible instrument of the play's work. Resisting a sense of the stage as totalized space, Brecht's writing also refuses to be organically digested into conventional performance. While Beckett's writing urges the rhetorical absorption of the stage directions into the authorial, authorized discourse of the "poetry," Brecht systematically locates and differentiates distinctive forms of textuality as having distinctive kinds of use: stage directions, narrative information for the placards, dialogue, chorus, song. In *Quad*, the actors create the fictive space through their means of inhabiting the dim square mapped by their movements. Much like Eliot or Yeats, who assigned different modes of performance to different forms of dramatic writing, Brecht's decomposing of the text enables, perhaps enforces, the use of writing in different registers, as not one instrument but several instruments for engaging different activities onstage, different slices of performance.

This is perhaps the lesson of a striking moment in *Life of Galileo*. After Galileo's recantation, Brecht's play calls for a surprising engagement with writing in its most *archival* dimension, a *"reading before the curtain"* (48) of Galileo's famous recognition in *The Discorsi*: "The common assumption that a large and small machine are equally durable is apparently erroneous" (49). Here, the play questions the confidence that any *archive* can provide unmediated access to "history," setting "the text" against Brecht's masterful use of performance to shape a moment of historical fantasia, a scene that spurs its audiences to desire something – a performance commodity, Galileo heroic in torture – that can, unhappily enough, never really satisfy us. How is this text performed, materialized in our performance with the play? Many productions project this text on the curtain, modern technology providing the illusion that writing projects the past into the present unchanged, unmediated by the *repertoire* of its transmission. And yet one lesson of *Life of Galileo* is that writing, and the books or screens that contain it, is material; hidden in a globe, traded for a goose, secretly transported out of Italy, *The Discorsi* undergoes several performances in the play, returning from the dramatic "past" to the "present" of theatrical performance as light itself. The alienating climax of Brecht's greatest play insists on the value of writing, but insists as well that writing alone cannot determine our relation to history, to the temporal and spatial meanings of the social world we perform in and out of the theatre.

Brecht was an inveterate reviser, rewriting his own and others' plays to sharpen their use in the *scene* at hand. Staging the text of *The Discorsi*, Brecht locates a crucial recognition. Poetry is deployed as one instrument in the making of dramatic performance. While it has a specific shape, it gains its power, its significance as action through the means of its use. Projecting the text as light, *The Discorsi* performs its implication in the "advancement of science"; writing with radiation, the play stages a dialogue between Galileo's ethics and those behind the physics of nuclear holocaust (see *Brecht on Theatre* 158). *Antigone, Hamlet, Life of Galileo, Quad* all belong, now, to the *archive*, but the sense that writing can govern the theatre, that writing unchanged by its means of embodiment and ways of inhabiting space, is nowhere more brilliantly challenged than here. Beckett may have longed for a theatre of pure textuality, but as Brecht suggests dramatic performance necessarily confronts the materiality of writing with the matter of the stage. The technology that transforms writing into an instrument of performance, the *repertoire* of theatre, defines the affordance of its tools, taking the poetry and shaping how it speaks to us, what it can say and do as performance.

Notes

Preface: Drama, Poetry, and Performance

1 Unless otherwise noted, references to Shakespeare are to *The Norton Shakespeare*.
2 Aristotle, *Poetics*, trans. M. E. Hubbard 53. See also Gerald F. Else's translation, "with all the persons who are performing the imitation acting, that is carrying on for themselves" 18.
3 A list of general studies discussed in *Drama: Between Poetry and Performance* that might be of interest for further reading can be found on page 259.

Introduction: Between Poetry and Performance

1 See Stern.
2 See Erne, *Shakespeare*. For a wider discussion of the impact of a print-centered understanding of Shakespearean authorship on the modern sense of drama, see Worthen, *Force* chapter 1.
3 On the economics of play publication, see Blayney, "Publication," the subsequent challenge by Farmer and Lesser, and Blayney's response, "Alleged Popularity."
4 Laertes' leap is noted in all three early texts: he *Leaps in the grave* in Q2 and F versions, while *Laertes leaps into the grave* in the Q1 text. See all three versions of *Hamlet*, ed. Thompson and Taylor; all references to *Hamlet* are to these editions.
5 See Thomas Keneally's novel *The Playmaker*, and Timberlake Wertenbaker's dramatic version, *Our Country's Good*, as well as Louis Nowra's play, *The Golden Age*.
6 We can see the persistence of Lamb's views in Harold Bloom's sense that "In the theater, much of the interpreting is done for you, and you are victimized by the politic fashions of the moment" (Harold Bloom 720). See

also Harry Berger's lively understanding of how "imaginary audition" attempts to preserve the dialogical character of dramatic writing while not limiting the reader to the material meanings of the stage. Michael Bristol's revealing phrase for the theatre is "derivative creativity" (61).

7   As Jerome McGann argues, the "critical possibilities of digital environments require that we revisit what we know, or what we think we know, about the formal and material properties of the codex," the book, to which we might add, of texts and textuality, and the relation between texts and other means for the representation of writing, such as the stage (19).

8   In 2003, at a symposium sponsored by the University of Western Sydney to commemorate the fiftieth anniversary of *Waiting for Godot*, Edward Beckett walked out on a production of *Godot* that used a background score as accompaniment to the play. The addition of music as a point of protest is long-standing; JoAnne Akalaitis had used a Philip Glass score in the 1984 *Endgame* at the American Repertory Theatre, and had also drawn protests from Beckett's legal agents. Matthew Rimmer reports, however, that while the Australian government had recently passed a law protecting the right "to object to derogatory treatment of a work that is prejudicial to the honour and reputation of the author," it was unlikely that the Sydney production – directed by Neil Armfield and performed by Company B – would be actionable, in that the "acclaimed production could be seen to enhance the reputation of the playwright." See also Marks.

9   See Elizabeth Dyrud Lyman's fine discussion of the contradictory impulses in the scores of contemporary composers; she persuasively notes "No artists this century have been as daring in interrogating and expanding their own notational forms as have composers" (224).

10   I've adapted this example from Weaver (11). Perhaps a numerical example would be clearer for some readers. If one message is considerably more probable than the other, its information value is relatively low. In the series 2–4–6–8–___, the probability that 10 follows so exceeds the probability of not-10 that there's relatively little information implied when 10 appears next (though if 11 were to appear, a new binary would arise: is the 11 surprising "information" or the result of static or interference in the system?). If there is only one message to choose from, there is no information to communicate: adding 1 to the series 1–1–1–1–___ conveys little information.

11   Norbert Wiener – the inventor of cybernetics, control-via-feedback – argues that the "transmission of information is impossible save as a transmission of alternatives. If only one contingency is to be transmitted, then it may be sent most efficiently and with the least trouble by sending no message at all. The telegraph and the telephone can perform their function only if the messages they transmit are continually varied in a manner not

completely determined by their past, and can be designed effectively only if the variation of these messages conforms to some sort of statistical regularity" (*Cybernetics* 10). See also John R. Pierce's rather different discussion of entropy (21–4). Pierce also notes that the decision to represent the most frequently used letter in the English language – E – with the simplest signal in Morse code – a single dot – was made not by counting the actual frequency of letters used, but "by counting the number of types in the various compartments of a printer's type box" (25).

12   The New Bibliography of W. W. Greg, A. W. Pollard, Fredson Bowers, and others, in its effort to lift the "veil of print" from the underlying, integral "work" of the author, in this sense regards print as at once guaranteeing the identical transmission of the work, and as inserting distortion into the signal, degrading the authorial work as it passes into materiality itself. The phrase "veil of print" is from Bowers (87); see also Greg. The critique of the New Bibliography is now relatively familiar, but an excellent summary can be found in Maguire. The Hinman collator, a device superimposing reflected images of the same page of different versions of a text in order to locate where words have been changed, is the perfected image of print culture: a difference engine designed to purify the code.

13   The clearest, and perhaps most controversial, statement of this position is de Grazia and Stallybrass, "Materiality." See also Gary Taylor, "Renaissance," and "c:wp\file.txt 04:41 10–07–8," and McGann. On the "polynomial" aspect of Shakespeare's plays, the fact that the same "character" is often represented in the text by different speech prefixes, see McLeod.

14   J. L. Styan's effort to bring about a colloquy between critical and directorial practice might also be seen in these terms; see also Worthen, *Authority* chapter 3.

15   Predictably enough, a critical backlash against the supposed domination of "theatrical" Shakespeare in the contemporary classroom has set in as well, in which the "imaginative labor of turning words on the page of the Shakespeare text into the discourse of criticism" is set against a supposedly naive and enervating appeal to "the authority of performance" (McLuskie 249).

16   See Norman's discussion of *affordance, constraint, mapping* (12–13).

17   For a brief, engaging critique of theatre semiotics, see Sauter 23–31. See also Fischer-Lichte, *Semiotics*.

18   See Geertz; Greenblatt; Whigham; Lentricchia. Burke is mentioned in passing by Shannon Jackson (12); Jon McKenzie lists "Kenneth Burke's 'dramatistic pentad'" among paradigms of performance derived from social sciences (Victor Turner, Erving Goffman, Milton Singer, John J. MacAloon) in the 1950s (*Perform* 33–4, 86); Marvin Carlson has a slightly fuller discussion, linking Burke to folklore studies (17), and summarizing

"dramatism" (36–7). Yet Burke's way of conceiving Shakespeare, as Scott L. Newstok suggests, "looks a lot like what scholars of recent decades do when they attempt to meditate on 'the body'; blend psychoanalytic and materialist critiques; retheorize genre on philosophically formal grounds; create a sociological account for the existence of literature; draw plays into a troubled dialogue with their historical situations; and articulate the social basis for an audience's response to a performance" ("Editor's" xxiii). Finally, as Fredric Jameson suggests, despite Burke's systematicity, we don't need to submit to "a rage for patterns and symmetries and the mirage of the metasystem" to find Burke's critique of action suggestive (Jameson, "Symbolic" 138).

19   Austin's deployment in cultural theory in the 1990s was marked by Judith Butler, *Gender Trouble*, and expanded in the collection *Performativity and Performance*, ed. Parker and Sedgwick. On the application and misapplication of Austin and the "performative" to dramatic performance, see Worthen, *Force* chapter 1.

20   The anxiety of Burke's 1975 essay on Austin is audible three decades earlier in the more confident tones of "The Philosophy of Literary Form" (1941) – the essay that laid the groundwork for his massive theory of "motives." Burke takes poetry "as the adopting of various strategies for the encompassing of situations" ("Philosophy" 1), noting that while the "symbolic act" performed by the poem is "the *dancing of an attitude*," in "this attitudinizing of the poem, the whole body may finally become involved" (8). The poem's rhythm, assonance, consonance, the ways it demands engagement with its formal and conceptual processes imply that "the whole body is involved in an enactment" (11). At the same time, this ascription of embodiment to reading raises a problem bypassed in Burke's general bypassing of theatre. Doesn't this materialization of literature particularize it too much, denying its general significance, or, in the terms raised by the New Critics, predicate the meaning of the poem on factors external to it, in the particularities of the history of reading, embodiment, enactment? It's for this reason, I think, that Burke opens "The Philosophy of Literary Form" by claiming that his poem-as-strategy "point of view does not, by any means, vow us to personal or historical subjectivism. The situations are real; the strategies for handling them have public content; and in so far as situations overlap from individual to individual, or from one historical period to another, the strategies possess universal relevance" ("Philosophy" 1). Burke lends the physical engagement with the sound and vocal production of words considerable rigor in "Musicality in Verse"; see also Altieri.

21   Burke's remarks might be compared with Victor Turner's famous braiding of social drama and stage drama in *From Ritual to Theatre*, which developed in dialogue with Richard Schechner's "restoration of behavior"

("Restoration"); his comments on the mystification of identity also resonate with, for instance, Judith Butler's "performative" critique in *Gender
Trouble*.

22   Burke calls this distinctive tension the "paradox of substance": for things
to be "consubstantial," sharing something in common, they must actually
be different, be of different substance; otherwise, they would be the same.
An apple and an orange are different (different substance); they are consubstantial as fruits; two oranges are two instances of one substance.

23   "Antony in Behalf of the Play," it's worth recalling, takes its place alongside other essays on public manipulation – the rhetoric of the press in
"Reading While you Run: An Exercise on Translating from English to
English," "The Nature of Art under Capitalism," and the brilliant analysis
of *Mein Kampf*, "The Rhetoric of Hitler's 'Battle.'"

Chapter 1: From Poetry to Performance

1   Shannon Jackson briefly discusses Brooks and Heilman, Bentley, Fergusson,
and Williams, chapter 3.

2   These terms are from: Diana Taylor, *Archive*; Schechner, "Restoration";
Roach, *Cities*; Phelan, *Unmarked*; Turner, *Ritual to Theatre*; Jon McKenzie,
Perform.

3   On the critical impact of poetic drama in modernism and modern drama,
see Puchner, *Stage Fright*, and Worthen, *Modern Drama*.

4   Walker convincingly notes the ways Eliot's "early critical writings helped
to define the category of the literary in specifically anti-performative
terms," despite the "more ambivalent stance toward performance" of his
later career ("Why" 154); at the same time, the potential for a revision of
the inertness of contemporary *performance* the New Critics attributed to
"poetic drama" also strikes me as a theme of Eliot's poetics throughout
his career. On Eliot, see also Julia A. Walker, "Text/Performance" 24.

5   From as early as *The Waste Land*, Eliot had been fascinated by the work of
the so-called "Cambridge School," classicists – F. M. Cornford, Jane Ellen
Harrison, Gilbert Murray – who variously worked to locate the patterns
of "ritual" (derived most directly from Sir James Frazer's *The Golden Bough*
[1890]) in the designs of Greek mythology and culture. Characterizing
Fergusson as "perhaps one of the more insightful and widely-read drama
critics of the period," Jackson suggests that while Fergusson's "approach
reproduced the primitivist and structural reductions of [...] earlier anthro-
pological models," it is nonetheless "noteworthy that the contingencies of
the dramatic event served as a bridge between New Criticism and classical
anthropology. As such, his drama scholarship can be located on a discon-

tinuous genealogy in literary and cultural studies, indirectly anticipating the mutual enthusiasms between literature and anthropology that would underpin the 'blurred genres' and 'new historicisms' of a later generation" (*Professing* 95). For a more plausible critique of the "ritual," see Jameson, "Symbolic Inference" 148–9. Fergusson was also openly indebted to Burke, and richly reviewed *A Grammar of Motives*; see "Kenneth Burke's *Grammar of Motives*."

6   The challenge of framing New Critical "depth" and "ambiguity" was posed by the emerging canon of modern drama as Bentley, Fergusson, and Williams defined it: *Thinker* has chapters on Shaw, Ibsen, Strindberg, Pirandello, Brecht, and Sartre; *Idea* on Ibsen, Chekhov, Pirandello, Cocteau, Obey, and Eliot; *Ibsen to Eliot* on Ibsen, Strindberg, Chekhov, Shaw, Synge, Hauptmann, Toller, Pirandello, Anouilh, Yeats, Eliot, Auden and Isherwood, Fry, and "The Faber Dramatists."

7   The antitheatricalism of *Understanding Drama* is pervasive: the first usage of the word *theatre* in any form occurs in a footnote on page 27: ("It is beyond the scope of this book to investigate whether the conventional length of drama has some justification more fundamental than theatrical practice"); the word occurs only a few more times in the main study – the undescribed "theatrical conventions" of Plautus' day (141); in *The London Merchant*, George Lillo was "aiming at tragedy, and in terms of the theater he was once very successful. [...] In reading the play, the student will find it useful to try to discover the reason why the play is no longer the popular theater piece it once was" (146); "With the decline of the drama, the Roman theatre finally came to house a form of entertainment comparable to that of modern circuses, burlesque, and vaudeville" (Appendix B, 29); and "some Romantic work – plays by Goethe, Schiller, and Victor Hugo, for instance – had considerable influence upon the theatre" (Appendix B, 32).

8   Shannon Jackson rightly assimilates Williams's early and ongoing interest in drama to his formative role in "cultural studies"; although this "legacy" is "often ignored or unknown, particularly in the US context," Williams "preceded and interspersed his foundational scholarship in cultural studies with his less famous series in dramatic criticism between 1952 and 1968" (97–8). Perhaps begging the question (unknown to whom?), Jackson at once sees Williams's notion of "convention" prefiguring and sustaining a more dynamic "cultural" function for literature, while failing to seize the stage performance of drama itself as the site of cultural work. Rather than implying Williams's "hypocrisy" (101) for failing to deal more energetically with theatre, we might attend more carefully to his work on drama itself.

9   See Fergusson's review of Boleslavsky, *Human* 105–14.

10 On the dynamics of role and character in Shakespeare, see Bruster and Weimann.
11 I have in mind R. P. Blackmur's *Language as Gesture*, see also Julia A. Walker's discussion of Brooks and Heilman on gesture, "Why" 154.
12 It should be noted that Williams's sense of "convention" departs in other ways from Brooks and Heilman's, notably when it comes to "character." Williams regards "character" as a fully conventional structure: "There are no characters to have 'unspoken thoughts'; they are simply conventions of expression. The artist needs characters as a convention, and the other conventions he needs are for further communications of the experience, not for amplifying the characters" (20 n.2). Elsewhere, Bentley notes, "A character is not a role until, to begin with, it can be put across in a few acted scenes. Any idea for a character which cannot be put across at that velocity and by that method is unsuited to dramatic art" (*Life* 171).
13 In "Why Performance?" Julia A. Walker presents a reading of Brooks and Heilman in the context of emerging notions of literature and performance that jibes with mine here in several respects; see her reading of Brooks's metaphorical invocation of "drama" here, 172 n.19. Note also Ransom's comment that Burke "conceives of poetry as drama, whether completely realized or not" ("Address" 143).
14 Taylor relies on several pieces by Dwight Conquergood to locate the resistance of performance: "Rethinking"; "Ethnography, Rhetoric"; and "Of Caravans and Carnivals." The principal object of this critique is Clifford Geertz's work, notably the sense "that cultural forms can be treated as texts, as imaginative works built out of social materials"; see Geertz 449.
15 These now-familiar terms for the analysis of performance are taken from Schechner, "Restoration of Behavior"; Roach, *Cities*; Phelan, *Unmarked*; Victor Turner, *Ritual to Theatre*; and McKenzie, *Perform*. For the materialist critique of writing and print, see McGann, and Grigely. For an application of this work to drama and performance, see Worthen, *Print*.
16 David Román, in an elegant reading of Taylor, suggests that "Taylor's promotion of the *repertoire* not as the *archive's* antagonistic opposite, but as a separate repository of cultural memory, allows for that memory to be reembodied, reperformed, and thus restored," a position that assimilates Taylor's work more directly to Joseph Roach's *surrogation*, and ameliorates the occasionally more antagonistic rhetoric of both books toward the oppressive force of writing in the *archive* (see 139).
17 See Steiner; and see Worthen, "Convicted Reading."
18 As Jon McKenzie has pointed out, while performance studies emerged from the constellation of theatre and anthropology in the 1950s and 1960s, the formal paradigms of the field shifted "from theater to theory" in the later 1970s and 1980s. See McKenzie, *Perform* 36–42.

19   I refer here to Parker and Sedgwick, eds., *Performativity*. Although Austin's understanding of "performativity" is indeed applicable to dramatic performance, it requires us to understand the constitutive work of performance in determining the potential agency or affordance of the text; see Worthen, *Force* chapter 1.

20   I have in mind here such studies as Taplin; Wiles, *Tragedy in Athens*; Winkler and Zeitlin; Styan; Holland.

21   Goldman cites Richard Schechner, "Actuals: Primitive Ritual and Performance Theory," *Theatre Quarterly* 1.2 (April–June 1971); for the ease of readers here, I refer to "Actuals," chapter 2 of *Performance Theory*. One might note, *pace* Jackson on Fergusson, that the "primitivizing" gesture consigned to the "drama" phase of the "drama-to-culture" genealogy persists well into the era of "performance studies."

22   On phenomenology, for example, see States; on the spatial configurations of drama and theatre, see Chaudhuri, *Staging*; and Chaudhuri and Fuchs, eds., *Land/Scape/Theater*.

23   Despite Blau's deep comment to contemporary theory and performance, his work also develops in dialogue with an earlier tradition: his account of the disappearance of the public in *The Audience* draws both Kenneth Burke and Francis Fergusson into the discussion – "an earlier critical work to which recent thinking about the theater remains indebted, Francis Fergusson's *The Idea of a Theater*" (45) – and a post-show discussion of Heiner Müller's *Hamletmachine* at New York University in 1986 recalls Eric Bentley's remarks in *The Playwright as Thinker* on a performance of Ibsen at Yale: "there were questions about the acting, staging, music, lighting, and even, this time, about the director's obligation to the text, but not a single question about what the text meant, nor its politics, nor anything to Müller – who might have evaded it – on how he felt about that" (392 n.8). For Blau, theatre is hardly the illustration of textuality, but the utility of dramatic writing in exploring the thinking of performance remains a powerful lure.

24   Like Blau, Garner, and Goldman, and indeed like Fergusson, Bentley, and Williams, Bennett also finds a touchstone of theoretical inquiry in Eliot's investigation of the possibility of a poetic drama; see *Revolutionary* 8, 89–92.

25   Bennett puts this very well, if schematically: "All that is needed, in performance space, is our recognition of an *interpretive* relation between the performance (P) and its inferred text (T). No force of 'understanding' is required to keep that relation open; it is always already opened by the categorical separation between T and the living bodily materiality of P" (*Revolutionary* 186).

26   Schechner slightly but significantly altered this passage from its earlier 1982 version, perhaps pulling the punch: "Performance is not merely a

selection from data arranged and interpreted; it is behavior itself and carries with it a kernel of originality, making it the subject for further interpretation, the source of further *history*" (emphasis mine). The paragraph continued, "That is why ritual is so much more powerful than myth. Ritual lives – is performed – or it isn't, while myths die and lie around libraries" ("Collective Reflexivity" 43). My thanks to Richard Schechner for pointing out this alteration.

27   See also Walker's extensive qualification of Judith Butler's account of the *performative*, "Why" 161–9.

28   Among the many differences between European and North American academic practices, it might be noted that the incorporation of artists as producers of critical and theoretical discourse characteristic of the formation of performance studies (the appearance of Eugenio Barba, Augusto Boal, Guillermo Gómez-Peña, and Ngugi wa Thiong'o as contributing editors of *TDR* is one mark of this institutionalization, apart from the extensive impact of their critical writing) has long been part of the horizon of European theatre studies: the Prague School, for example, included avant-garde director-theoreticians like Jindřich Honzl, among others.

29   On Lehmann, see Bennett, *Revolutionary* 201–2.

30   Hopkins and Reynolds energetically take issue with my use of the term "drama" elsewhere (see Worthen, "Drama, Performativity, Performance"); while I don't think they quite capture the situation either, they have correctly clarified a conceptual opacity in my own thinking, and I am very grateful for their careful and provocative reading.

31   McKenzie's summons was richly answered in Janelle Reinelt's response, "Is Performance Studies Imperialist? Part 2." Locating an Anglophone bias in the production of scholarship and the structure of scholarly organizations, and describing a differential relationship between performance studies and theatre studies in the US and European traditions, Reinelt notes "specific situated reasons that explain resistances among certain scholars to a proposed paradigm shift, or a resistance to its terminology as a brand" (12–13); such specific situated reasons perhaps also help to contextualize the sense of a possible paradigm shift as attractively opportune. While locating dramatic performance as part of a hegemonic archive may well both reflect its use in specific situations of performance, and help to provide the institutional leverage sometimes necessary for a paradigm shift to take place, in other historical, political, disciplinary, and institutional situations dramatic performance or – to speak in perhaps less pejorative, Eurocentric terms – performance using writing has an entirely different relation to dominant political, cultural, and/or academic formations.

32   See also Phelan, "Reconstructing Love."

Chapter 2: Performing Writing: *Hamlet*

1 Unless otherwise noted, references to *Hamlet* are to *Hamlet*, ed. Ann Thompson and Neil Taylor (this edition represents the 1604 second quarto); where noted, references to the 1603 first quarto or to the Folio texts are to *Hamlet: The Texts of 1603 and 1623*, ed. Ann Thompson and Neil Taylor. Other Shakespeare quotations are to Stephen Greenblatt et al., eds., *The Norton Shakespeare*.

2 On Hamlet's reading, see Craig.

3 For an informative, and surprising, discussion of the widespread use of erasable notebooks – or "tables" – in the early modern period, see Stallybrass, Chartier, Mowery, and Wolfe, "Hamlet's Tables."

4 On popular songs, ballads, and proverbs, see Harold Jenkins's Longer Notes to 2.2.399, 3.2.265–6, and 4.5, in his edition of *Hamlet*.

5 Polonius' lines are among those marked out for "commonplacing" in the Q1 version of *Hamlet*, where they are spoken by Corambis, perhaps highlighting their "textual" quality even in performance. See Lesser and Stallybrass.

6 See Mack.

7 The relationship between writing and performance in *Hamlet* has been suggestively explored by Rowe. For a superb reading of the impact of print on what might be called the ideology of writing, see Ayers, who notes that the play is "much concerned with the issue of documents and the different kinds of significance that are attached to them by different kinds of readers and writers" (423).

8 On the use of title pages, even in quartos, to establish claims to the literary identity of drama, see Douglas A. Brooks chapter 1, and Erne's vivid rejoinder, *Shakespeare* 44–57. And while Erne, and following him Patrick Cheney, find the publication of Shakespeare's plays in quarto in the final decade of the sixteenth century to point to an assertion of print-based "literary" status for plays and playwrights, David Scott Kastan suggests that printed drama may have remained, for a time, in a "category of its own, competing in the marketplace with other recognizable categories of reading material" (45).

9 The 1604 quarto title page is reproduced in G. R. Hibbard's edition of *Hamlet* (90).

10 I cite here from Thompson and Taylor's edition, which preserves original punctuation. Jenkins's edition, however, points the line differently: "… Plautus too light. For the law of writ, and the liberty, these are the only men" (2.2.383–4).

11 There is considerable debate about the displacement of reading aloud by silent reading as the dominant practice, and its relation to print; see Ong chapter 5 *passim*, and Ayers 425–30.

12   Courtney Lehman has noticed this sense of *Hamlet*'s inflection by print, while arguing that Hamlet, "mimicking the proliferation of infinitely repeatable, identical texts made possible by the invention of moveable type," is alienated by print's emerging culture, a world that is "too fixed, too repeatable" (94–5).

13   Walter Ong's sense that drama "from antiquity had been controlled by writing" is perhaps overstated here; the sense that "Until print, the only linearly plotted lengthy story line was that of the drama" (133) perhaps has more to do with the conditions of its public performance, constrained by occasion in ways that did not as readily enable the performance of serial or episodic narrative. Charlotte Scott also notes the tactical uses of reading in the play, suggesting that "the book emerges as Hamlet's platform for performance; it enables his 'madness' to emerge, and stands between him and his observers" (141).

14   Bednarz's detailed study argues that the "War" involved a series of plays produced at both the public outdoor amphitheatres and the indoor "private" theatres: Jonson's *Every Man Out of His Humour* (1599), *Cynthia's Revels* (1600), and *Poetaster* (1601), Marston's *Histriomastix* (1599), *Jack Drum's Entertainment* (1600), and *What You Will* (1601), Dekker's *Satiromastix* (1601), and Shakespeare's *As You Like It* (1600), *Twelfth Night* (1601), *Hamlet* (1601), and *Troilus and Cressida* (1601), and taking in several other plays more peripherally. He develops a complex reading of this controversy, encompassing professional rivalries among individuals, critical contestation on the purposes of poetry, drama, and performance, and concerns – possibly reflected in *Hamlet* – about the possible loss of some elite playgoers to the children's companies. Given the nature of this now-lost struggle, Bednarz recognizes that some elements of his reconstruction are conjectural, but he provides a scrupulous and tenacious account of its possible development; on *Hamlet*, see especially chapter 9, and also the "Chronological Appendix." For an alternative account of the "little eyases," placing this allusion outside the War of the Theatres, see Knutson chapter 5. Both the introduction and annotations to Tom Cain's edition of *Poetaster* are informative as well.

15   Shakespeare's company had produced Jonson's *Every Man Out of His Humour*, and as Bednarz remarks, comedy of humours was strongly identified with Jonson (246).

16   As most commentators note, the distinction here is not entirely clear: the Players may be versatile enough both for plays composed according to (classical) rules and for plays disregarding them, or for scripted as well as unscripted or improvisational performance. See Jenkins's annotation to this line and his Longer Note, as well as Hibbard's, both of which point to the difficulties of this distinction. Jeffrey Knapp notes that while

Hamlet "may indeed bear witness to the 'fashion' for a theater where authors clash with players [...] that is pointedly *not* the stage for which Shakespeare writes" (12); Shakespeare's theatre, like the Players', is one in which "author's writ becomes theater only through the willing collaboration of players" (16).

17 Bednarz (247–8) discusses the significance of this passage, and relates it to the texts of *Hamlet*. He also suggests that "in Hamlet's formulation of theatrical mimesis there is a significant shift in emphasis: it is the players, not their scripts, who mirror life by reflecting the form and pressure of the time" (253).

18 Recently, Lukas Erne and others have worked to reclaim the notion that Shakespeare wrote as a "literary dramatist": "Shakespeare was acutely aware of and cared about his rise to prominence as a print-published dramatic author" ("Reconsidering" 29). While we should be sensitive to the potentially antitheatrical dimension of this case, the sense that Shakespeare may have written his plays with literary preservation in mind would not necessarily hedge an awareness of their mutable *agency* as instruments in performance.

19 On the "antitheatrical" literature and its invocation in early-modern theatre generally, and in *Hamlet*, see Barish; Howard.

20 As Barbara Hodgdon suggests, too, stage and film acting "share a frame of reference and exist in dialogue with one another"; see "Spectacular Bodies" 97.

21 Harold Jenkins's Arden edition of *Hamlet* 1.2.126–32 places 7 lines of text on the page and one line of stage direction; the passage is accompanied by 37 double-column lines of gloss in smaller font, three lines of textual apparatus, and one and a half pages of additional summary in the "Longer Notes."

22 The reading of Q2 "sallied" as "sullied" is urged most effectively only in the twentieth century; see Wilson, *Manuscript* 309–15.

23 In his 1934 discussion of *The Manuscript of Shakespeare's Hamlet*, J. Dover Wilson listed the play's thirty-two cruxes; this passage is not among them. See Vol. 2: *Editorial Problems* 296–9.

24 Alexander Schmidt's *Shakespeare-Lexikon* does indeed connect the "defiled, filthy" meaning to hawking: "*Enseam* was the technical name for the whole process of cleansing the hawk from internal defilement," though Jenkins is surely correct that this reading is beside the point. Dover Wilson's reading emphasizes the *greasy* sense more elaborately: "For 'grainèd' and 'tinct,' being terms of wool-dyeing, have suggested 'enseamèd,' another technical word from the woollen industry meaning 'loaded with grease,' and that in turn, because the 'seam' employed in the greasing process was hog's-lard, has suggested the 'nasty sty.'" Wilson goes on to suggest that

"in this instance the associations are probably too remote to influence the imagination" (Wilson, ed., *Hamlet* xxxviii–xxxix).

25 On ways to "enseam and harden" horses, see Langbaine; on falconry, see Cox. For contemporary discussion of the possible merits of enseaming birds of prey, see *Falconry Forum* <falconryforum.co.uk> and *International Falconry* <www.intfalconry.com>.

26 See Thompson and Taylor's note to their edition of *Hamlet* 3.4.90.

27 I cite from George Chapman, *Bussy D'Ambois*, ed. Robert J. Lordi.

28 See notes to this line in Evans, ed., *Bussy D'Ambois* and the Glossary item in Hudston, ed., *George Chapman: Plays and Poems*.

29 See Bevington.

30 In "The Displaced Body of Desire," Lisa Starks persuasively argues that the Branagh film tends to "sanitize" (177) the play of unruly sexual desire, in order to resituate "Shakespeare's text in a new age of taboos and repression, symptoms, and traumas," notably valorizing the "paternal law and its dictates for normalcy through disavowals and displacements" (178).

31 In an email to the author, Russell Jackson reports that this error apparently intruded itself in the transmission of the shooting script to the publisher of the screenplay; email to author 22 June 2007 and 2 July 2007. Jackson notes in the screenplay that the basic text used was the Oxford *Complete Works*, edited by Stanley Wells and Gary Taylor (Branagh 174), but he notes elsewhere that he also had recourse to both the Jenkins and Hibbard editions; see Russell Jackson, "Kenneth Branagh's Film of *Hamlet*."

32 I refer to two performances of the Wooster Group, *Hamlet*, directed by Elizabeth LeCompte, Public Theatre, 7 and 8 November 2007; Hamlet: Scott Shepherd; Claudius/Marcellus/Ghost/Gravedigger: Ari Fliakos; Gertrude/Ophelia: Kate Valk; Polonius: Bill Raymond; Laertes/ Rosencrantz/Guildenstern/Player King: Casey Spooner; Horatio: Judson Williams; Bernardo/Rosencrantz/Guildenstern/Player Queen: Daniel Pettrow; Nurse: Dominique Bosquet; Attendant/Soldier/Banister: Alessandro Magania; Stage Manager: Ruth E. Sternberg.

33 Sellars's *Merchant of Venice* opened at the Goodman Theatre, Chicago, in 1994 before touring extensively; Castorf's *Master and Margarita* opened in 2002, and has remained in the repertoire of the Berlin Volksbühne; Smeds's *Three Sisters* premiered at the Kajaani City Theatre in 2004, before touring to the Tampere Theatre Festival the following year; van Hove's *Misanthrope* had a successful run in New York in 2007.

34 On Piscator, Svoboda, and the history of recording media in the theatre, see Dixon 77–85.

35 The production rehearsed in 2006, and was shown in Paris and Berlin in November; it then reopened at St. Ann's Warehouse in New York in March 2007, before playing in Amsterdam, returning to the Public Theatre in New

York in November, and then traveling to Los Angeles in early 2008. See archive section of the Wooster Group website <www.thewoostergroup. org>, which contains dates of development, rehearsal, and production as well.

36 The phrase "dancing with technology" is from a program note to *To You, The Birdie! (Phèdre)* (2001), qtd. Causey 43. There is a substantial body of work on the Wooster Group, much of it considering the group's ongoing engagement with recording media in performance. In addition to Matthew Causey's discussion, see especially Savran; Aronson; Monks; and Bell.

37 On remediation as "the representation of one medium in another," see Bolter and Grusin 45. For the notion of the Almereyda *Hamlet*'s preoccupation with remediation, see Rowe; Donaldson; Worthen, "Fond Records"; Almereyda, dir., *Hamlet*.

38 Although the Wooster Group program and subsequent reviews claim that the film was shown "in 2000 movie houses across the United States," 1964 news reports put the number at 976 theatres (Crowther). See the Wooster Group, *Hamlet*, Program 7 November 2007, "Program Note." On the provenance of the film, see Morley.

39 For a reading of Electronovision that draws some different conclusions about the Wooster Group's *Hamlet*, see Cartelli.

40 I take the notion that "historically, the live is actually an effect of mediatization" from Auslander 51.

41 Susan Sontag qtd. in Dixon 129. See *Richard Burton's Hamlet*, "Trailer" for the theatrical trailer circulated in advance of the film's release. The trailer is also available as "Richard Burton in Hamlet TV Commercial Rare," *YouTube*, accessed 6 December 2007.

42 *Richard Burton's Hamlet*, "Richard Burton Discusses 'Electronovision.'" The interview is also available as "Richard Burton talks Electronovision," *YouTube*, accessed 6 December 2007.

43 See "The Met on Demand"; the live-recorded broadcasts, transmitted to movie theatres, will be available to on-demand television subscribers in the US "within 30 days of theatrical release."

44 As Philip Auslander argues, "Television's specific ability to position itself as theatre's replacement has its origins in the claims of immediacy made on behalf of television throughout its development, and in television's claim to replicate theatrical discourse" (23).

45 Laurie E. Osborne has noted that despite the producers' desire to produce a "live" film event – she usefully compares the fortunes of the recordings made of Shakespeare productions shown on the *Live from Lincoln Center* program – Burton's film is "now *only* a DVD production which includes the interview and the ad extolling the 'liveness' and immediacy of the experience" (52).

46 It might be noted, though, that the Wooster Group has its own investment in the propriety of the text; as the "Technical Note" in the Program suggests: "We have digitally reedited the Burton film so that the lines of verse, which were spoken freely in the 1964 production, *are delivered according to the original poetic meter*" (emphasis mine). This emphasis on spoken verse, if it still persists in the production, escaped my notice on the performances I attended.

47 On "surrogation," his adaptation of Schechner's "restored behavior," see Roach, *Cities* 1–11.

48 For a detailed, though somewhat unsympathetic, account of this aspect of Stelarc's work, see Jones 106–8. Jones also discusses a similar installation by Mona Hatoum, in which a recording made by arthroscopic camera was used as the basis of an installation.

49 My thanks to Teresa Hartmann of the Wooster Group for this information about the various reverb and tremolo effects applied to Kate Valk's voice when it overdubs Linda Marsh's in the film; email to author 5 December 2007.

50 For a fascinating reading of the phonographic archive of Shakespeare, and its relation to liveness, see Lanier.

51 As Causey notes, in the Wooster Group's work and elsewhere in contemporary performance, "works of mediatized performance established as a separate aesthetic object to theatre, a para-performative, tele-theatrical artifact wherein the immediacy of performance and the digital alterability of time and space through technology converge" (6); Causey discusses *embeddedness* on 4 and *passim*.

52 My thanks to Clay Hapaz of the Wooster Group for this information, and for his very kind assistance in assembling the photographs here; email to author 6 December 2007.

53 Fredric Jameson's critique of postmodern representation as "pastiche" is at once apposite and yet inadequate here. While postmodern artworks "no longer 'quote' such 'texts' as a Joyce might have done, or a Mahler; they incorporate them," this activity – in the Wooster Group *Hamlet* – is hardly a kind of blank parody, but instead an urgent effort to assess the nature of the text's authority in performance; see "Postmodernism and Consumer Society" 112.

Chapter 3: Embodying Writing: Ibsen and Parks

1 As Ibsen asked those in attendance at a banquet in Christiania in 1898, "perhaps you have been expecting that I would make a speech about my books?" See Ibsen, *Letters and Speeches* 331.

2 Unless otherwise noted, all references to Ibsen's plays are to *The Complete Major Prose Plays*, trans. Rolf Fjelde. Phrases in Norwegian are taken from the 1932 *Samlede Verker*.

3 As Chaudhuri remarks, "Again and again in Ibsen, the crisis of the concept of home appears as the collision therein of two incommensurable desires: the drive for a stable container for identity and the desire to deterritorialize the self" (*Staging* 8). In "The Sociology of Modern Drama," Georg Lukács remarks, "For only this much-heightened sense of the significance of milieu enables it to function as a dramatic element; only this could render individualism truly problematic" (434).

4 This challenge is traced brilliantly in Cavell.

5 On bodies and setting in melodrama, see Simon Shepherd 154; on melodramatic aspects of *Rosmersholm*, see Moi 270, and in Ibsen more generally, see Goldman, *Ibsen* 11–12.

6 Ibsen's speech to the workers of Trondhjem, 14 June 1885, is often compared with the language of *Rosmersholm*:

> An element of *nobility* must enter into our national life, our administration, our representative bodies, and our press.
> Of course I am not thinking of a nobility of *birth*, nor of that of *wealth*, nor of that of *knowledge*, neither of that of *ability* or talent. I am thinking of a nobility of character, of a nobility of will and spirit.
> Nothing else can make us free. (*Letters and Speeches* 249)

7 One aspect of Freud's reading of the play is that Kroll's revelation then provides a concrete cause for Rebecca's final confession to Kroll and Rosmer: "After she has learnt that she has been the mistress of her own father, she surrenders herself wholly to her now overmastering sense of guilt. She confesses to Rosmer and Kroll that she was a murderess; she rejects for ever the happiness to which she has paved the way by crime; and prepares the way for departure. But the true origin of her sense of guilt, which wrecks her at the moment of attainment, remains a secret. We have seen that it is something quite other than the atmosphere of Rosmersholm and the refining influence of Rosmer" ("Some Character-Types" 176). While Freud's insight into the incest motif is now widely acknowledged, it does tend to narrow and specify motive in a way that the play seems to resist: locating Rebecca's confession in a specific motive rather than the "atmosphere of Rosmersholm."

8 As Stanislavski asks in his famous reading of the role of Roderigo at the opening of *Othello*, "What is the *past* which justifies the *present* of this scene?" ("From the Production Plan" 131).

9   The humility of these words is important, as Brendel's specific use of the word *gladelig*, the word that informs so much of the final dialogue. I follow Goldman's keen perception here, that Brendel's words give "us a taste of the disturbing sensations to which pleasure can be linked" (*Ibsen* 135).

10   I have Mouth's famous refrain in mind, "what? .. who? .. no! .. she!" (Beckett, *Complete Dramatic Works* 379).

11   Insofar as a felicitous confession would require that it "be executed by all participants both correctly and … completely," most of Rosmer's and Rebecca's disclosures "misfire" (Austin 15); in some cases, the disclosure is incomplete, but in others – Rosmer's various avowals of "innocence" come to mind – the agent seems unaware of his own motives and actions.

12   Moi points out that Fjelde underplays Rosmer's (and Ibsen's) clear emphasis here, omitting the word "second" in his translation; see 280 n.18.

13   For Freud's comment, see Templeton 358 n.5. Templeton suggests "Rosmer's sexual innocence is related to an overriding need to consider himself unfallen. His belief in his ability to ennoble his fellow citizens rests on the certainty of his unblemished goodness, and thus the news of Beata's accusation constitutes an 'overwhelming burden' that crushes his notion of himself as a moral leader" (187). Elizabeth Hardwick has an even more skeptical view, which nonetheless takes in both the tone and action of Rosmer's behavior in the play: "In *Rosmersholm*, the husband is unusually dense and mild. He courteously refuses to understand the drama that has exploded around him, to take in the violent sweeps of feeling in himself and in the two women. Rosmer leans as long as he can on the stick of 'friendship' and 'innocence' to protect himself from his love for Rebecca and his complicity in his wife's suicide" (76).

14   It should be emphasized that some of Parks's orthographic inventions – *thuh*, for example – are not readily assimilable to the use of scripted dialect to mark racialized representation: regardless of the racial or ethnic identification of the performer, *thuh* is spoken by both African American *and* white/European characters in Parks's work: addressing **The Bride-to-Be** after she has doffed her "Hottentot" disguise in *For the Love of the Venus*, the inset play in *Venus*, **The Young Man** says "Shrug all you want but keep thuh core" (*Venus* 154).

15   Elam and Rayner see Parks's use of footnotes in particular as a purely textual, nearly parodic, aspect of her writing (see "Echoes" 186).

16   Given Parks's attention to the appearance of her plays on the page, I have attempted to reproduce the formality of lineation, capitalization, and other stylistic features in citations; since I also suggest that speech prefixes do not function as "names," I use the prefix instead of a "name," when necessary, and so retain the typographical style used in the original published

version of the play, usually small caps (THE FOUNDLING FATHER) or bold face (**The Baron Docteur**).

17 Geis notes that from Frederick Douglass ("Lincoln was not, in the fullest sense of the word, either our man or our model. In his interests, in his associations, in his habits of thought, and in his prejudices, he was a white man") onward, Lincoln has had a controversial reputation among African Americans (98). In this sense, Parks "signifies" – repeating "dominant discourse … in a subversive way that lets the (knowing) listener or reader understand how that discourse is being mimicked, undermined, reinscribed, revised, and reused for purposes that may run counter to the original, authoritarian intent" (13). My sincere thanks to LeAnn Fields of the University of Michigan Press for providing me with an advance copy of this fine overview of Parks's career.

18 As Elam and Rayner suggest, these scenes help to reframe the ways that the "perpetuation of the Lincoln myth has created real scars for African Americans" ("Echoes" 183).

19 Fabian notes that while it may be impossible to take measurements of this kind with a sextant, Galton told versions of this story repeatedly (Fabian 48 n.13). Dalton was Charles Darwin's cousin, and invented the word *eugenics* (Holmes 101).

20 In an essay that "focuses on Parks's representation of Saartjie Baartman as an accomplice in her own exploitation" (699), Jean Young argues that *Venus* replicates the English court's treatment of Baartman by staging her as willingly complicit in both the decision to be displayed in Europe and in continuing to do so. In Young's view, then, Parks's play contributes to the objectification of African women in general, and more extensively to their alleged complicity as signifiers of "primitive" and primitivizing sexuality, which the work of anatomists like Georges Cuvier, who measured and dissected Baartman and is figured in the role of The Baron Docteur in the play, used to distinguish the Hottentot from full humanity. In "Body Parts," Harry Elam, Jr. and Alice Rayner develop a parallel reading of the play's spectacle as politics, to which I am indebted at several points here. Sara L. Warner takes a related position, contrasting the "restoration of Baartman's dignity through proper burial" to her sense of Parks's purposes, which avoid a "transformational teleology. Parks is not only uninterested in restoring Baartman's dignity, she goes so far as to create a drama in which it is almost impossible for audiences to do so by making Venus complicit in her captivity. Parks's *Venus* does not deny Baartman dignity so much as it takes the loss of her dignity as its premise" (193).

21 The Egyptian Hall was later one of the first London movie theatres; my thanks to Barbara Hodgdon for pointing this out to me, and for many timely suggestions. In *Destination Culture*, Barbara Kirshenblatt-Gimblett

usefully situates Bullock's London Museum in the history of ethnographic display (41–6).

22   Kirby provides this account from the court records: "The decency of the exhibition was not called in question; it appearing that the woman had proper clothing adapted to the occasion; but from some expressions which had been uttered by those who had brought her over to this country, and with whom she had continued, and some apparent indications of reluctance on her part during her exhibition, there was reason to believe, and affidavits were accordingly laid before the Court to that effect, by the secretary of a society, denominated the African Institution, that she had been clandestinely inveigled from the Cape of Good Hope, without the knowledge of the British Governor, (who extends his peculiar protection in nature of a guardian over the Hottentot nation under his government, by reason of their general imbecile state;) and that she was brought to this country and since kept in custody and exhibited here against her consent" ("Hottentot Venus" 58).

23   *The Times* report of the proceedings provides a summary of Baartman's deposition: "This examination took up almost three hours: the questions were put by persons who spoke Dutch, and no person immediately connected with the exhibition was present. The Hottentot said, she had left her own country when extremely young. She was brought down to the Cape by the Dutch farmers, and served Peter Cezar. She then agreed with Hendrich Cezar, to come over to England for six years. She appeared before the Governor at the Cape, and got his permission. Mr. Dunlop promised to send her back rich. She was under no restraint. She was happy in England. She did not want to go back, nor to see her two brothers and three sisters, for she admired this country. She went out in a coach on Sunday for two or three hours together. Her father was a drover of cattle, and in going up the country was killed by the Bushmen. She had a child by a drummer at the Cape, where she lived two years. The child was dead. She has two black boys to attend her, and would like warmer clothes. The man who shews her never comes till she is just dressed, and then only ties a ribbon round her waist." To these comments, "the affidavit of a notary was added, who had read the agreement to her in Dutch, and thought she seemed perfectly to understand it, and be pleased with the prospect of getting back the profits." Baartman's competence is at once marked and denied ("seemed to understand it"), as the court trained its attention not on the "decency" of the case, but on the propriety of the contract: while "the Hottentots were supposed so incapable of managing their own concerns, that no contract among them was valid unless it was made before a Magistrate," nonetheless "This contract between the Hottentot and Cezar was made as usual" ("Law Report"). Rosemary Wiss notes the difficulty

of finding Baartman's "voice" in this testimony, and the difficulty the court seems to have had in understanding her; though she could apparently speak some English, she was interviewed in the "original colonizer's language" of Dutch (Wiss 17–18).

24 I have summarized these details from Wiss's fine article, and from Altick 268–73, Warner 183–4, and Holmes *passim*. Wiss argues that the court's decision that Baartman could and did consent to be exhibited denotes a particular view of her agency: "Saartjie Baartman's freedom was evaluated by the possibility of her receiving an income for having her body exhibited, a body perceived as private property not in the sense of determining its contested meaning, but in the sense of receiving value for its alienation" (18). Cuvier notes that his observations confirm "the cruel law" which seems to have condemned such races "to an eternal inferiority" (Cuvier 7, my translation).

25 Although on a visit to the Musée de l'Homme in 1998 I was informed that accounts of the Venus Hottentot's remains were entirely fictitious, they had been widely reported, most recently in connection with a 1995 exhibition documenting racist attitudes toward aboriginal peoples, which was protested by representatives of the Khoi-San and Griqua (see Young 707 n.1; and Elam and Rayner, "Body Parts" 266, 270). Kirby reported in 1949 that "a cast of her body was made, and her skeleton prepared and mounted. Both of these objects are now, as I have said, in Case No. 33 in the Musée de l'Homme," and included a photograph of the cast in his article ("Hottentot Venus" 61). In a useful discussion of the anatomical – and racial – controversies centered on "Hottentot" anatomy, Stephen J. Gould also reports seeing, on a shelf above the shelf holding the brain of Paul Broca, "a little exhibit that provided an immediate and chilling insight into nineteenth-century *mentalité* and the history of racism: in three smaller jars, I saw the dissected genitalia of three Third-World women. I found no brains of women, and neither Broca's penis nor any male genitalia grace the collection. The three jars are labelled *une négresse, une péruvienne*, and *la Vénus Hottentotte*" (20). After extensive negotiation, Baartman's remains were returned to South Africa in 2002 (see Warner 186; and Holmes 103–11).

26 Not, of course, that this prosthesis prevents the kind of eroticization that defined Baartman's career; John Lahr's review of the 1996 New York production notes "Here the illusion of the Hottentot's enormous butt is created by well-padded mocha-colored tights, which give her swaying backside a monstrous allure" (98), while at the same time noting that "From the play's first beat, when the Venus appears before an ogling crew of top-hatted upper-class fops, she is defined by the gaze of others."

27 In this play, a young Frenchman Adolphe is convinced by his world-traveling uncle that French women have become over-civilized, and so refuses to marry a French woman; claiming that American Indian and Hottentot women are the most beautiful, the uncle determines to find a suitable bride for Adolphe. Meanwhile a young widow, Amélie, has fallen in love with Adolphe; dismissing her other suitor Le Chevalier, she decides instead to costume herself *à la Hottentote* to seduce Adolphe. When she makes her appearance in disguise, however, the uncle is at first dumbfounded, as is Adolphe, since neither can speak Hottentot; however, since both the "Hottentot Venus" and the uncle are conveniently fluent in "Iroquois," he is able to interpret between Amélie and Adolphe, who are married on the spot. When Le Chevalier bursts in and says that he has just left the real Hottentot Venus in Paris, she is forced to doff her disguise, and "Adolphe, forgiving Amélie for her roguery, looks forward to a blissful future with his Parisian Venus" (see Kirby, "More" 131–3; and Holmes 78–9).

28 Parks makes the parallels explicit in a series of verbal echoes as well: **The Venus**'s "Unloved" (36) is echoed by The Bride-to-Be (39); **The Mother Showman**'s carnival cry "Presenting" (59) is echoed by the Uncle when he presents The Bride/Venus to The Young Man (132); **The Baron Docteur** and The Young Man each present their Venus with a box of chocolates.

29 This specular relationship is also represented in the many cartoons, often on political subjects, in which Baartman appears; in some respects, much as these cartoons stereotype Baartman, they also emphasize the English and French obsession with observing her. See Altick 270 and 271, and Kirby, "More" 131–2.

30 In "Femme de Race Bochismanne," Cuvier at first describes examining Baartman, who is unnamed in his account, in 1815 in the Jardin du Roi, noting the grace of her posture, and her finely formed hand and foot (3).

31 I am indebted here again to Rayner and Elam's fine discussion of the work of history in *The Death of the Last Black Man in the Whole Entire World*, especially to their sense that Parks's theatre demands "an encounter with its signifiers *as* signifiers" ("Unfinished" 459). In "Body Parts," Elam and Rayner suggest that "Baartman never fully coincides with her multiple meanings, and in that sense is a sign as well as an instance of the loss that history entails" (270).

32 For a somewhat more novelistic account of this meeting, see Holmes 3–7.

33 Geis outlines the padded/unpadded treatment of The Venus's body, and some of the critical consequences of this decision (83). Warner makes an analogous suggestion regarding the final lines of the play, "*Kiss* me / *Kiss* me / *Kiss* me / *Kiss*," arguing that the "protagonist's" – a word nicely

blending actor and role – "final gesture is extremely undignified and extremely generous: an invitation to return the kiss and to participate in a radical new form of fleshy communalism" (199).

34 As Holmes reports, Étienne Geoffroy Saint-Hilaire intervened with the police to have Baartman's body transferred directly to the Museum of Natural History, which was not otherwise allowed to receive bodies for scientific use (see 93–5). Holmes discusses the dissection and preservation of Baartman (95–102), and notes that Cuvier's body was also dissected according to his instructions (100–1).

Chapter 4: Writing Space: Beckett and Brecht

1 All references to Beckett's plays are to *The Complete Dramatic Works*.
2 Beckett had eliminated the Auditor when he directed Madeleine Renaud in the play, and advised directors in 1986, "simply to omit the auditor. He is very difficult to stage (light – position) and may well be of more harm than good. For me the play needs him but I can do without him. I have never seen him function effectively" (*Theatrical Notebooks* 4: xxiv)
3 See Stanton B. Garner's superb discussion of the phenomenology of space in Beckett's dramaturgy, chapter 2.
4 See Worthen, *Print* 159–75 for a fuller discussion of the competing authority of various zones of Beckett's page.
5 Describing *Quad* as the "choreography of madness" lacking "the recitation of any spoken dialogue, strange, poetic, or otherwise," Enoch Brater also reminds us that "one of the origins of Western theater lies in the dithyramb and the choral dance" (107).
6 *Quad* has become something of a site of experiment, as have other Beckett works, on *YouTube*. One elegant black-and-white version shows an open weed-filled square, in what seems to be a housing estate in the suburbs; each figure materializes and begins to trace the "course" and then fades out, to be replaced by a subsequent figure. The figures often appear superimposed on one another, among other technical experiments with the play. See Morello and Donet, *Quad*. See also the Katsura Kan elegant double *Quad*. It might also be noted that Beckett's play resembles Oskar Schlemmer's *Space Dance*, performed in the 1920s at the Bauhaus: three figures, each unidentifiable and clothed in a primary color (red, blue, yellow) enter separately to different musical/percussion accompaniment. A square playing area is marked on the floor, with lines bisecting the square from opposite corners and from the midpoint of each side.
7 On these controversies, see entries on *adaptation, censorship,* and *law* in Ackerley and Gontarski; on Akalaitis and the ART, see Kalb 165–84, and

Rabkin; on the Warner–Shaw *Footfalls*, see Worthen, *Print* 159–75; on the 2006 *Godot* production in the Italian courts, see McMahon.

8   I cite from the Performance License Rider attached to a license to perform several of Beckett's short plays at the University of California, Berkeley, under the direction of Patrick Anderson. The agreement is dated 24 February 2000, and, based on other accounts of the Beckett estate's intervention in productions, I assume it is standard. My sincere thanks to Katherine Mattson, Production Manager in the Department of Theater, Dance, and Performance Studies, for her assistance in this, and many other, matters. See also Jacobs.

9   On Lefebvre, and theatrical space more generally, see David Wiles's discussion in *Tragedy* 20, and *Short* 9–13.

10   See Brantley, "When a Universe Reels"; and Isherwood, "Words Fail Him."

Works Cited

Ackerley, C. J., and S. E. Gontarski. *The Grove Companion to Samuel Beckett: A Reader's Guide to His Works, Life, and Thought*. New York: Grove, 2004.

Albright, Daniel. *Beckett and Aesthetics*. Cambridge: Cambridge University Press, 2003.

Almereyda, Michael, adapt. *William Shakespeare's Hamlet*. London: Faber and Faber, 2000.

Almereyda, Michael, dir. *Hamlet*. 2000. DVD Buena Vista, n.d.

Altick, Richard D. *The Shows of London*. Cambridge, MA: Harvard University Press, 1978.

Altieri, Charles. "Taking Lyrics Literally: Teaching Poetry in a Prose Culture." *New Literary History* 32 (2001): 259–81.

Aristotle. *Poetics*. Trans. Gerald F. Else. Ann Arbor: University of Michigan Press, 1967.

Aristotle. *Poetics*. Trans. M. E. Hubbard. *Classical Literary Criticism*. Ed. D. A. Russell and Michael Winterbottom. Oxford: Oxford University Press, 1993.

Arnold, Matthew. "Memorial Verses." *Empedocles on Etna and Other Poems*. London: Fellowes, 1852.

Aronson, Arnold. *Looking into the Abyss: Essays on Scenography*. Ann Arbor: University of Michigan Press, 2005.

Artaud, Antonin. *The Theater and Its Double*. Trans. Mary Caroline Richards. New York: Grove, 1958.

Auslander, Philip. *Liveness: Performance in a Mediatized Culture*. London: Routledge, 1999.

Austin, J. L. *How to Do Things with Words*. 2nd ed. Ed. J. O. Urmson and Marina Sbisà. Cambridge, MA: Harvard University Press, 1997.

Ayers, P. K. "Reading, Writing, and *Hamlet*." *Shakespeare Quarterly* 44 (1993): 423–39.

Bair, Deirdre. *Samuel Beckett*. New York: Harcourt Brace Jovanovich, 1978.

Barish, Jonas. *The Antitheatrical Prejudice*. Berkeley: University of California Press, 1981.

Bart, Peter. "Filmed 'Hamlet' Gets Costly Push." *New York Times* 19 September 1964.

Bart, Peter. "Stage-Film Group Maps New Plans." *New York Times* 5 August 1964.

Barthes, Roland. "The Tasks of Brechtian Criticism." *Critical Essays*. Trans. Richard Howard. Evanston: Northwestern University Press, 1972. 71–6.

Beckerman, Bernard. *Dynamics of Drama: Theory and Method of Analysis*. New York: Drama Book Specialists, 1979.

Beckett, Edward. *Letter to The Guardian*. 24 March 1994.

Beckett, Samuel. *The Complete Dramatic Works*. London: Faber, 1986.

Beckett, Samuel. *The Theatrical Notebooks of Samuel Beckett*. Gen. ed. James Knowlson. 4 vols. London: Faber; New York: Grove, 1992–9.

Beckett, Samuel. *The Theatrical Notebooks of Samuel Beckett. Volume IV: The Shorter Plays*. Ed. S. E. Gontarski. London: Faber; New York: Grove, 1999.

Bednarz, James P. *Shakespeare and the Poets' War*. New York: Columbia University Press, 2001.

Bell, Phaedra. "Fixing the TV: Televisual Geography in the Wooster Group's *Brace Up!*" *Modern Drama* 48 (2005): 565–84.

Bennett, Benjamin. *All Theater Is Revolutionary Theater*. Ithaca: Cornell University Press, 2005.

Bennett, Benjamin. *Theater as Problem: Modern Drama and its Place in Literature*. Ithaca: Cornell University Press, 1990.

Bennett, Rodney, dir. *Hamlet*. 1980. *The BBC TV Shakespeare Plays*. DVD Ambrose, n.d.

Bentley, Eric. *The Life of the Drama*. New York: Atheneum, 1967.

Bentley, Eric. *The Playwright as Thinker: A Study of Drama in Modern Times*. 1946. New York: Meridian, 1960.

Bentley, Eric, ed. *The Theory of the Modern Stage: An Introduction to Modern Theatre and Drama*. Harmondsworth: Penguin, 1978.

Berger, Harry, Jr. *Imaginary Audition: Shakespeare on Page and Stage*. Berkeley: University of California Press, 1989.

Bevington, David. "Modern Spelling: The Hard Choices." *Textual Performances: The Modern Reproduction of Shakespeare's Drama*. Ed. Margaret Jane Kidnie and Lukas Erne. Cambridge: Cambridge University Press, 2004. 143–57.

Blackmur, R. P. *Language as Gesture: Essays in Poetry*. New York: Harcourt, Brace, and Co., 1952.

Blau, Herbert. *The Audience*. Baltimore: Johns Hopkins University Press, 1990.

Blau, Herbert. *Take Up the Bodies: Theater at the Vanishing Point*. Urbana: University of Illinois Press, 1982.

Blayney, Peter M. "The Alleged Popularity of Playbooks." *Shakespeare Quarterly* 56 (2005): 33–50.

Blayney, Peter M. "The Publication of Playbooks." *A New History of Early English Drama*. Ed. John D. Cox and David Scott Kastan. New York: Columbia University Press, 1997. 383–42.

Bloom, Gina. *Voice in Motion: Staging Gender, Shaping Sound in Early Modern England*. Philadelphia: University of Pennsylvania Press, 2007.

Bloom, Harold. *Shakespeare: The Invention of the Human*. New York: Riverhead, 1998.

Bolter, Jay David, and Richard Grusin. *Remediation: Understanding New Media*. Cambridge, MA: MIT Press, 1999.

Bowers, Fredson. *On Editing Shakespeare and the Elizabethan Dramatists*. Philadelphia: University of Pennsylvania Library for the Philip H. and A. S. W. Rosenbach Foundation, 1955.

Branagh, Kenneth. *Hamlet, by William Shakespeare. Screenplay, Introduction and Film Diary*. Film Diary by Russell Jackson. New York: Norton, 1996.

Branagh, Kenneth, dir. *Hamlet*. 1996. DVD Warner Brothers, 2007.

Brantley, Ben. "Looks It Not Like the King? Well, More Like Burton." *New York Times* 1 November 2007: B1.

Brantley, Ben. "When a Universe Reels, a Baryshnikov May Fall." *New York Times* 19 December 2007.

Brater, Enoch. *Beyond Minimalism: Beckett's Late Style in the Theater*. New York: Oxford, 1987.

Brecht, Bertolt. *Brecht on Theatre: The Development of an Aesthetic*. Ed. and Trans. John Willett. New York: Hill and Wang, 1964.

Brecht, Bertolt. *Life of Galileo*. Trans. John Willett. Ed. John Willett and Ralph Manheim. New York: Arcade, 1994.

Bristol, Michael. *Big-Time Shakespeare*. London: Routledge, 1996.

Brook, Peter. *The Empty Space*. 1968. New York: Atheneum, 1978.

Brook, Peter, dir. *Hamlet*. 2001. DVD Facets Multi-Media, 2005.

Brooks, Cleanth. *The Well Wrought Urn: Studies in the Structure of Poetry*. New York: Harcourt, Brace, 1947.

Brooks, Cleanth, and Robert B. Heilman. *Understanding Drama: Eight Plays*. New York: Henry Holt, 1945.

Brooks, Douglas A. *From Playhouse to Printing House: Drama and Authorship in Early Modern England*. Cambridge: Cambridge University Press, 2000.

Brown, John Russell. *Discovering Shakespeare: A New Guide to the Plays*. New York: Columbia University Press, 1981.

Bruster, Douglas, and Robert Weimann. *Shakespeare and the Power of Performance: Stage and Page in the Elizabethan Theatre*. Cambridge: Cambridge University Press, 2008.

Burke, Kenneth. "Antony in Behalf of the Play." *The Philosophy of Literary Form* 329–43.

Burke, Kenneth. "Foreword." *The Philosophy of Literary Form* xvii–xxiv.

Burke, Kenneth. *A Grammar of Motives*. 1945. Berkeley: University of California Press, 1969.

Burke, Kenneth. "Literature as Equipment for Living." *The Philosophy of Literary Form* 293–304.

Burke, Kenneth. "Musicality in Verse." *The Philosophy of Literary Form* 369–78.

Burke, Kenneth. "The Nature of Art Under Capitalism." *The Philosophy of Literary Form* 314–22.

Burke, Kenneth. "*Othello*: An Essay to Illustrate a Method." Newstok, *Kenneth Burke on Shakespeare* 65 100.

Burke, Kenneth. *The Philosophy of Literary Form: Studies in Symbolic Action*. 1941. 3rd ed. Berkeley: University of California Press, 1973.

Burke, Kenneth. "The Philosophy of Literary Form." *The Philosophy of Literary Form* 1–137.

Burke, Kenneth. "Reading While You Run: An Exercise on Translating from English to English." *The Philosophy of Literary Form* 323–8.

Burke, Kenneth. *A Rhetoric of Motives*. 1950. Berkeley: University of California Press, 1969.

Burke, Kenneth. "The Rhetoric of Hitler's 'Battle.'" *The Philosophy of Literary Form* 191–220.

Burke, Kenneth. "Twelve Propositions on the Relation between Economics and Psychology." *The Philosophy of Literary Form* 305–13.

Burke, Kenneth. "Words as Deeds." *Centrum* 3.2 (Fall 1975): 147–68.

Butler, Judith. *Excitable Speech: A Politics of the Performative*. New York: Routledge, 1997.

Butler, Judith. *Gender Trouble: Feminism and the Subversion of Identity*. New York: Routledge, 1990.

Carboni, Alessandro. "ABQ: From Quad to Zero: Mathematical and Choreographic Processes – between Number and Not Number." *Performance Research* 12.1 (2007): 50–6.

Carlson, Marvin. *Performance: A Critical Introduction*. London: Routledge, 1996.

Carson, Anne. "Preface: Tragedy – A Curious Art Form." *Grief Lessons: Four Plays by Euripides*. Trans. Anne Carson. New York: New York Review of Books, 2006. 7–9.

Cartelli, Thomas. "Channeling the Ghosts: The Wooster Group's Remediation of the 1964 Electronovision *Hamlet*." *Shakespeare Survey* 61 (2008): 147–60.

Causey, Matthew. *Theatre and Performance in Digital Culture: From Simulation to Embeddedness*. London: Routledge, 2006.

Cavell, Stanley. *Must We Mean What We Say?* New York: Scribner, 1969.

Chambers, Robert, ed. *The Book of Days: A Miscellany of Popular Antiquities in connection with The Calendar including Anecdote, Biography, & History,*

Curiosities of Literature, and Oddities of Human Life and Character. London: W. & R. Chambers, 1864. Rpt. 1906.

Chapman, George. *Bussy D'Ambois*. Ed. Robert J. Lordi. Lincoln: University of Nebraska Press, 1964.

Chaudhuri, Una. *Staging Place: The Geography of Modern Drama*. Ann Arbor: University of Michigan Press, 1995.

Chaudhuri, Una, and Elinor Fuchs, eds. *Land/Scape/Theater*. Ann Arbor: University of Michigan Press, 2003.

Cheney, Patrick. *Shakespeare's Literary Authorship*. Cambridge: Cambridge University Press, 2008.

Conquergood, Dwight. "Rethinking Ethnography: Towards a Critical Cultural Politics." *Cultural Monographs* 58 (1991): 179–94.

Conquergood, Dwight. "Ethnography, Rhetoric, and Performance." *Quarterly Journal of Speech* 78 (1992): 80–123.

Conquergood, Dwight. "Of Caravans and Carnivals: Performance Studies in Motion." *TDR: The Drama Review – The Journal of Performance Studies* 39.4 (1995): 137–41.

Cornford, F. M. *The Origin of Attic Comedy*. London: E. Arnold, 1914.

Cox, Nicholas. *The Gentleman's Recreation: Being a Treatise of Hawking and Falconry*. London, 1686.

Craig, Hardin. "Hamlet's Book." *The Huntington Library Bulletin* No. 6 (November 1934): 17–37.

Crowther, Bosley. "Electronic Cameras Record Play." *New York Times* 24 September 1964.

Cuvier, G., "Femme de Race Bochismanne." *Histoire Naturelle des Mammifères, avec des figures originales, coloriées, dessinées d'après des animaux vivants*. Ed. Geoffrey Saint-Hilaire and Frédéric Cuvier. Paris: A. Belin, 1824. 1–7.

de Grazia, Margreta. *Hamlet without Hamlet*. Cambridge: Cambridge University Press, 2007.

de Grazia, Margreta, and Peter Stallybrass. "The Materiality of the Shakespearean Text." *Shakespeare Quarterly* 44 (1993): 255–83.

Dent, Alan, ed. *Hamlet: The Film and the Play*. Designs by Roger Furse. London: World Film Publications, 1948.

Dent, Alan. "Text-Editing Shakespeare with Particular Reference to 'Hamlet.'" Dent, *Hamlet: The Film and the Play*.

Derrida, Jacques. "La Parole Soufflée." *Writing and Difference*. Trans. Alan Bass. Chicago: University of Chicago Press, 1978. 169–95.

Derrida, Jacques. "The Theater of Cruelty and the Closure of Representation." *Writing and Difference* 232–50.

Derrida, Jacques. *Paper Machine*. Trans. Rachel Bowlby. Stanford: Stanford University Press, 2005.

Diamond, Elin. *Unmaking Mimesis: Essays on Feminism and Theater*. London: Routledge, 1997.

Diderot, Denis. *The Paradox of Acting*. Trans. Walter Herries Pollock. London: Chatto and Windus, 1883.

Dixon, Steve, with contributions by Barry Smith. *Digital Performance: A History of New Media in Theater, Dance, Performance Art, and Installation*. Cambridge, MA: MIT Press, 2007.

Donaldson, Peter S. "Remediation: Hamlet among the Pixelvisionaries: Video Art, Authenticity, and 'Wisdom' in Almereyda's *Hamlet*." Henderson, *A Concise Companion to Shakespeare on Screen* 216–37.

Elam, Harry, Jr. *Taking It to the Streets: The Social Protest Theater of Luis Valdez and Amiri Baraka*. Ann Arbor: University of Michigan Press, 1997.

Elam, Harry, Jr., and Alice Rayner. "Body Parts: Between Story and Spectacle in *Venus* By Suzan-Lori Parks." *Staging Resistance: Essays on Political Theater*. Ed. Jeanne Colleran and Jenny S. Spencer. Ann Arbor: University of Michigan Press, 1998. 265–82.

Elam, Harry, Jr., and Alice Rayner. "Echoes from the Black (W)hole: An Examination of *The America Play* by Suzan-Lori Parks." *Performing America: Cultural Nationalism in American Theater*. Ed. Jeffrey D. Mason and J. Ellen Gainor. Ann Arbor: University of Michigan Press, 1999. 178–92.

Eliot, T. S. *The Complete Poems and Plays 1909–1950*. New York: Harcourt Brace & World, 1971.

Eliot, T. S. "Introduction." *Shakespeare and the Popular Dramatic Tradition*. By S. L. Bethell. London: P. S. King and Staples, 1944. n.p. [7–9].

Eliot, T. S. "Marie Lloyd." *Selected Prose of T. S. Eliot* 172–4.

Eliot, T. S. *Murder in the Cathedral. The Complete Poems and Plays 1909–1950* 173–221.

Eliot, T. S. "Poetry and Drama." *Selected Prose of T. S. Eliot* 132–47.

Eliot, T. S. *Selected Prose of T. S. Eliot*. Ed. and Introd. Frank Kermode. New York: Harcourt Brace Jovanovich, 1975.

Eliot, T. S. "Tradition and the Individual Talent." *Selected Prose of T. S. Eliot* 37–44.

Eliot, T. S. "*The Waste Land*: Text of the First Edition." *The Waste Land: A Facsimile and Transcript of the Original Drafts including the Annotations of Ezra Pound*. Ed. Valerie Eliot. New York: Harcourt Brace Jovanovich, 1971. 133–49.

Erickson, Jon. "The Ghost of the Literary in Recent Theories of Text and Performance." *Theatre Survey* 47.2 (November 2006): 245–51.

Erne, Lukas. "Reconsidering Shakespearean Authorship." *Shakespeare Studies* 36 (2008): 26–36.

Erne, Lukas. *Shakespeare as Literary Dramatist*. Cambridge: Cambridge University Press, 2003.

Esslin, Martin. *The Theatre of the Absurd*. Garden City, NY: Doubleday, 1961.

Evans, Maurice, ed., *George Chapman: Bussy D'Ambois*. London: Ernest Benn, 1965.

Farmer, Alan B., and Zachary Lesser. "The Popularity of Playbooks Revisited." *Shakespeare Quarterly* 56 (2005): 1–32.

Fabian, Johannes. "Hindsight: Thoughts on Anthropology Upon Reading Francis Galton's *Narrative of an Explorer in Tropical South Africa*." *Critique of Anthropology* 7.2 (1987): 37–49.

Falconry Forum. <falconryforum.co.uk>.

Farmer, Alan B., and Zachary Lesser. "The Popularity of Playbooks Revisited." *Shakespeare Quarterly* 56 (2005): 1–32.

Feenberg, Andrew. *Critical Theory of Technology*. New York: Oxford University Press, 1991.

Fergusson, Francis. *The Human Image in Dramatic Literature*. New York: Doubleday, 1957.

Fergusson, Francis. *The Idea of a Theater: A Study of Ten Plays. The Art of Drama in Changing Perspective*. Princeton: Princeton University Press, 1949.

Fergusson, Francis. "Kenneth Burke's *Grammar of Motives*." Rueckert, *Critical Responses to Kenneth Burke 1924–1966* 173–82.

Fischer-Lichte, Erika. "The Avant-Garde and the Semiotics of Antitextual Gesture." Trans. James Harding. Harding, *Contours of the Theatrical Avant-Garde* 79–95.

Fischer-Lichte, Erika. *The Semiotics of Theatre*. Trans. Jeremy Gaines and Doris L. Jones. Bloomington: Indiana University Press, 1992.

Fischer-Lichte, Erika. "Theaterwissenschaft." *Metzler Lexikon Theatertheorie*. Ed. Erika Fischer-Lichte, Doris Kolesch, and Matthias Warstat. Stuttgart: P J. B. Metzler, 2005. 351–8.

Foucault, Michel. "Of Other Spaces." Trans. Jay Miskowiec. *Diacritics* 16.1 (Spring 1986): 22–7.

Frazer, Sir James. *The Golden Bough: A Study in Magic and Religion*. 2nd ed. London: Macmillan, 1900.

Freud, Sigmund. "Some Character-Types Met with in Psycho-analytic Work." Trans. E. Colburn Mayne. *Character and Culture*. New York: Collier, 1963. 157–81.

Freud, Sigmund. "The 'Uncanny.'" Trans. David McClintock. *The Uncanny*. Harmondsworth: Penguin, 2003. 121–62.

Frye, Northrop. *Anatomy of Criticism: Four Essays*. Princeton: Princeton University Press, 1957.

Fugard, Athol, John Kani, and Winston Ntshona. *The Island*. In *Statements: Three Plays*. Oxford: Oxford University Press, 1974. 45–77.

Garner, Stanton B., Jr. *Bodied Spaces: Phenomenology and Performance in Contemporary Drama*. Ithaca: Cornell University Press, 1994.

Garrett, Shawn-Marie. "Figures, Speech and Form in *Imperceptible Mutabilities in the Third Kingdom*." Wetmore and Smith-Howard, *Suzan-Lori Parks: A Casebook* 1–17.

Garton, Janet. "The Middle Plays." McFarlane, *Cambridge Companion to Ibsen* 106–25.

Geertz, Clifford. *The Interpretation of Cultures: Selected Essays*. New York: Basic Books, 1973.

Geis, Deborah R. *Suzan-Lori Parks*. Ann Arbor: University of Michigan Press, 2008.

Gilman, Sander L. "Black Bodies, White Bodies: Toward an Iconography of Female Sexuality in Late Nineteenth-Century Art, Medicine, and Literature." *"Race," Writing, and Difference*. Ed. Henry Louis Gates, Jr. Chicago: University of Chicago Press, 1986. 223–61.

Goffman, Erving. *Frame Analysis: An Essay on the Organization of Experience*. New York: Harper, 1974.

Goldman, Michael. *The Actor's Freedom: Toward a Theory of Drama*. New York: Viking, 1975.

Goldman, Michael. *Ibsen: The Dramaturgy of Fear*. New York: Columbia University Press, 1999.

Goldman, Michael. *On Drama: Boundaries of Genre, Borders of Self*. Ann Arbor: University of Michigan Press, 2000.

Goodman, Nelson. *Languages of Art: An Approach to a Theory of Symbols*. Indianapolis: Bobbs-Merrill, 1968.

Gould, Stephen Jay. "The Hottentot Venus." *Natural History* 91.10 (1982): 20–7.

Gottscheff, Dimiter, dir. *Ivanov*. Volksbühne Theater, Berlin, January 2005.

Granville-Barker, Harley. *Prefaces to Shakespeare*. 2 vols. Princeton: Princeton University Press, 1978.

The Great McGinty. Dir. Preston Sturges. Paramount, 1940.

Greenaway, Peter, dir. *Prospero's Books*. VHS. Troy, MI: Media Home Entertainment, 1993.

Greenblatt, Stephen. *Renaissance Self-Fashioning: From More to Shakespeare*. Chicago: University of Chicago Press, 1980.

Greg, W. W. *The Editorial Problem in Shakespeare: A Survey of the Foundations of the Text*. Oxford: Clarendon Press, 1951.

Grigely, Joseph. *Textualterity: Art, Theory, and Textual Criticism*. Ann Arbor: University of Michigan Press, 1995.

Grosz, Elizabeth. *Volatile Bodies: Toward a Corporeal Feminism*. Bloomington: Indiana University Press, 1994.

Grotowski, Jerzy. *Towards a Poor Theatre*. Ed. Eugenio Barba. Pref. Peter Brook. New York: Routledge, 2002.

Gussow, Mel. "Stage: Disputed 'Endgame' in Debut." *New York Times* 20 December 1984.

Halpern, Richard. *Shakespeare Among the Moderns*. Ithaca: Cornell University Press, 1997.

Hapaz, Clay. Email to author 6 December 2007.

Harding, James M., ed. *Contours of the Theatrical Avant-Garde: Performance and Textuality*. Ann Arbor: University of Michigan Press, 2000.

Hardwick, Elizabeth. *Seduction and Betrayal: Women and Literature*. New York: Vintage, 1975.

Haring-Smith, Tori. "Dramaturging Non-Realism: Creating a New Vocabulary?" *Theatre Topics* 13 (2003): 45–54.

Harrison, Jane Ellen. *Themis: A Study of the Social Origins of the Greek Religion, with an Excursus on the Ritual Forms Preserved in Greek Tragedy by Professor Gilbert Murray and a Chapter on the Origin of the Olympic Games by Mr. F. M. Cornford*. Cambridge: Cambridge University Press, 1912.

Hartmann, Teresa. Email to author 5 December 2007.

Hayles, N. Katherine. *How We Became Posthuman: Virtual Bodies in Cybernetics, Literature, and Informatics*. Chicago: University of Chicago Press, 1999.

Hayles, N. Katherine. *Writing Machines*. Designer Anne Burdick. Editorial Director Peter Lunenfeld. Cambridge, MA: MIT Press, 2002.

Henderson, Diana, ed. *A Concise Companion to Shakespeare on Screen*. Oxford: Blackwell, 2006.

Herren, Graley. *Samuel Beckett's Plays on Film and Television*. New York: Palgrave Macmillan, 2007.

Hershock, Peter D. *Reinventing the Wheel: A Buddhist Response to the Information Age*. Albany: State University of New York Press, 1999.

Hibbard, G. R., ed. *Hamlet*. Oxford: Oxford University Press, 1987.

Hodgdon, Barbara. "Spectacular Bodies: Acting + Cinema + Shakespeare." Henderson, *A Concise Companion to Shakespeare on Screen* 96–111.

Hodgdon, Barbara, and W. B. Worthen, eds. *A Companion to Shakespeare and Performance*. Oxford: Blackwell, 2005.

Holland, Peter. *Ornament of Action: Text and Performance in Restoration Comedy*. Cambridge: Cambridge University Press, 1979.

Holmes, Rachel. *African Queen: The Real Life of the Hottentot Venus*. New York: Random House, 2007.

Hopkins, D. J., and Bryan Reynolds. "The Making of Authorships: Transversal Navigation in the Wake of *Hamlet*, Robert Wilson, Wolfgang Wiens, and Shakespace." *Shakespeare After Mass Media*. Ed. Richard Burt. New York: Palgrave, 2002. 265–86.

Howard, Jean. *The Stage and Social Struggle in Early Modern England*. London: Routledge, 1994.

Hudston, Jonathan, ed. *George Chapman: Plays and Poems*. Texts prepared by Richard Rowland. London: Penguin, 1998.

Ibsen, Henrik. *The Complete Major Prose Plays*. Trans. and Introd. Rolf Fjelde. New York: Plume, 1978.

Ibsen, Henrik. *Letters and Speeches*. Ed. Evert Sprinchorn. [London]: MacGibbon and Kee, 1965.

Ibsen, Henrik. *Rosmersholm. Samlede Verker.* Oslo: Norske Forlag, 1932. 10: 311–547.

International Falconry. <www.intfalconry.com>.

Ionesco, Eugène. *Four Plays: The Bald Soprano, The Lesson, Jack; or, The Submission, The Chairs*. Trans. Donald M. Allen. New York: Grove, 1958.

Irace, Kathleen O., ed. *The First Quarto of Hamlet*. Cambridge: Cambridge University Press, 1998.

Isherwood, Charles. "Keeping the Old Off Off Broadway Spirit Alive." *New York Times* 27 April 2007.

Isherwood, Charles. "Words Fail Him, but Memories Can't Be Silenced." *New York Times* 19 July 2008.

Jackson, Russell. Email to author, 22 June 2007 and 2 July 2007.

Jackson, Russell. "The Film Diary." *Hamlet*. By William Shakespeare. Screenplay and Introduction by Kenneth Branagh. New York: Norton, 1996.

Jackson, Russell. "Kenneth Branagh's Film of *Hamlet*: The Textual Choices." *Shakespeare Bulletin* 25.2 (1997): 37–8.

Jackson, Shannon. *Professing Performance: Theatre in the Academy from Philology to Performativity*. Cambridge: Cambridge University Press, 2004.

Jacobs, Leonard. "Beckett Estate Ends 'Godot,' Cites Casting Concerns." *Backstage* 29 November 2002.

Jameson, Fredric. "Postmodernism and Consumer Society." *The Anti-Aesthetic: Essays on Postmodern Culture*. Ed. Hal Foster. Port Townsend: Bay Press, 1983. 111–25.

Jameson, Fredric. "Symbolic Inference; or, Kenneth Burke and Ideological Analysis." *The Ideologies of Theory: Essays 1971–1986. Volume 1: Situations of Theory*. Theory and History of Literature Volume 48. Minneapolis: University of Minnesota Press, 1988. 137–52.

Jenkins, Harold, ed. *Hamlet*. The Arden Shakespeare third series. London: Methuen, 1982; rpt. Walton-on-Thames, Surrey: Thomas Nelson, 1997.

Jiggetts, Shelby. "Interview with Suzan-Lori Parks." *Callaloo* 19 (2006): 309–17.

Johnson, Samuel, ed. *The Plays of William Shakespeare, in Eight Volumes, with the Corrections and Illustrations of Various Commentators; To which are added Notes by Sam. Johnson*. Vol. VI. London: J. and R. Tonson, et al., 1765.

Johung, Jennifer. "Figuring the 'Spells'/Spelling the Figures: Suzan-Lori Parks's 'Scene of Love (?).'" *Theatre Journal* 58 (2006): 39–52.

Jones, Amelia. "Stelarc's Technological 'Transcendence'/Stelarc's Wet Body: The Insistent Return of the Flesh." *Stelarc: The Monograph*. Ed. Marquard Smith. Foreword William Gibson. Cambridge, MA: MIT Press, 2005. 87–123.

Jonson, Ben. *Poetaster*. Ed. Tom Cain. Manchester: Manchester University Press, 1995.

Kalb, Jonathan. *Beckett in Performance*. Cambridge: Cambridge University Press, 1989.

Kastan, David Scott. "'To think these trifles some-thing': Shakespearean Playbooks and the Claims of Authorship." *Shakespeare Studies* 36 (2008): 37–48.

Katsura Kan and Saltimbanques. *Beckett Butoh Notation W-Quad 07*. <www.youtube.com/watch?v=QPHkpcyO9CE&feature=rec-HM-r2> 12 July 2009.

Keneally, Thomas. *The Playmaker*. London: Hodder and Stoughton, 1987.

Kernan, Alvin. *Printing Technology, Letters & Samuel Johnson*. Princeton: Princeton University Press, 1987.

Kirby, Percival R. "The Hottentot Venus." *Africana Notes and News* 6 (1949): 55–62.

Kirby, Percival R. "More About the Hottentot Venus." *Africana Notes and News* 10 (1953): 124–34.

Kirshenblatt-Gimblett, Barbara. *Destination Culture: Tourism, Museums, Heritage*. Berkeley: University of California Press, 1998.

Knapp, Jeffrey. "What Is a Co-Author?" *Representations* 89 (Winter 2005): 1–29.

Knight, G. Wilson. *The Wheel of Fire: Interpretations of Shakespearian Tragedy with Three New Essays*. Rev. ed. London: Methuen, 1949.

Knutson, Roslyn Lander. *Playing Companies and Commerce in Shakespeare's Time*. Cambridge: Cambridge University Press, 2001.

Krasner, David, and David Z. Saltz, eds. *Staging Philosophy: Intersections of Theater, Performance, and Philosophy*. Ann Arbor: University of Michigan Press, 2006.

Kubiak, Anthony. *Agitated States: Performance in the American Theater of Cruelty*. Ann Arbor: University of Michigan Press, 2002.

Lahr, John. "Lowdown Sensations." *New Yorker* 20 May 1996: 98–100.

Lamb, Charles. "On the Tragedies of Shakespeare, Considered with Reference to their Fitness for Stage Representation." 1811. *Works in Prose and Verse*. By Charles and Mary Lamb. Ed. Thomas Hutchinson. London: Henry Frowde for Oxford University Press, n.d. [1908].

Langbaine, Gerald. *The Hunter: A discourse of horsemanship directing the right way to breed, keep, and train a horse for ordinary hunting*. Oxford: Nicholas Cox, 1685.

Lanier, Douglas. "Shakespeare on the Record." Hodgdon and Worthen, *A Companion to Shakespeare and Performance* 415–36.

"Law Report – The Hottentot Venus." *The Times* 29 November 1810.

Lefebvre, Henri. *The Production of Space*. Trans. Donald Nicholson-Smith. Oxford: Blackwell, 1991.

Lehman, Courtney. *Shakespeare Remains: Theater to Film, Early Modern to Modern.* Ithaca: Cornell University Press, 2002.

Lehmann, Hans-Thies *Postdramatic Theatre.* Trans. Karen Jürs-Munby. London: Routledge, 2006.

Lentricchia, Frank. *Criticism and Social Change.* Chicago: University of Chicago Press, 1983.

Lesser, Zachary, and Peter Stallybrass. "The First Literary *Hamlet* and the Commonplacing of Professional Plays." *Shakespeare Quarterly* 59 (2008): 371–420.

Longenbach, James. *The Resistance to Poetry.* Chicago: University of Chicago Press, 2004.

Luhrmann, Baz, dir. *William Shakespeare's Romeo + Juliet.* Screenplay by Craig Pearce and Baz Luhrmann. Twentieth Century Fox, 1996.

Lukács, Georg. "The Sociology of Modern Drama." Trans. Lee Baxandall. Bentley, *Theory of the Modern Stage* 421–50.

Lyman, Elizabeth Dyrud. "Visible Language in Theatrical Texts: Present, Past, and Future Forms of Stage Direction." PhD dissertation. Department of English, University of Virginia, 2003.

Mack, Maynard. "The World of *Hamlet*." *Yale Review* 41 (1952): 502–23.

Maguire, Laurie E. *Shakespearean Suspect Texts: The "Bad" Quartos and Their Contexts.* Cambridge: Cambridge University Press, 1996.

Malpica, Javier. *Our Dad is in Atlantis.* *American Theatre* 25.6 (July/August 2008): 69–82.

Marks, Kathy. "Director Calls Beckett Heir an 'Enemy of Art' after Godot Censure." *Independent* 11 January 2003 <independent.co.uk> 20 October 2008.

McFarlane, James, ed. *The Cambridge Companion to Ibsen.* Cambridge: Cambridge University Press, 1994.

McFarlane, James, ed. and trans. *Rosmersholm. The Oxford Ibsen.* Vol. 6. London: Oxford University Press, 1960.

McGann, Jerome. *Radiant Textuality: Literature after the World Wide Web.* Houndmills: Palgrave, 2001.

McKenzie, Jon. "Is Performance Studies Imperialist?" *TDR: The Drama Review – The Journal of Performance Studies* 50.4 (2006): 5–8.

McKenzie, Jon. *Perform or Else: From Discipline to Performance.* London: Routledge, 2001.

McLeod, Randall. "UN *Editing* Shak-speare." *Sub-Stance* 33 (1982): 26–55.

McLuskie, Kathleen. "Shakespeare Goes Slumming: Harlem '37 and Birmingham '97." Hodgdon and Worthen, *Companion to Shakespeare and Performance* 249–66.

McMahon, Barbara. "Beckett Estate Fails to Stop Women Waiting for Godot." *Guardian* 4 February 2006.

"The Met on Demand." *New York Times* 29 November 2007.

Moi, Toril. *Henrik Ibsen and the Birth of Modernism: Art, Theater, Philosophy.* Oxford: Oxford University Press, 2006.

Monks, Aoife. " 'Genuine Negroes and Real Bloodhounds': Cross-Dressing, Eugene O'Neill, the Wooster Group, and *The Emperor Jones.*" *Modern Drama* 48 (2005): 540–64.

Morello, Élisa, and Yannick Donet, adapt. *Quad* <www.youtube.com/watch?v=wl-GwUBnlg&feature-related> 12 October 2008.

Morley, Sheridan. Liner notes. *Richard Burton's Hamlet.*

Mowat, Barbara A., and Paul Werstine, eds. *The Tragedy of Hamlet Prince of Denmark.* Folger Shakespeare Library. New York: Washington Square Press, 1992.

Murray, Gilbert. "Excursus on the Ritual Forms Preserved in Greek Tragedy." Harrison, *Themis* 341–63.

Newstok, Scott L., ed. "Editor's Introduction: Renewing Kenneth Burke's 'Plea for the Shakespearean Drama.'" *Kenneth Burke on Shakespeare* xvii–l.

Newstok, Scott L., ed. *Kenneth Burke on Shakespeare.* West Lafayette, IN: Parlor Press, 2007.

Norman, Donald A. *The Design of Everyday Things.* New York: Basic Books, 2002.

The Norton Shakespeare, Based on the Oxford Edition. Gen. ed. Stephen Greenblatt. New York: W. W. Norton, 1997.

Nowra, Louis. *The Golden Age: Australia Plays.* Introd. Katherine Brisbane. London: Nick Hern Books, 1989.

Olivier, Laurence. "Foreword." Dent, *Hamlet: The Film and the Play.*

Olivier, Laurence, dir. *Hamlet.* 1948. DVD. Criterion Collection, 2000.

Ong, Walter J. *Orality and Literacy: The Technologizing of the Word.* London: Routledge, 1982.

Osborne, Laurie E. "Speculations on Shakespearean Cinematic Liveness." *Shakespeare Bulletin* 24.3 (2006): 49–65.

Parker, Andrew, and Eve Kosofsky Sedgwick, eds. *Performativity and Performance.* London: Routledge, 1992.

Parks, Suzan-Lori. *The America Play and Other Works.* New York: Theatre Communications Group, 1995.

Parks, Suzan-Lori. *The America Play. America Play and Other Works* 157–99.

Parks, Suzan-Lori. *The Death of the Last Black Man in the Whole Entire World. America Play and Other Works* 99–132.

Parks, Suzan-Lori. "from Elements of Style." *The America Play and Other Works* 6–18.

Parks, Suzan-Lori. *Fucking A. Red Letter Plays* 113–240.

Parks, Suzan-Lori. "Possession." *The America Play and Other Works* 3–5.

Parks, Suzan-Lori. *The Red Letter Plays*. New York: Theatre Communications Group, 2001.

Parks, Suzan-Lori. *Venus*. New York: Theatre Communications Group, 1997.

Paulin, Tom. *The Riot Act: A Version of Sophocles' Antigone*. London: Faber, 1985.

Pearce, Craig, and Baz Luhrmann. *William Shakespeare's Romeo + Juliet. The Contemporary Film, the Classic Play*. New York: Bantam, 1996.

Pennington, Michael. *Hamlet: A User's Guide*. London: Nick Hern Books, 1996.

Performance License Rider: Samuel Beckett's Plays. Samuel French, Inc.

Phelan, Peggy. "Reconstructing Love: *King Lear* and Theatre Architecture." Hodgdon and Worthen, *A Companion to Shakespeare and Performance* 13–35.

Phelan, Peggy. *Unmarked: The Politics of Performance*. London: Routledge, 1993.

Pierce, John R. *An Introduction to Information Theory: Symbols, Signals & Noise*. 2nd rev. ed. New York: Dover, 1980.

Protopapa, Efrosini. "A Phantom in Contemporary European Choreography." *Performance Research* 12.1 (2007): 20–34.

Puchner, Martin. "Entanglements: The Histories of *TDR*." *TDR: The Drama Review – The Journal of Performance Studies* 50.1 (T189; Spring 2006): 13–27.

Puchner, Martin. *Stage Fright: Modernism, Anti-Theatricality, and Drama*. Baltimore: Johns Hopkins University Press, 2002.

Rabkin, Gerald. "Is There a Text on This Stage?: Theatre/Authorship/ Interpretation." *Performing Arts Journal* 9.2/3 (1985): 142–59.

Ransom, John Crowe. "An Address to Kenneth Burke." Rueckert, *Critical Responses to Kenneth Burke 1924–1966* 141–58.

Ransom, John Crowe. *The New Criticism*. Norfolk, CT: New Directions, 1941.

Raphael, Timothy. "Mo(u)rning in America: Hamlet, Reagan, and the Rights of Memory." *Theatre Journal* 59 (2007): 1–20.

Rayner, Alice, and Harry J. Elam, Jr. "'Unfinished Business': Reconfiguring History in Suzan-Lori Parks's *The Death of the Last Black Man in the Whole Entire World*." *Theatre Journal* 46 (1994): 447–64.

Reinelt, Janelle. "Is Performance Studies Imperialist? Part 2." *TDR: The Drama Review – The Journal of Performance Studies* 51.3 (2007): 7–16.

Reinelt, Janelle G., and Joseph R. Roach, eds. *Critical Theory and Performance*. Ann Arbor: University of Michigan Press, 1992.

"Richard Burton Discusses 'Electronovision.'" *Richard Burton's Hamlet*.

Richard Burton's Hamlet. Stage dir. John Gielgud, 1964. Film dir. Bill Colleran. Atlantic Programmes Ltd. 1964. Onward Productions Ltd. and Paul Brownstein Productions Inc., 1995. DVD Image Entertainment, 1999.

Richards, I. A. *Practical Criticism: A Study of Literary Judgment*. 1929. London: Kegan Paul, Trench, Trubner and Co., 1930.

Richards, Nathaniel. *Tragedy of Messallina the Roman Empress. As it hath beene acted with generall applause divers times, by the Companie of his Majesties Revells.* London: Printed by Tho. Cates for Daniel Frere, 1640.

Rimmer, Matthew. "Damned to Fame: The Moral Rights of the Beckett Estate." *Australian Library and Information Association* <www.alia.org.au/publishing/incite/2003/05/beckett.html> 20 October 2008.

Roach, Joseph. *Cities of the Dead: Circum-Atlantic Performance.* New York: Columbia University Press, 1996.

Roach, Joseph. "The Great Hole of History: Liturgical Silence in Beckett, Osofisan, and Parks." *South Atlantic Quarterly* 100 (Winter 2001): 307–17.

Román, David. *Performance in America: Contemporary US Culture and the Performing Arts.* Durham, NC: Duke University Press, 2005.

Rouse, John. "Textuality and Authority in Theater and Drama: Some Contemporary Possibilities." Reinelt and Roach, *Critical Theory and Performance* 146–57.

Rowe, Katherine. " 'Remember Me': Technologies of Memory in Michael Almereyda's *Hamlet.*" *Shakespeare, the Movie, II.* Ed. Richard Burt and Lynda E. Boose. London: Routledge, 2003. 37–55.

Rudnitsky, Konstantin. *Meyerhold the Director.* Trans. George Petrov. Ed. Sydney Schultze. Introd. Ellendea Proffer. Ann Arbor: Ardis, 1981.

Rueckert, William H., ed. *Critical Responses to Kenneth Burke 1924–1966.* Minneapolis: University of Minnesota Press, 1969.

Sauter, Willmar. *The Theatrical Event: Dynamics of Performance and Reception.* Iowa City: University of Iowa Press, 2000.

Savran, David. *Breaking the Rules: The Wooster Group.* New York: Theatre Communications Group, 1988.

Schechner, Richard. "Actuals." *Performance Theory.* Rev. ed. New York: Routledge, 1988. 35–67.

Schechner, Richard. "Collective Reflexivity: Restoration of Behavior." *A Crack in the Mirror: Reflexive Perspectives in Anthropology.* Ed. Jay Ruby. Philadelphia: University of Pennsylvania Press, 1982. 39–81.

Schechner, Richard. "Interview with Richard Schechner." Conducted by James M. Harding. Harding, *Contours of the Theatrical Avant-Garde* 202–14.

Schechner, Richard. *Performance Theory.* London: Routledge, 2003.

Schechner, Richard. "Restoration of Behavior." *Between Theater & Anthropology.* Foreword Victor Turner. Philadelphia: University of Pennsylvania Press, 1985. 35–116.

Schmidt, Alexander. *Shakespeare-Lexikon: A Complete Dictionary of all the English words, phrases and constructions in the Works of the Poet.* Berlin, 1901. Rev. and enlarged Gregor Sarrazin. New York: Benjamin Blom, 1968.

Scott, Charlotte. *Shakespeare and the Idea of the Book.* Oxford: Oxford University Press, 2007.

Shannon, Claude E. "The Mathematical Theory of Communication." Shannon and Weaver, *The Mathematical Theory of Communication* 29–125.

Shannon, Claude E., and Warren Weaver. *The Mathematical Theory of Communication*. 1949. Urbana: University of Illinois Press, 1964.

Shepherd, Simon. *Theatre, Body and Pleasure*. London: Routledge, 2006.

Smith, Anna Deavere. *Fires in the Mirror: Crown Heights, Brooklyn and Other Identities*. New York: Doubleday, 1993.

Smith, Anna Deavere. "Introduction." *Fires in the Mirror* xxiii–xli.

Soja, Edward. *Postmodern Geographies: The Reassertion of Space in Critical Social Theory*. London: Verso, 1989.

Stallybrass, Peter, Roger Chartier, J. Franklin Mowery, and Heather Wolfe. "Hamlet's Tables and the Technologies of Writing in Renaissance England." *Shakespeare Quarterly* 55 (2004): 379–419.

Stanislavski, Constantin. *An Actor's Work: A Student Diary*. Ed. and Trans. Jean Benedetti. London: Routledge, 2008.

Stanislavski, Constantin. "From the Production Plan of *Othello*." *Acting: A Handbook of the Stanislavski Method*. Ed. Toby Cole. New York: Crown, 1979.

Starks, Lisa. "The Displaced Body of Desire: Sexuality in Kenneth Branagh's *Hamlet*." *Shakespeare and Appropriation*. Ed. Christy Desmet and Robert Sawyer. London: Routledge, 1999. 166–78.

States, Bert O. *Great Reckonings in Little Rooms: On the Phenomenology of Theater*. Berkeley: University of California Press, 1985.

Steiner, George. *Antigones*. New York: Oxford University Press, 1984.

Stern, Tiffany. *Rehearsal from Shakespeare to Sheridan*. Oxford: Clarendon Press, 2000.

Stevens, Wallace. "The Emperor of Ice Cream." *The Palm at the End of the Mind*. Ed. Holly Stevens. New York: Random House, 1972. 79–80.

Styan, J. L. *The Shakespeare Revolution: Criticism and Performance in the Twentieth Century*. Cambridge: Cambridge University Press, 1977.

Taplin, Oliver. *Greek Tragedy in Action*. Berkeley: University of California Press, 1978.

Taylor, Diana. *The Archive and the Repertoire: Performing Cultural Memory in the Americas*. Durham, NC: Duke University Press, 2003.

Taylor, Gary. "c:\wp\file.txt 04:41 10–07–8." *The Renaissance Text: Theory, Editing, and Textuality*. Ed. Andrew Murphy. Manchester: Manchester University Press, 2000. 44–54.

Taylor, Gary. "General Introduction." *William Shakespeare: A Textual Companion*. By Stanley Wells and Gary Taylor, with John Jowett and William Montgomery. Oxford: Clarendon, 1987. 1–68.

Taylor, Gary. "The Renaissance and the End of Editing." *Palimpsest: Editorial Theory in the Humanities*. Ed. George Bornstein and Ralph G. Williams. Ann Arbor: University of Michigan Press, 1993. 121–49.

Taylor, Mark C. *The Moment of Complexity: Emerging Network Culture.* Chicago: University of Chicago Press, 2001.

Templeton, Joan. *Ibsen's Women.* Cambridge: Cambridge University Press, 1997.

Thompson, Ann, and Neil Taylor, eds. *Hamlet.* London: Arden Shakespeare, 2006.

Thompson, Ann, and Neil Taylor, eds. *Hamlet: The Texts of 1603 and 1623.* London: Arden Shakespeare, 2006.

Thompson, Howard. "Treat for Teen-Agers." *New York Times* 28 January 1965.

Toole-Stott, R. *Circus and Allied Arts: A World Bibliography 1500–1962.* 3 vols. Derby: Harpus & Sons Distributors, 1962.

"Trailer." *Richard Burton's Hamlet.*

Turner, Victor. *From Ritual to Theatre: The Human Seriousness of Play.* New York: Performing Arts Journal Publications, 1982.

van Itallie, Jean-Claude. *America Hurrah and Other Plays.* New York: Grove, 1978.

Vanden Heuvel, Michael. " 'Mais je dis le chaos positif': Leaky Texts, Parasited Performances, and Maxwellian Academons." Harding, *Contours of the Theatrical Avant-Garde* 130–53.

Walker, Julia A. "The Text/Performance Split across the Analytic/Continental Divide." Krasner and Saltz, *Staging Philosophy: Intersections of Theater, Performance, and Philosophy* 19–40.

Walker, Julia A. "Why Performance? Why Now? Textuality and the Rearticulation of Human Presence." *Yale Journal of Criticism* 16.1 (Spring 2003): 149–75.

Warner, Sara L. "Suzan-Lori Parks's Drama of Disinterment: A Transnational Exploration of *Venus.*" *Theatre Journal* 60 (2008): 181–99.

Weaver, Warren. "Recent Contributions to the Mathematical Theory of Communication." Shannon and Weaver, *The Mathematical Theory of Communication* 1–28.

Weber, Samuel. *Theatricality as Medium.* New York: Fordham University Press, 2004.

Weiler, A. H. "Broadway 'Hamlet' to Be Filmed For Short Run in 1,000 Houses." *New York Times* 27 June 1964.

Weimann, Robert. "Mimesis in *Hamlet.*" *Shakespeare and the Question of Theory.* Ed. Patricia Parker and Geoffrey Hartman. New York: Methuen, 1985. 275–91.

Weingust, Don. *Acting from Shakespeare's First Folio: Theory, Text and Performance.* New York: Routledge, 2006.

Wells, Stanley, and Gary Taylor, with John Jowett and William Montgomery. *William Shakespeare: A Textual Companion.* Oxford: Clarendon, 1987.

Wertenbaker, Timberlake. *Our Country's Good: Based on the Novel "The Playmaker" by Thomas Keneally.* London: Methuen, 1988.

Wess, Robert. *Kenneth Burke: Rhetoric, Subjectivity, Postmodernism.* Cambridge: Cambridge University Press, 1996.

Wetmore, Kevin, Jr., and Alycia Smith-Howard. *Suzan-Lori Parks: A Casebook.* London: Routledge, 2007.

Whigham, Frank. *Ambition and Privilege: The Social Tropes of Elizabethan Courtesy Theory.* Berkeley: University of California Press, 1984.

Wiener, Norbert. *Cybernetics or Control and Communication in the Animal and the Machine.* 2nd ed. Cambridge, MA: MIT Press, 1962. First ed. 1948.

Wiener, Norbert. *The Human Use of Human Beings: Cybernetics and Society.* 2nd. ed. Boston: Houghton Mifflin, 1954; rpt. [Cambridge]: DaCapo Press, n.d. [1988].

Wiles, David. *Tragedy in Athens: Performance Space and Theatrical Meaning.* Cambridge: Cambridge University Press, 1997.

Wiles, David. *A Short History of Western Performance Space.* Cambridge: Cambridge University Press, 2003.

Williams, Raymond. *Drama from Ibsen to Brecht.* London: Hogarth Press, 1987.

Williams, Raymond. *Drama from Ibsen to Eliot.* London: Chatto and Windus, 1952.

Wilson, J. Dover. *The Manuscript of Shakespeare's Hamlet and the Problem of its Transmission.* Vol. 2: *Editorial Problems and Solutions.* 1934. Cambridge: Cambridge University Press, 1963.

Wilson, J. Dover, ed. *Hamlet.* 1934. 2nd ed. 1936. Cambridge: Cambridge University Press, 1964.

Winkler, John J., and Froma I. Zeitlin, eds. *Nothing to Do with Dionysos? Athenian Drama in its Social Context.* Princeton: Princeton University Press, 1990.

Wise, Jennifer. *Dionysus Writes: The Invention of Theatre in Ancient Greece.* Ithaca: Cornell University Press, 1998.

Wiss, Rosemary. "Lipreading: Remembering Saartjie Baartman." *Australian Journal of Anthropology* 5.1–2 (1997): 11–40.

Wooster Group. *Hamlet.* Dir. Elizabeth LeCompte. Public Theatre, 8–9 November 2007.

Wooster Group. The Wooster Group *Hamlet.* Program. Public Theatre, 8–9 November 2007.

Worthen, W. B. "Convicted Reading: *The Island*, Hybridity, Performance." *Crucibles of Crisis: Performance and Social Change.* Ed. Janelle Reinelt. Ann Arbor: University of Michigan Press, 1996. 165–84.

Worthen, W. B. "Drama, Performativity, Performance." *PMLA* 113 (1998): 1093–107.

Worthen, W. B. "Fond Records: Remembering Theatre in the Digital Age." *Shakespeare, Memory, and Performance.* Ed. Peter Holland. Cambridge: Cambridge University Press, 2006. 281–304.

Worthen, W. B. *Modern Drama and the Rhetoric of Theater.* Berkeley: University of California Press, 1992.

Worthen, W. B. *Print and the Poetics of Modern Drama.* Cambridge: Cambridge University Press, 2006.

Worthen, W. B. *Shakespeare and the Authority of Performance.* Cambridge: Cambridge University Press, 1997.

Worthen, W. B. *Shakespeare and the Force of Modern Performance.* Cambridge: Cambridge University Press, 2003.

Young, Jean. "The Re-Objectification and Re-Commodification of Saartjie Baartman in Suzan-Lori Parks's *Venus.*" *African American Review* 31 (1997): 699–708.

Zeffirelli, Franco, dir. *Hamlet.* 1990. DVD. Warner Brothers, 2004.

Zola, Émile. "Naturalism in the Theatre." Trans. Albert Bermel. Bentley, *Theory of the Modern Stage* 347–72.

Zolotow, Sam. "Stage's 'Hamlet' Becomes a Film." *New York Times* 3 July 1964.

Further Reading

Although all references are listed in the Works Cited, readers of *Drama: Between Poetry and Performance* might wish to consult these general studies of drama, theatre, and performance.

Austin, J. L. *How to Do Things with Words.* 2nd ed. Ed. J. O. Urmson and Marina Sbisà. Cambridge, MA: Harvard University Press, 1997.

Beckerman, Bernard. *Dynamics of Drama: Theory and Method of Analysis.* New York: Drama Book Specialists, 1979.

Bennett, Benjamin. *All Theater Is Revolutionary Theater.* Ithaca: Cornell University Press, 2005.

Bennett, Benjamin. *Theater as Problem: Modern Drama and its Place in Literature.* Ithaca: Cornell University Press, 1990.

Bentley, Eric. *The Playwright as Thinker: A Study of Drama in Modern Times.* 1946. New York: Meridian, 1960.

Blau, Herbert. *The Audience.* Baltimore: Johns Hopkins University Press, 1990.

Blau, Herbert. *Take Up the Bodies: Theater at the Vanishing Point.* Urbana: University of Illinois Press, 1982.

Bolter, Jay David, and Richard Grusin. *Remediation: Understanding New Media.* Cambridge, MA: MIT Press, 1999.

Brook, Peter. *The Empty Space.* 1968. New York: Atheneum, 1978.

Brooks, Cleanth, and Robert B. Heilman. *Understanding Drama: Eight Plays.* New York: Henry Holt, 1945.

Burke, Kenneth. *A Grammar of Motives.* 1945. Berkeley: University of California Press, 1969.

Burke, Kenneth. *The Philosophy of Literary Form: Studies in Symbolic Action.* 1941. 3rd ed. Berkeley: University of California Press, 1973.

Burke, Kenneth. *A Rhetoric of Motives.* 1950. Berkeley: University of California Press, 1969.

Burke, Kenneth. "Words as Deeds." *Centrum* 3.2 (Fall 1975): 147–68.

Butler, Judith. *Excitable Speech: A Politics of the Performative*. New York: Routledge, 1997.

Butler, Judith. *Gender Trouble: Feminism and the Subversion of Identity*. New York: Routledge, 1990.

Carlson, Marvin. *Performance: A Critical Introduction*. London: Routledge, 1996.

Causey, Matthew. *Theatre and Performance in Digital Culture: From Simulation to Embeddedness*. London: Routledge, 2006.

Chaudhuri, Una. *Staging Place: The Geography of Modern Drama*. Ann Arbor: University of Michigan Press, 1995.

Derrida, Jacques. *Writing and Difference*. Trans. Alan Bass. Chicago: University of Chicago Press, 1978.

Diamond, Elin. *Unmaking Mimesis: Essays on Feminism and Theater*. London: Routledge, 1997.

Dixon, Steve, with contributions by Barry Smith. *Digital Performance: A History of New Media in Theater, Dance, Performance Art, and Installation*. Cambridge, MA: MIT Press, 2007.

Eliot, T. S. *Selected Prose of T. S. Eliot*. Ed. and Introd. Frank Kermode. New York: Harcourt Brace Jovanovich, 1975.

Fergusson, Francis. *The Idea of a Theater: A Study of Ten Plays. The Art of Drama in Changing Perspective*. Princeton: Princeton University Press, 1949.

Foucault, Michel. "Of Other Spaces." Trans. Jay Miskowiec. *Diacritics* 16.1 (Spring 1986): 22–7.

Frye, Northrop. *Anatomy of Criticism: Four Essays*. Princeton: Princeton University Press, 1957.

Garner, Stanton B., Jr. *Bodied Spaces: Phenomenology and Performance in Contemporary Drama*. Ithaca: Cornell University Press, 1994.

Goldman, Michael. *The Actor's Freedom: Toward a Theory of Drama*. New York: Viking, 1975.

Goldman, Michael. *On Drama: Boundaries of Genre, Borders of Self*. Ann Arbor: University of Michigan Press, 2000.

Goodman, Nelson. *Languages of Art: An Approach to a Theory of Symbols*. Indianapolis: Bobbs-Merrill, 1968.

Grigely, Joseph. *Textualterity: Art, Theory, and Textual Criticism*. Ann Arbor: University of Michigan Press, 1995.

Hayles, N. Katherine. *How We Became Posthuman: Virtual Bodies in Cybernetics, Literature, and Informatics*. Chicago: University of Chicago Press, 1999.

Jackson, Shannon. *Professing Performance: Theatre in the Academy from Philology to Performativity*. Cambridge: Cambridge University Press, 2004.

Lefebvre, Henri. *The Production of Space*. Trans. Donald Nicholson-Smith. Oxford: Blackwell, 1991.

Lehmann, Hans-Thies. *Postdramatic Theatre*. Trans. Karen Jürs-Munby. London: Routledge, 2006.

McGann, Jerome. *Radiant Textuality: Literature after the World Wide Web.* Houndmills. Palgrave, 2001.

McKenzie, Jon. *Perform or Else: From Discipline to Performance.* London: Routledge, 2001.

Norman, Donald A. *The Design of Everyday Things.* New York: Basic Books, 2002.

Phelan, Peggy. *Unmarked: The Politics of Performance.* London: Routledge, 1993.

Roach, Joseph. *Cities of the Dead: Circum-Atlantic Performance.* New York: Columbia University Press, 1996.

Schechner, Richard. *Performance Theory.* London: Routledge, 2003.

Schechner, Richard. *Between Theater & Anthropology.* Foreword Victor Turner. Philadelphia: University of Pennsylvania Press, 1985.

States, Bert O. *Great Reckonings in Little Rooms: On the Phenomenology of Theater.* Berkeley: University of California Press, 1985.

Taylor, Diana. *The Archive and the Repertoire: Performing Cultural Memory in the Americas.* Durham, NC: Duke University Press, 2003.

Turner, Victor. *From Ritual to Theatre: The Human Seriousness of Play.* New York: Performing Arts Journal Publications, 1982.

Williams, Raymond. *Drama from Ibsen to Eliot.* London: Chatto and Windus, 1952.

Williams, Raymond. *Drama from Ibsen to Brecht.* London: Hogarth Press, 1987.

Worthen, W. B. *Print and the Poetics of Modern Drama.* Cambridge: Cambridge University Press, 2006.

Index